Paranormal Realities

Keith Johnson

Summer Wind Press
ATTICA, NEW YORK

Paranormal Realities

ISBN 978-0-615-29744-6

Cover design by Emmi Gossard

Foreword
by Lisa Dowaliby

Every so often, you meet someone who really stands out in the vast sea of new acquaintances. There's *just* something about the person that is extraordinary and you can feel it from the first moment you meet. My initial impressions of Keith Johnson: Deeply intelligent. Quietly observational. Tactfully honest. Emanating positive energy. These impressions proved to be accurate, but I soon discovered that there was so much more to know and learn from my dear friend Keith. He is a devoted husband and father, an *amazing* teacher, and an exemplary investigator and I *am* very honored to have been asked to write the foreword for his book.

I began to have an interest in the paranormal at young age after my father gave me a book on paranormal and supernatural events. That growing interest, combined with a degree in anthropology, a fascination with cultural belief systems and their relation to the afterlife has led me to become a paranormal investigator. Once in the field, I was fortunate enough to become acquainted with Keith Johnson and his amazing wife, Sandra. Working with this husband/wife team has been a great learning experience for me, both as an investigator and as a human being. They each bring different qualities to the table yet complement each other perfectly. They approach cases with an organized, professional demeanor that is both intriguing and admirable.

It is my privilege to be Case Manager for their paranormal group, New England Anomalies Research. As an investigator of any kind, it is vital to possess common sense, objectivity, empathy, humility and mindfulness. Lacking even one of these qualities can mean misinterpretation of data, conflict with others and failure to bring legitimacy to the field you are working in.

Keith approaches each potential case with the open mindedness of a beginner yet with the wisdom of a veteran. Many of the cases Keith is called upon for consist of potentially negative situations, which may involve genuine paranormal activity, psychological issues on the part of the client, or both.

No matter how awkward, difficult, or nasty the situation may be, Keith remains grounded and focused, never panicking or falling into dramatics.

As a scientifically minded and skeptical person, I find that these qualities are not only remarkable but also invaluable. Keith's wide array of knowledge in many areas—the scientific, historic, folklore, religious, psychological, and so on, is vital to his skills as an investigator. As a fellow investigator and personal friend of Keith Johnson, I am both excited and proud to see his amazing experiences put into writing. This is a book I've been waiting a long time for and it's well worth the wait. Sit back, get comfortable, open your mind, and prepare to be impressed. The following stories will take you on a fascinating journey and you are very likely to finish this book with more questions than you had when beginning it. If you find this to be the case, you are in very good company; the paranormal field continues to excite, baffle, confound and intrigue all of us who choose to explore it.

Lisa Dowaliby
Case Manager New England Anomalies Research
Former cast member of 'Ghost Hunters'

Foreword
by David Manch

Paranormal investigation has truly come a long way. From the earliest formation of an organized group 147 years ago, the hunt for things that go bump-in-the night has continually evolved to include new ideas, new gadgets, and new personalities.

The Ghost Club was formed in London in 1862 with the specific goal of exposing fraudulent spirit mediums and investigating authentic psychic phenomena. In 1938, renowned ghost hunter Harry Price remarked that The Ghost Club was a "body of extremely skeptical men and women who get together every few weeks to hear the latest news of the psychic world and to discuss every facet of the paranormal." Although the methods of hunting and investigating paranormal activity may have changed over the years, that one particular ideal has stood the test of time, and has been the binding force in nearly every modern investigative group.

Whereas many groups of the past relied on psychic intuition to foster their theories on the paranormal, the driving force behind today's investigative research is science. We have at our disposal fascinating advances in audio, video, thermic, and electromagnetic science to aid us in our search for the elusive mysteries surrounding the paranormal realm. In a growing field that has witnessed many remarkable phenomena, it is only a matter of time before someone comes along with a new concept that will again revolutionize the way in which we all conduct our research.

Going forward, it is a privilege to participate in the investigation of paranormal phenomena and to add our name's to the hallowed list of researchers that have come before us. By continuing to use new concepts in the field, we move ever closer to discovering exactly what it is that so many people experience daily around the world, and possibly uncovering the answer to the question, "Is there life after death?"

We soon shall see

David Manch
Case Manager, New England Paranormal
Author, *There Are Ghosts In Our World But Are They Real?*

Dedication

This book is dedicated to my dear wife Sandra, whose love, patience and support have proven invaluable to me, both in the writing of this book and in the *work* itself. Sandra is a devoted wife and mother of our only son, Keith Jr., whose autism causes him to struggle to fit into this world each and every day. Sandra is also my helpmate in every facet of my career in dealing with the paranormal. This includes presenting lectures, teaching classes, traveling to conventions, reviewing hours and hours of data collected during investigations and sometimes even the potentially very dangerous task of confronting demonic entities. Never once have I known her faith to falter or have I ever seen her retreat in fear. Her faith, courage, and devotion are qualities to be greatly admired and I feel truly blessed that God has brought us together!

Keith and Sandra are interviewed on the McLovin & Fender Show.

Contents

CHAPTER 1

Paranormal Beginnings-Thirsty Ghost

OFTEN I AM ASKED what first sparked my interest into the field of paranormal research and investigation. My response is simple; I grew up in a haunted house. Now, when I say haunted, I'm not referring to the activity akin to "The Amityville Horror," nor was it by any means something constant just sporadic. Neither was the house I lived in an old, cavernous, Gothic-style mansion.

The house was actually a raised ranch, built for our family, on property given to my parents as a wedding gift by my maternal grandfather. We were the first family ever to live in this house, located along Hartford Pike in the rural town of North Scituate, Rhode Island. Yet every once in awhile in this normal, unobtrusive looking house, unexplained activity would occur.

Our family moved into the newly finished house when my twin brother Carl and I were six months old. Two years and four months later, our new baby sister Cynthia arrived to join our family. Carl and I were absolutely thrilled with the new addition, and enjoyed a certain feeling of importance and responsibility when told by our mother that we were expected to help out with the care of our little sister.

The first event I can recall, which might in *any* way be considered paranormal, was when Carl and I were five years of age and Cynthia about three. We were just finishing eating supper early on a Saturday evening, with Carl and I seated at the kitchen table and our little sister Cindy in her high chair. My mother had risen to start on the dishes, when, in the middle of a sentence, she began to choke slightly, as if something had simply gone down the wrong way. Fortunately it was no emergency. Nonetheless, my father quickly filled a glass of water from the faucet and handed it to her. My mother took a couple of sips, which seemed sufficient to clear her throat. The glass was still at her lips, when a loud slurping sound was suddenly heard, causing her eyes to widen in surprise. The next thing my mother knew, she was holding an empty glass in her hand. "What just happened?" she asked in astonishment. "Where did the rest of the water go?"

"What the heck?" my father Lenny asked, equally puzzled.

Completely baffled, all my mother could say was, "It just went away!"

Although our little sister was much too young to have noticed what had just happened, both Carl and I had witnessed this brief event, and listened to our parent's inability to come up with any logical explanation.

My parents' only explanation was that we had a "thirsty ghost" in the house with us.

CHAPTER 2

Outside The Bedroom Window

THE NEXT EVENT I recall also took place when I was five years old. It was sometime during the middle of the night in the bedroom which Carl and I shared. I awoke to the sounds of a heavy downpour just outside our window. Intermingled with the sounds of the rain coming down in torrents were the sounds of laughter and animated voices. At first I thought it might be the rain merely sounding like voices. But soon, it was unmistakably the familiar sound of my mom and dad socializing with their friend. At least it was a comforting thought to know that my parents had just arrived home from an evening out. I knew too that I'd soon hear them coming through our front door from out of the rain and greeting the baby sitter whoever that may be. After several minutes of listening to this lively chatter, I began to grow a bit impatient, wondering what was taking them so long, especially since they were obviously being drenched outside there in the heavy downpour.

Meanwhile, my brother Carl remained sound asleep, breathing rhythmically, probably because his bed was not next to the window. Glancing over to the window to my immediate right, to where the driveway was outside, I could see no trace of the expected headlights through the curtain. The voices then became significantly louder. Another peculiar thing I noticed was that although I could hear the

3

conversation loud and clear, I could not understand a single word being said. In fact, it was as if the adults outside were speaking some sort of foreign language with which I was totally unfamiliar.

And then with a shock of realization, I remembered that my parents had *not* gone out that night after all. But, if it wasn't my parents and their friend making all that noise outside in the rain, then who the heck was it? At that moment, the voices suddenly stopped. It was some time though before I was able to get back to sleep that night.

The following morning I of course related my experience of the previous night to my mother. Not surprisingly, she dismissed it as my having simply dreamt the whole occurrence. I insisted that I had been fully awake, and that I remembered looking through the curtain and not seeing any headlights. Still mother insisted that it must have been my imagination, probably having mistaken the rain against the roof for the sound of people talking outside. "But Mom", I protested, "I could hear people right outside the window, talking and laughing in the rain. It's just that I couldn't understand anything they were saying. But I *did* hear them out there."

Remaining unconvinced, my mother then simply attributed the experience to my over-active imagination. When I reminded her of our "thirsty ghost" incident, she insisted that it had been just an isolated occurrence. After all, spooky things like that just don't keep on happening... do they?

CHAPTER 3

The 'Haunted House' of Little Compton

MY BROTHER CARL, my sister Cindy and I regularly attended church with our parents throughout our childhood, and made our church confirmation at the expected time. Our dad had been a soloist with the choir since the age of nineteen and our mom was a Sunday school teacher. Carl and I were both trumpet players in both the junior high band, and later in the high school band. For the most part our childhood and teenage years were normal. There were of course the expected teenage pranks and pratfalls, especially with Carl and I being identical twins.

Admittedly we did switch a few classes at school, and there were times after Church, when our dad would take us to visit our cousins in Cranston, that Carl and I would squeeze into the same Sunday jacket. We'd then walk down the street together, creating the illusion to all of our neighbors who happened to be outside, that we were actually conjoined twins.

No harm no foul.

The years in our own home in North Scituate were good and genuinely quiet, paranormally speaking that is. There would be the occasional unexplained rapping or creaking of the cellar stairs. At times even a family member would think they'd just heard their name called when no one had, but otherwise, not much which could be defined as "paranormal."

In fact, my next significant experience occurred during the summertime of my tenth year. One of our family traditions was to stop by the "haunted house" in Little Compton on our way back from visiting the beach. In reality, we hadn't a clue as to whether or not this long-abandoned house was actually haunted; it just looked like it was. It was large and *spooky* looking, and it was in rather good condition despite being abandoned for who knew how long. In fact, it rather resembled the "Addams Family" house.

And since there were never any "no trespassing" signs posted in front of it, and no one there to prevent us from gaining access, we'd annually avail ourselves of a brief tour inside the house. This tradition was originally the brainchild of my mom and her cousin Virginia, who both loved a good potential thrill. It was during this, our last visit to the "haunted house" that I momentarily lingered behind inside by myself. Mom, Virginia, Carl and seven-year-old Cindy were already on their way out to the car. My dad unfortunately had to work this day. Since I'd been right behind my brother Carl on our way out, it was relatively easy to take a step backwards at the front door and simply walk back in, while no one was watching.

Back upstairs on the second floor for a last look around, I could hear my mother, growing in impatience, calling me from outside. "C'mon, Keith, we're waiting! You shouldn't be in there by yourself."

"Yep. I'm on my way," I called back while biding my time.

"Keith," my mom called again, "if we have to come back in after you, you're in trouble!" I then overhead her telling my brother Carl to go in and get me.

While heading towards the staircase on my way out, I suddenly had the peculiar feeling that if I just turned back and peered into one of the nearby rooms, I'd see something unusual. Following this premonition, I took a few steps back and glanced into the nearest doorway…and there, in the middle of this otherwise empty room, was an old wooden rocking chair, which I'd seen in that room many times before. Only now, it was rhythmically rocking back and forth by itself, just as if someone were sitting in it contentedly rocking away.

It took only a couple of seconds to find my footing, and dash the length of the hallway, down the stairs, and out of the house just as fast as my little sunburned legs could carry me. "It's about time," said my mom as I raced to the car and hopped in the back seat. "We were about to send your brother to come collect you."

"But listen," I excitedly exclaimed to everyone while catching my breath, "I just saw a rocking chair rocking by itself upstairs! No one was in it!"

"Yeah. Sure you did," said my mom, while backing the car out of the driveway. Once again, she chalked-up what I'd just experienced to my over-active imagination. No one else in the car seemed all that impressed with my tale, either.

"No, it's true!" I protested. "The 'haunted house' really IS haunted! That chair was rocking all by itself, really fast. I swear!"

"You better *not* swear," is all mom advised me.

In retrospect, I realize that whatever spirit may have inhabited that old abandoned house may have merely been demonstrating its farewell to me as well. After all, my family and I had given it quite a bit of recognition each summer, even if none of us had ever experienced anything unusual up until that one final incident. Each year I'd always wanted to experience at least some sign that the old place really was haunted, and it had graciously obliged. In fact, I even grew to feel honored that it had chosen me to convey the message of "I really am here." Inadvertently at ten years of age I'd conducted my first successful paranormal investigation!

Years later, whoever bought this house in Little Compton, had it beautifully restored, to its original grandeur. Perhaps someday, I'll work up the nerve to place my self-consciousness aside, and walk up to their front door and ask if they've ever experienced anything unusual... and if they ever kept that old antique wooden rocking chair.

CHAPTER 4

The Voices Return

I T WAS WHILE I was in my fifteenth year, that I was awakened sometime in the middle of the night by the beginnings of a violent, early spring thunderstorm. As the storm rapidly approached, flashes of lightning periodically illuminated the bedroom, followed by increasingly loud rumbles of thunder. Although my brother Carl still seemed to be breathing evenly in the next bed over to mine, I could tell there'd be no getting back to sleep for me until the thunderstorm abated, however long that might turn out to be. Guess I'd just have to wait it out, I figured. It was then that I heard a high-pitched voice speaking from somewhere outside in the storm. The voice had a feminine quality to it, almost cooing. Just as when I was five years old, although this time I could hear the voice plainly, I was unable to distinguish any of the words. Silently I thought to myself, "At least now I know for certain that I'm wide awake, and I'm not imagining this."

Before long, there was a blinding flash of lightning, immediately followed by a terrific crash of thunder, which caused the entire bedroom to shake. In that instant our phonograph, which Carl had switched off just before going to bed, suddenly switched back on by itself, once again beginning to play the LP which had been left on the turntable.

The following morning, I reasoned that since the phonograph had still been plugged in, the jolt from the lightning had somehow caused it to be to be switched back on, even though the switch itself had still been in the off position. However, this did not help to explain the voices I'd heard…voices that were eerily similar to the ones I heard outside my bedroom window all those years before.

This was the first of three occasions, within a span of three months that I was to hear these voices outside of my bedroom window. All three times it was on a night when the weather outside was stormy, and the atmosphere felt charged with static energy. Each time the voices sounded closer, as if becoming increasingly emboldened. By the third occasion, high-pitched laughter mingled with chattering could be heard directly outside the farthest right window, where the voices had always been heard. There could even be heard the deliberate, almost playful sound of splashing of feet in the muddy ground directly below our window.

As I lay in bed listening, wide-awake and terrified, the laughter and chattering sounds flitted to the window in front of me and then over to the third window, directly to my left. And then the sounds finally ceased. While this had been going on, I'd felt a great 'now or never' temptation to suddenly leap out of bed and throw back the one of the shades to see just what was out there. But somehow I was unable to force myself to do so.

In retrospect, I found it strange that even though my brother Carl and I shared the same bedroom we never simultaneously shared an experience. On the other hand, he would soon begin experiencing things, which I myself did not. So much had happened to me that I was under the distinct impression I was being toyed with, and therefore I became determined to investigate the source of the phenomenon. I began leaving a tape recorder on the dresser near the bedroom windows at night, in case the voices ever returned. Unfortunately they never did.

One thing I feel is significant is the fact that on the last occasion I heard these voices, they were moving from window to window in a counter-clockwise direction. *This,* as I came to learn is a telltale sign of the demonic.

CHAPTER 5

Ouija Board Experiences

IT WAS WHILE CARL, Cynthia and I were teenagers, that we began experimenting with spirit contact though the use of an Ouija board. Ours was the typical game board type, which is mass-produced by Parker Brothers just like any other board game. My brother and sister seemed to have somewhat more of an interest in playing with the board than I did, and would often hold nightly sessions after supper. We certainly considered it a relatively harmless pastime back then, and saw no real potential danger in attempting to communicate with whatever 'friendly' spirits might be willing to come though the board and communicate with us. In fact, our mother mentioned to us that she herself occasionally played with an Ouija board back when she was a teenager, and she'd never experienced anything really frightening while using it.

It wasn't long before Carl and Cindy began getting some noticeable results from using the Ouija board. Not surprisingly, they initially accused each other of intentionally moving the planchette around. "You're moving it, I know you are!" Cindy regularly told Carl.

"No, I'm not," Carl insisted. "I'm hardly even touching it, my fingers are only resting lightly on the edge of it."

Half seriously, Cindy said, "Maybe it's Tilly." Well 'Tilly' was the 'family ghost' our step-grandmother would dress up as, to playfully scare the children of the family every Halloween.

They then decided to ask the spirit if it had a name.

"Can you please tell us your name?" Carl asked.

Their fingers then seemed to be guided, as the planchette spelled out the name S-Y-L-V-I-A. Carl asked, "Sylvia...is *that* your name?"

With the tips of their fingers resting lightly upon it, the planchette moved to YES.

As Cindy and Carl continued asking questions of 'Sylvia' the planchette began moving so fast it felt as though it was about to fly out of their hands. During this session they ascertained from their new spirit friend 'Sylvia' that she was the spirit of a woman who had died at the age of 32, and who was glad to be able to communicate with someone after all these years. Near the end of the session Carl asked 'Sylvia' where she was right now. In response the planchette spelled out "In this house."

"Where in this house?" asked Cindy.

The planchette spelled out the word C-E-L-L-A-R. Carl then asked 'Sylvia' if she could do something to prove that she was real, 'Sylvia' said yes.

Cindy and Carl then ended their session and promptly went over to the stairs leading to the cellar, to see if 'Sylvia' would actually give them a sign of her presence. They waited together on the third cellar step for about twenty minutes – and as Carl states, when you're 15 and 13 years old prospectively, twenty minutes is certainly a long time to wait. Finally deciding to give up, they turned and were about to head back upstairs, when suddenly three distinct raps could be heard on one of the cellar walls. Carl and Cindy glanced first at each other, then down into the darkness of the empty cellar. Carl then suggested that this was simply too much a coincidence, and that it must be some kind of rodent tapping on the wall. No sooner had he said this, than three louder, resounding knocks were heard against the cellar wall.

Cindy and Carl rushed upstairs to switch the cellar light on. Together, they went downstairs and walked through the entire basement, only to find it completely empty.

Throughout the next few weeks, my brother and sister began holding almost nightly communication sessions with their new spirit friend 'Sylvia' through the Ouija board. One evening as I sat there watching, Carl asked 'Sylvia' if she could further prove her reality by prompting his girlfriend Suzie to call him. Less than ten seconds later the telephone rang, causing both Carl and Cindy to glance up at each other, open-mouthed. Carl then rushed over to the phone, and sure enough *it* was Suzie calling for him.

One evening soon afterwards, while Cindy and Carl were using the Ouija board, their session suddenly took on a bizarre new twist. To their surprise, a new, not so pleasant male spirit whom identified himself as 'Nick' was now present; 'Sylvia' had been replaced. Unlike 'Sylvia', 'Nick' refused to exchange pleasantries or engage in personable conversation. His manner seemed gruff, and his conversation was even crude and repulsive at times. Another strange development was the fact that Cindy and Carl now found the planchette difficult to move, whereas before while communicating with 'Sylvia' it would slide across the board quickly and easily. And when the planchette did move, with some resistance, Carl and Cindy also felt an icy sensation on top of their fingers, almost as if it were a chill breeze.

Also in contrast to 'Sylvia', 'Nick' seemed more reluctant to divulge personal information pertaining to himself. When Carl asked for a last name, the spirit of 'Nick' eventually did cooperate to a small extent. The planchette was guided to six different letters on the board, which Carl rearranged to spell out the name R-U-B-E-N-S. Upon doing some historical research on variations of "Nick Rubens," the closest name Carl came across was that of Nicholas Rubenstien, who was a friend and mentor of the famous Russian composer Peter Ilyich Tchaikovsky, and who had also helped to found the Moscow Conservatory of Music. Although Nicholas Rubenstien had shared a close friendship with Tchaikovshy, he later severely criticized some of Tchaikovsky's compositions. Nicholas Rubenstein died in Moscow in March of 1881...although what his spirit might now be doing in the town of Scituate, Rhode Island, Carl could not guess, and 'Nick' was not telling.

Before long, another nameless entity came through, which refused to identity itself. This one began giving portents of local tragedies and other mishaps through the Ouija board. A few of these predictions would later prove to be true, while others did not. This particular entity even began spelling out insults and gutter talk to Carl and Cindy, until they finally decided to cease their Ouija board session's altogether for a while.

However, my brother and sister and I had some teenage friends at the time that were also quite interested in Ouija board communications. One of these friends in particular was a classmate of Carl's and mine named Jay. Jay had his own Ouija board at home, and was apparently very adept at using the board for spirit contact. In fact, unlike Carl and Cindy who always used the Ouija board, Jay was just as comfortable using the board by himself, by lightly placing one index finger on the planchette and allowing it to quickly slide and spell out messages. Jay also had his own personal spirit guide on the board. Coincidentally, this spirit also went by the first name of 'Nicholas', although the surname of Jay's 'Nicholas' was 'Selegrad'.

From what Jay related to us, his spirit friend 'Nicholas' would provide him with endless hours of companionship and brilliant conversation. 'Nicholas' would often give Jay friendly advice concerning his home and school life. He also assured Jay that he deeply appreciated his friendship, and promised to always be with him.

Several years later my sister Cindy revived her interests in spirit communication through the Ouija board. One of her reasons for doing so was because she'd recently ended a long-term relationship with a boyfriend, and as a result was experiencing a deep sense of depression and loneliness. Only now, like our friend Jay, she felt comfortable enough to try using the board all by herself, in the privacy of her bedroom. Once again she was soon able to establish contact with an unseen friend, this time claiming to be the spirit of a sweet young woman named 'Gail'. Cindy eventually became so emotionally dependant upon her new friend that she would leave the Ouija board next to her bed so she could begin communicating again as soon as she woke up in the morning.

During this time Cindy also became intensely interested in 1950's matinee idol James Byron Dean, who's life had tragically been cut short at age 24 in a car crash, which took place on September 30, 1955, in Cholame, California. Cindy began researching the life of the actor, memorizing every detail of the actor's personal life. One evening, Cindy decided to ask her spirit friend if she could do her a favor, and put her in touch with the spirit of James Dean. After all, since 'Gail' herself was a spirit, maybe she had *connections* in the spirit world. Positioning her fingers lightly on the edge of the planchette, Cindy asked, "Gail…would it be possible for you to put me in touch with the spirit of actor James Byron Dean? If you are able to, I'd be eternally grateful."

Slowly, the plastic indicator began moving towards, the center of the board, then abruptly stopped. Cindy again repeated her question, with no response. "Gail? Are you still there?" asked Cindy.

With a sharp tug, the planchette then moved to 'No.'

Recalling the negative experience that she and Carl had with the Ouija board years before, Cindy became alarmed. Cautiously she asked, "Who is this?"

The indicator promptly responded by spelling out a vulgarity. "What?" Cindy asked in shock. "Who is this, and why are you saying that? Is… is this the spirit of 'Nicholas' from years ago?"

Once more the planchette refused to communicate, aside from spelling out vulgarities and filthy names, adding a prediction of a car crash involving me that very night. Cindy then immediately decided to end the session. Thankfully, the prediction proved to be false but after this, she could not bear the thought of ever using the Ouija board again, or even having it in her room another night. She promptly packed the board up along with the planchette, and then placed the cardboard box outside on the stonewall in front of our house. Cindy had heard of the potential dangers of burning an Ouija board, she decided against risking any sort of backlash by attempting to destroy it.

First thing the following morning, Cindy went outside to see if the Ouija board was still there. To her relief, she saw that it was now gone. Although this was not the morning for trash pick-up, someone had presumably spotted it while driving by and had helped him or herself to it. "Good riddance," she thought.

Unfortunately, whoever took the Ouija board with them may well have wound up with more than they'd bargained for. Also, I feel my sister's experience is a perfect example of an entity coming through over the Ouija board and attempting to gain an individual's trust. Once it has gained *that* person's trust, it will do anything to deceive this person into willingly allowing it to gain further access into his or her life. And an unholy spirit will have no reservations about taking advantage of an individual's personal vulnerabilities, such as loneliness or depression. In fact, there are certain parasitic entities, which actually feed off of negative human emotions.

Usually only after the point where the person using the Ouija board 'crosses the line' by asking the spirit to manifest itself in some way, will the entity will begin to reveal its true nature. The unseen entity that may formerly have pretended to be such a nice 'spirit friend' will suddenly begin spelling out language that is coarse, vulgar and even sometimes downright threatening. Often at this point the individual will take the hint and wisely cease using the Ouija board altogether.

CHAPTER 6

The Problems Persist

I T WAS LATE one Friday afternoon during the month of October that my sister Cindy and brother Carl happened to be standing in the dining room sharing casual conversation. Suddenly while in mid-sentence, Cindy was shoved from behind by an unseen hand, causing her nearly to lose her balance. Perhaps not so coincidentally for Cindy happened to be standing beside the dining room table where she and Carl conducted their Ouija board sessions.

Less than a week later as our family was getting ready for bed, we heard what sounded like incredibly heavy footsteps treading upon the roof of our house. In fact, the footsteps were so heavy; they actually caused the house to vibrate. "What the heck is that?" my dad asked in astonishment. The noise then abruptly stopped. An investigation by Carl outside revealed no sign of anything having fallen upon the roof, or of any intruder. Although my dad insisted that there must be at least some damage from a racket such as that, a daylight inspection the following morning revealed no trace of any damage whatsoever. Carl and Cindy later described the sound as that of a giant stomping across the rooftop, weighing at least 500lbs or more.

There was another occasion when Carl and Cindy discovered a small, woman's glove lying in the hallway, which seemed somewhat old-fashioned in appearance. No one in our family had ever seen it before. Carl picked it up to examine it closer, then placed it upon the dining room table. A minute or so later, when he went to retrieve it, the glove had mysteriously vanished from sight.

Around this time, Carl, being a chronic insomniac decided to set up his own bedroom space in a corner of our basement. Another reason Carl wished to have his own personal space was to have a place to socialize with a select group of friends, who were also interested in exploring various aspects of paranormal phenomena. During one of these discussion sessions, which took place in the basement on a Saturday afternoon, our friend Jay suddenly had an inkling to point his index finger at one of the overhead light bulb, which promptly exploded.

One evening, Carl decided to tape record one of these basement paranormal chats for the sake of posterity. Present during this discussion were my brother and myself, Jay, and two other teenage friends of ours. After about an hour or so, Carl began playing back the audiotape to go over certain topics that had been discussed. Suddenly, while we were listening to our discussion, a low voice could be heard during a momentary break in the conversation. "What the heck was that?" asked Carl, glancing at the rest of us.

"It certainly wasn't any of us," said Jay.

"In fact, it sounded like someone speaking in slow motion."

Carl rewound the tape and played it again. Sure enough, a low yet distinct voice could be heard saying something in slow motion and making the words difficult to understand. We could only conjecture that whatever *had* spoken, had imprinted its voice onto the audiotape at an increased speed compared to normal conversation. After listening to this section of the recording several times, we could seemingly decipher the words: "Somebody...help me," spoken in a low, masculine sounding voice.

We then listened to the rest of the audiotape, which was recorded on only one side, but no other mysterious voices were discernable. Mark, a member of our paranormal discussion group, fortunately owned a tape recorder, which could be adjusted to different speeds. We suggested he take the audio cassette tape home with him, and increase the playing speed of the voice to that of normal conversation.

Mark returned the next day with his findings. When speeded up, the voice that had been recorded in slow motion no longer sounded male; rather it had a distinctly female quality to it. This female voice now clearly seemed to be saying: *"Carl... help me. Help."* A few light taps could then be heard.

Quite by accident, we had recorded our first authentic example of Electronic Voice Phenomenon, or 'EVP'. We were later to learn that the tapping sound we heard accompanying the voice is not uncommon with EVP recordings.

Carl did attempt further communication with this entity by employing what is known as 'spirit rescue.' The technique he employed was simply to remain in the basement with the tape recorder going. While either by himself or with a few of our friends, he verbally offered to help this spirit and asked in what way he could be of assistance. Although Carl received no further communication from this spirit in the form of EVP, it was soon to make its presence known in another manner.

CHAPTER 7

'Sylvia' Appears

WHILE CONTINUING to sleep downstairs in the cellar, Carl would often awake to find various items of furniture rearranged in the immediate area around him. Even though he happened to be an extremely light sleeper, he attributed this to other family members having come downstairs during the night and moved some of the furniture around.

Then one morning shortly before dawn, Carl had awoken and was lying in bed for some time, waiting for the sunrise, when he caught sight of someone walking through the darkened cellar. Realizing he was no longer alone downstairs, he assumed this to be one of the family quietly walking around in the darkness, being careful not to disturb him. "Hello?" he called out. "Who is that?"

Carl watched, the shadowy figure continue to slowly glide by in silence without replying. With his vision now adjusted to the darkness, Carl could now make out the distinct silhouette of a woman wearing a long dress, with her hair pulled back into a bun. Clearly she did not appear to be from the present century. Also noticeable was the fact that the woman made no sound of footsteps as she passed by. And then she was gone. Instantly Carl jumped out of bed and switched on the overhead light, but there was no trace at all of anyone else in the cellar.

Carl's immediate reaction was to dash upstairs. However, this female spirit form would appear to him in the basement at several more times. In time he learned to brace himself and objectively observe these appearances. On one occasion, as Carl watched her slowly gliding by in the semi-darkened basement, he observed just how seemingly solid she appeared to be, though clearly she was no living person. By the time he called out to her, she had once again vanished.

It was dawn on a spring morning and Carl was alone downstairs in his basement room, wide-awake lying in bed. Since nothing of a paranormal nature had occurred in the basement for some months, *it* was the farthest thing from his mind, when suddenly he caught a glimpse of someone standing nearby his bed. Turning to his right, he noticed what appeared to be a woman wearing a long, gray, frock-like dress. "Hello?" he reflexively asked her. When she did not answer Carl propped himself up on one elbow. It was then Carl recognized her as the spirit form, which he'd seen before in the basement. Only now, she was standing there staring directly at him with a very steady, motionless gaze. What must have been only a matter of seconds seemed to Carl like minutes as he observed the details of her appearance... the disheveled hair pulled back and the dark, expressionless eyes. After they'd intensely stared at each other for a moment, the woman in the gray dress seemed to evaporate from the bottom up until she had vanished completely.

Carl remained in the same position for the better part of an hour, wondering just who this spirit form might have been. He hadn't even thought to ask her if her name might be Sylvia. And even if he had asked, would she have answered him? Carl also wondered whether most people would even believe him, if he were to share this experience. After all, Carl, our sister, our friends and I had already experienced years of ridicule in our hometown and beyond, because of our interest in paranormal research.

We never did find out anything more about the possible identity of Sylvia. Since we were the first family to live in our house, and there was a pony corral on the property before the house was built she certainly couldn't have been someone who'd once lived there. To my grandfather's knowledge, no house had ever stood in that exact spot.

His house next door happened to be one of the oldest historic houses in North Scituate. In fact, it was the first house in town to have had plumbing installed. My own personal opinion was that the manifestation of Sylvia represented someone who had lived next in my grandfather's house many years ago, and that this spirit may have been drawn over to our house though the Ouija board.

CHAPTER 8

Studying Spirit Activity

EVEN AS A YOUNG CHILD, I had always been fascinated by stories of angels in the Bible, which my parents would read to me. They were powerful and highly intelligent spirit creatures, created by God to directly serve Him and to watch over His human creation. Quite often they'd function as messengers, as the very name angel denotes. When I was between the age of four and five years, I would sometimes experience lucid dreams just prior to waking, during which I'd find myself in the company of large, tantalizingly beautiful spirit guides which I referred to as "friends." They would hold me in their arms and give me words of encouragement, telling me I had a special mission and that they would always be with me. Sometimes they would even take me with them to unknown places that I would not remember, and then return me to safely to my bed. Often just prior to awakening, I would suddenly feel the sensation of being "whooshed" back down into my body.

On the other hand, the thought of some of these powerful spirit beings falling from Heaven and becoming demons seemed truly frightening. Carl and I had learned about Satan at an early age, and were taught by our parents that Jesus Christ had authority over Satan and his minions of evil spirits. At about age nine, both Carl and I began a very rudimentary study of demons as well as angels.

During our teenage years, most of our paranormal investigations consisted of visiting local cemeteries or abandoned buildings with a reputation for being haunted, such as the long abandoned inn on Darby Road in North Scituate. Since on more than one occasion we'd been apprehended by local authority figures while at these locations, more often than not our investigations began to take place during the dead of night, often in adverse weather conditions.

Often our rudimentary investigations took place in our own home. Carl and I of course also studied the work of such pioneers in the paranormal research field as Hans Holzer and J.B. Rhine, as well as books concerning the life and prophecies of Edgar Cayce, among others. As our research continued, Carl and I became increasingly interested not only in human spirits, but inhuman spirits as well... specifically, the realms of the angelic and the demonic. Not only did we delve into the study of the supernatural, but also the preternatural as well. Carl also began taking an interest in studying the works of Anton Szandor LaVey, who had authored "The Satanic Bible" and "The Satanic Witch." Carl eventually began leaning toward the theory that some of the spirits entities involved in hauntings may in fact be manifestations of displaced human energy. Carl and I both agreed with the theory that these entities were most probably trans-dimensional as well.

There was a wooded area about two miles from our house, located along Hunting House Brook, which seemed to me as if it might be conducive to some sort of mild paranormal activity. While spending extended amounts of my free time there, I would often begin to experience a sort of presence with me, which sometimes seemed to be attempting to communicate with me. It was a comforting sensation, not in the least unnerving. Of course, may well have been just my own youthful imagination at the time. But then again, running water is a powerful energy source, and paranormal phenomena has been known to occur in some areas where an energy current produced by flowing water is present. Many old, abandoned mill sites throughout New England are noted spots of haunting activity.

There were a few occasions when we'd been asked to speak in some of our classes at school on the topic of paranormal investigation, although at the time it seemed that few of our classmates took the subject matter seriously. There was one time, however, when my brother Carl was lecturing on the occult to one of our English classes. As soon as he began speaking on the topic of Satanism, one of the girls in class suddenly happened to slip out of her chair onto the floor. Although she was uninjured, she was apparently convinced that Carl had placed a hex upon her, and caused her to fall.

Another time, during a break in an agriculture class, some of my classmates asked me to speak for a while on the topic of werewolves. I briefly explained what I knew of the European belief in lycantropy, including the folklore of "shape-shifters" stripping themselves naked underneath the full moon. Well, by the following day, the rumor had spread all over the school how "Johnson believes that he's a were-wolf, and he strips naked underneath the full moon!" After that incident, I pretty much kept my research into the supernatural to myself.

Quite often, especially in times of teenage turmoil, I would seclude myself in my bedroom and pray. During these times I often felt comforted by the presence of angels, and vividly recalled my early childhood dreams of them. This, combined with my Christian upbringing, began leading me more and more in the direction of assisting others who were living in fear of the paranormal. I had empathy for people who were suffering, and wanted to help mend broken lives and change the world. And yet, I also had very little idea, *if* any, of how I'd be able to pursue this field of study in any sort of practical terms. All I could do was to trust in God to lead me according to His will.

At the age of seventeen, Carl and I were both feeling somewhat frustrated about just how to actively apply our interest in paranormal investigation. Aside from a few of our closest friends, there was seemingly no one who shared our interest, at least not to the same extent. Fortunately, we were soon to meet some very special people, who would let us know that we were by far not the only ones in New England conducting paranormal research.

CHAPTER 9

Meeting Other Paranormal Researchers

I T WAS ON A DRIZZLY evening in April that Carl, Jay, my girlfriend Angie and I attended a lecture held at Rhode Island College. The lecturers were two well known and world traveled paranormal investigators from Monroe, Connecticut. They were a husband and wife team, by the name of Ed and Lorraine Warren. Out in the lobby, there was a poster of Mr. and Mrs. Warren advertising them as 'Professional Ghost Hunters' who had investigated hauntings throughout the United States and all over the world as well. I commented, "They sound interesting. Maybe we're not so crazy, after all."

We then took our seats inside Roberts Auditorium, which was filling up fast with nervous and excited college students. To add to the atmosphere of anticipation, background music from "Dark Shadows" and "The Day The Earth Stood Still" was being piped through the speaker system. The lights then dimmed, as an attractive, stylishly dressed middle-aged couple took center stage.

With microphone in hand, Ed Warren – a large framed man with dark, slightly graying hair and a serious facial expression – addressed the audience in a clear, resonant voice. "Good evening, ladies and gentlemen; we'd like to welcome you to all here this evening. Let me begin by introducing ourselves. My name is Ed Warren, and this is my wife Lorraine. For over thirty years now we have been exploring the realm of the supernatural. However, my personal experience with the supernatural actually began years before Lorraine and I were married, or even met. You see I grew up in what could be called a haunted house."

Carl and I shared a knowing look with each other. Certainly here was someone who could relate to our own personal experiences as well, and not accuse us of being unbalanced or of merely hallucinating.

Ed Warren went on to explain that as a young child growing up Bridgeport, Connecticut, he would hear disembodied footsteps on the stairway and unexplained pounding on the walls. He'd even beheld the eerie apparition of an older woman, who had once lived and died in their house, manifesting inside his bedroom closet. Frightening as this was, it had also instilled in him a life-long desire to explore paranormal phenomena. Ed also explained that his wife Lorraine was a clairvoyant and a light trance medium, meaning that she possessed the ability to discern things beyond the normal five senses, as well as the ability to perceive the 'aura' surrounding an individual.

Mr. Warren then asked, unexpectedly asked the audience if there happened to be anyone present who was seriously involved in occult studies and experimentation. "Oh, no," I thought to myself, for I knew what was coming next. Instantly my brother Carl's hand shot up. "Yes, young man, would you please come down here to the front," Mr. Warren invited him. Carl rose from his seat and marched down the aisle to the front of the auditorium, his shoulder-length auburn hair set off by his dark suit and tie.

Once Carl had joined Mr. and Mrs. Warren on the stage Mr. Warren asked him to introduce himself and to state his age. "My name is Carl Johnson, and I'm currently seventeen years old," Carl said in his best public speaking voice.

"Nice to meet you, Carl," said Mr. Warren. "Now, would you mind relating some of your personal experiences involving occult studies?"

Without hesitation, Carl began detailing his personal encounters with paranormal phenomena, beginning with his apparently successful spirit communication through the Ouija board. As Carl related his experiences – including his experimentation into the occult - audible gasps could be heard from the mostly college age audience. Carl concluded by saying, "So, I guess you could say that I was at least partly responsible for my parents' house being haunted."

Mr. Warren added, "Or at least it seems to have intensified, after you and your sister inadvertently drew a spirit in by using the Ouija board." Ed Warren thanked Carl for candidly sharing his personal experiences and asked him to remain on stage for the moment. Then he turned back to the audience and asked if there was anyone else who'd be willing to share their experiences in paranormal experimentation.

Sitting there, I half expected our friend Jay to be the next person to raise his hand. Instead, my girlfriend Angie surprised me as her arm shot up. In a huffy tone of voice, she whispered to me, "I'm sorry, but I'm sick and tired of listening to your brother talking about the dark side of the supernatural."

Mr. Warren said, "Yes, the young lady with the blonde hair, would you mind coming down here to join us, please?"

After glancing at me and excusing herself, Angie rose from her seat next to mine and determinedly began making her way down the aisle, her long blonde hair sweeping behind her. Her slim figure in a white blouse, long peasant-style dress and black leather boots cut quite an attractive appearance as she took her place beside Carl on the stage with Ed and Lorraine Warren.

Ed Warren held the microphone for her, as Angie introduced herself as a "white witch," and related her own personal brushes with the paranormal. Once again, there were gasps of surprise and interest from the college audience. At the time, both Jay and I were quite content to simply sit there and listen to Carl and Angie without offering to share our own experiences. In fact, as it was, several people nearby were already beginning to point me out, whispering, "That must be Carl's brother," causing me to self-consciously slouch down in my seat.

When Angie had finished speaking about her own experiences, something of an on-stage debate began to ensue between both Carl and Angie. Whereas Carl was more of a mind for pursuing darker occult studies, Angie tended to concentrate specifically on "white magic." She declared that the spells and incantations she cast were only of a positive nature, and that she only summoned the aid of "benign" spirits.

Ed Warren suddenly took them both aback, by once again addressing the audience in a commanding voice, saying, "Ladies and gentlemen, these two lost lambs have no idea of the unseen forces they're dealing with. They are both playing with extremely dangerous spirits, which are beyond their ability to control."

After making a few more statements about the dangers of occult involvement, Ed thanked Carl and Angie for coming on stage and participating, and asked if they could please remain after the lecture, so he and Lorraine could speak with them both privately. Both Carl and Angie agreed that they would.

When Angie resumed her seat next to me, she whispered an apology, saying, "Sorry to get up and leave you so abruptly, but I just couldn't let your brother get up there and speak only about the dark forces. I had to get my own two cents in there."

"Quite alright," I said, relieved that she was sitting beside me once again. "After all, why let Carl steal the show?"

Ed and Lorraine Warren's presentation that night was truly captivating. Not only did they relate numerous stories of their investigations from all over the world, they showed slides of haunted locations they'd investigated, and of people who were the victims of some very frightening phenomena. They also wowed the audience by showing reputedly authentic photographs of spirit manifestations. Ed then played audio recordings of actual spirit voices, as well as the voices of individuals who were under demonic possession. He of course warned everyone in the audience to shut off any recording devices they might have, due the potential danger of attracting an unwanted spirit presence to themselves.

At the conclusion of their lecture, Ed and Lorraine Warren received a standing ovation, after which they were surrounded by dozens of enthusiastic students eager to speak to them in person. As Ed Warren had requested, Carl and Angie, along with Jay and I, came up on the stage to personally speak with both himself and Lorraine.

The Warren's turned out to be a surprisingly down-to-earth New England couple, despite their lengthy career of investigating paranormal phenomena all over the world. Lorraine was especially personable, referring to us as 'dear' and 'honey.' Ed Warren took a particular interest in Carl, and arranged for a private interview with him sometime in the near future.

Among the gathering of college students surrounding the Warren's, there were those who were also interested in meeting us. Several of these students introduced themselves as belonging to a parapsychology club associated with Rhode Island College. The founder and chairperson of the organization – an attractive brunette named Donna, who was a senior at Rhode Island College – extended a personal invitation to us to attend one of their weekly meetings. Donna explained that the name of their organization was P.I.R.O., which stood for 'Parapsychology Investigation and Research Organization.' We thanked Donna for her kind invitation. "No, I'd like to thank you," she told us. "You all seem to be very interesting people, and I'm looking forward to you sharing some of your experiences with us."

And so, we now knew that we were no longer alone in our quest to investigate the realm of the paranormal. At Donna's personal invitation, Carl, Jay, Angie and I attended the next two meetings of Parapsychology Investigation and Research Organization, after which we were invited by the group to become members. Thus it was that Carl and I joined our first official paranormal investigation organization. We also kept in regular touch with Ed and Lorraine Warren, who became personal friends of ours.

Over the next several months during our weekly meetings with Donna and the other members of P.I.R.O., our activities included various psychic experiments with telepathy, and the tapping into other latent abilities within the human psyche. We would sometimes invite various guest speakers to our meetings, one of which was the head of the science department at Rhode Island College. Other speakers included a self-described 'psychic witch' named Liz-Beth, as well as a proclaimed mystic visiting from Liverpool, England, known as Jason Radcliffe.

As a group, we eventually began conducting experiments involving astral projection and hypnotic regression. Quite often during these experiments, Carl, Jay and I would be the willing subjects. Of course, throughout our teenage years, Carl, Jay and I had frequently experimented with such things as astral projection, regression and remote viewing. However, we were now doing so in a semi-controlled environment, with so-called experienced experts in the field guiding us along.

During one of these experiments in past-life regression, with myself as the volunteer subject, the lights were turned low in our meeting room at Rhode Island College. With Liz-Beth's soft voice guiding me into a relaxed state as I reclined on a sofa, I attempted to tap into a 'past life' by returning to a moment before my birth. Eventually I did begin experiencing what seemed to be vague, trace memories. There were shadowy images of riding on horseback along some wooded trail, with a long cloak wrapped about my shoulders and carrying a pistol by my side. Next I felt myself dismounting, and tethering my horse at a nearby tree. As if from some near distance overhead, I overheard Liz-Beth telling the others in the room, "He's under." She then asked me, "Where are you? What are you seeing?"

"I'm in the woods somewhere," I replied. "I'm not sure where this is… but I know this place."

"Can you describe your surroundings?" asked Liz-Beth."

"It's just some wooded area," I said.

"I'm going to meet someone here," I added.

"Who are you going to meet?" asked Liz-Beth.

"Someone very important. It's an important meeting."

"Who are you?'

"I'm a general. A military general."

"Can you tell me your name?'

"Alex. Alexander."

Before we could go any further, however, one of the other members of the group named Bob, who was seated nearby me, began to quietly moan: "Aaaww… aaaww. He shot me!" Bob said. He then slumped out of his chair and onto the floor with a thud.

Donna whispered, "Bob? Are you alright?" In response, Bob exhaled with a loud gasp, and then seemingly 'expired.'

Liz-Beth then decided to end the session, and quickly brought me back to the present. The room lights were switched back on, and I glanced over to see Carl and another member assisting Bob back into his chair. It turned out that Bob was all right. He'd somehow been caught up "in the moment" of my regression session, and had become an active participant. Both Bob and I rapidly recovered our senses, after which I told him, "Gee, Bob, I'm sorry I shot you."

"Oh, no, that's quite alright," he said with a laugh. "I don't know what happened, but I guess that somehow I picked up on what you were experiencing. But I don't really remember much of it."

"What do you remember?" asked Donna.

Bob replied, "Well, it's extremely hazy. All I really remember is a gun being pointed at me, it being fired and the sensation of a bullet ripping through my chest. And then everything went totally black. That's all I remember."

We then stopped our regression sessions for the evening. However, there was another occasion when I was again the subject being regressed, and I was to be brought back to a Colonial New England setting. Although the details were once again quite scant, I was seemingly involved in of some sort of encounter of a sexual nature.

It was only later that I learned just how dangerous experimentation in past life regression could be, especially if the people conducting these experiments are not professionally trained. My girlfriend at the time ran into some trouble after submitting to a few regression sessions, when she began experiencing brief periods of lost time during her daytime school hours. Fortunately, we both discontinued our experimentation with past life regression soon afterwards.

CHAPTER 10

Early Investigation

OUR FIRST OVERNIGHT investigation was organized for as a summer evening. According to plan, it would actually begin as a social occasion, with the members of P.I.R.O. meeting together at the Johnson residence, Carl's and my house in North Scituate for dinner. The plan was to then walk a short distance to an abandoned barn located on the property bordering our house. Since this barn was rumored to be "haunted," with some mild paranormal activity having been experienced there by Carl, our investigation would center on the barn itself and the surrounding area.

Thus it was, that on the day of the investigation, after hours of working at my landscaping job, I was happy to arrive home and indulge in a soothing shower, while looking forward to the evening ahead. Carl was also especially looking forward with anticipation too seeing Donna, since a love interest had recently developed between the two of them.

Shortly after four other members of P.I.R.O. arrived at our house, we enjoyed a leisurely cookout in our backyard, which my parents graciously hosted. We then gathered together in our basement, for a brief meeting led our chairperson Donna. It was decided that we would split up into two groups, with Donna and Carl leading one and myself leading the other.

Due to the early summer season, it was still twilight when we arrived at the old, partially dilapidated barn following a brief walk. While Carl and Donna's group began their investigation inside the barn, I led my group throughout the grounds. Our plan was to switch after one half-hour. Not unexpectedly, my group did not experience anything in the way of paranormal activity in the outside area though we did try spirit communication.

When Carl and Donna's group came out from the barn, we quickly asked if they'd experienced anything. "Oh, yes," Carl said emphatically. "We seem to have made some spirit contact in there. But, I'll let you guys see if you experience anything similar, and then we can discuss it later."

Although I experienced nothing specific while we were in the barn, one of the more sensitive members of our team explained that she definitely sensed a female presence wandering through the rooms. After our investigation concluded, we gathered together in the basement of our house and compared notes. Carl and a couple of other members of his group reportedly sensed a strong spirit presence while in the barn, most probably of a malevolent nature. The sensitive member of *my* group shared that she had a definite feeling that a wandering female presence was in the barn, although she could not get a name. Bob, our self-proclaimed skeptic, claimed that he did not experience anything at all out of the ordinary.

It was not until the wee hours of the following morning, shortly before sunrise and hours after most of the others had left, that I spontaneously began feeling a sensation very similar to that which I'd experienced during some of my recent regression sessions. Rather than frightening, this feeling was almost exhilarating... so much so, that I felt compelled to greet the sunrise with an energetic walk around my neighborhood.

Later, when my rational thinking returned, I simply attributed this feeling to the result of sleep deprivation, since I'd been awake for the entire night. However, I did feel as if the experience did warrant further investigation, to discover whether it had truly been nothing more than a manifestation of my subconscious mind.

One early evening when Carl and I were still both 17 years old, not long after the overnight P.I.R.O. investigation, we were enjoying a social get-together at our house with several of our friends. It was about 7:00 PM, and my girlfriend Angie and I were seated at the kitchen table, casually chatting while sipping soft drinks. For a moment, we were smiling and gazing affectionately into each other's eyes. Suddenly, I could see what appeared to be the face of another somewhat older woman, with dark eyes, forming over my girlfriend's youthful features. The only way I can describe it was that a hazy, indistinct sort of mask seemed to be taking shape over her face. Angie was completely unaware of what was happening. As I sat there watching in silence, the woman's face slowly began to drift upwards, and then faded away.

Not many weeks later, Angie and I were seated on a sofa, when she turned to face me and suddenly let out a scream. When I asked her what was wrong, she told me that my face had just changed into someone else's. When I asked her to describe *the* face, all she could tell me was that it was the face of a stranger, with darker hair, darker eyes, and slightly older than myself. Naturally, at first I attributed this to merely being a trick of the rooms lighting.

However, one afternoon some months after this incident, I happened to be riding in the same car with my best friend and his wife, both of whom I'd known for years. In fact, I had introduced them to each other. At one point as we were riding along, my best friend's wife turned to say something to me, and suddenly let out a cry of alarm. When we both asked her what was wrong, she apologized, saying, "I'm sorry, Keith. It was just that for a moment, when I looked at you, your face looked like it was someone else's, someone *I* didn't know."

Her husband told her, "That's ridiculous, Ann. I think you're starting to see things." Of course, Ann knew nothing of my girlfriend's recent similar experience.

It was also around this time that my girlfriend experienced a snippet of "lost time," as well as the feeling that there was another presence nearby her, watching her and waiting for an opportunity to take over.

39

Fortunately, I eventually consulted with some fellow Christians with whom I'd recently been attending a weekly Bible study. Once I'd confided in them exactly what I'd been experiencing as a result of my psychic experimentation, they explained that a spirit had attached itself to me, most likely during one of my sessions with past-life regression. They also explained that this was not a spirit of human origin. Rather, it was a demonic entity masquerading as a human spirit. Together as a group, my fellow believers in Christ prayed over me, and rebuked this spirit.

There was just one other occasion where someone else experienced the apparent sudden transformation of my features. Some time had elapsed since the last episode had occurred, and I happened to be counseling a close friend of mine who had asked for spiritual advice. She also needed a friend to talk to about her ongoing relationship problems. As soon as I offered to pray with her, she suddenly looked at me in shock and gasped. "What is it?" I asked her.

She replied, "Keith, somehow your face just changed for a moment. You looked like someone else."

"What did I suddenly look like?" I asked.

"You suddenly looked like someone with darker hair and eyes, and maybe just a little bit older," she said.

Immediately, I rebuked whatever unholy spirit might be present in the name of Jesus Christ, asking in His name that it not be allowed to return.

And to this day, after nearly thirty years it has never happened again. In fact, I regarded that final appearance as an expulsion.

During the first year of Carl's, Jay's and my membership in P.I.R.O., most of our actual investigations were organized field trips to such well-known historic locations as Salem, Massachusetts. Occasionally we'd conduct a minor investigation of the Rhode Island College campus itself, especially since Jay felt energized by a particular maple tree on the campus grounds. We'd also sometimes attend lectures, especially if it was one given by our friends Ed and Lorraine Warren. My parents also became good friends with Ed and Lorraine, and I did have the opportunity to personally assist Ed during two separate investigations at our home in North Scituate.

With P.I.R.O., I would liked to have investigated the old Darby Road Inn in North Scituate, which was one of my original stomping grounds during my teen years. But, unfortunately, this building burnt to the ground close to a year before Carl and I ever joined P.I.R.O, so I never had the chance.

It must also be remembered that when P.I.R.O. existed as a college organization, paranormal groups were far from being generally accepted, in contrast to the way popular media has made them so today. In fact, we were sometimes not given the same basic respect that other campus organizations were. Occasionally we'd arrive for our weekly meeting, only to be informed that someone else would be using our usual meeting room. Whenever this happened, if there were no other spare rooms available, we'd be forced to hold our meetings out in the noisy lobby of the Student Union building. Also, almost all of our travel expenses had to be funded from our own treasury… *and* it certainly didn't help when one of our ex--members absconded with the dues.

However, during these early days of embarking on paranormal investigation, we were unexpectedly presented with one case in particular, which would help to set the course for my career in demonology. It involved a family in Rhode Island, which was under-going what turned out to be an actual demonic siege.

CHAPTER 11

Haunting In Harrisville

I T WAS SHORTLY before dawn on a May morning in 1885, as elderly Bathsheba Green crept unnoticed into the barn located in back of the Arnold farmhouse. Once inside the barns dark interior, Bathsheba first placed the small kerosene lantern she'd brought with her on a nearby table, before hastily setting about the task at hand. She'd certainly had to dress as quietly as possible that morning and leave her house in haste, taking special care not to awaken her husband and her personal black maid.

Soon the sun would rise, and she wanted to get this over with before anyone was up and about. Of course, as she said often, the hired farm hands here at the Arnold farm were a lazy lot, not a one of them worth his weight in spit. She needn't worry about being disturbed by *any* of them. Old man Arnold, however, was known to be an early riser and would often pay a quick morning visit to his barn prior to eating breakfast.

Fortunately, Bathsheba had lived on farms all of her life, and was still quite capable of being self-sufficient whenever the need arose. As quickly as the elderly woman's arthritic joints would allow, she dragged an old wicker chair over to the center of the floor, carefully positioning it directly underneath one of the rough-hewn, over head wooden beams. Next, despite her condition, it took the old woman less than twenty minutes to successfully sling and secure a rope around the beam directly above her. She then quickly tied the loose end of the rope into a makeshift noose, held together by an expertly done slipknot. Bathsheba gave the knot a snug pull to make certain that it would hold. It would be more than sufficient to support the weight of her short, plump body.

The old woman's attention was suddenly diverted, by the crowing of a rooster in the nearby hen house. Glancing over at the barn doorway, she perceived a thin, silvery shaft of morning sunlight streaming from underneath the door. Now she knew she really had to hurry. With a fierce determination, Bathsheba deftly slipped the noose over her bonnet, tucked it underneath her chin, and then pulled tightly on the knotted ball of the rope, making certain that it was snugly around her neck. She could now even feel the coarse thread of the rope beginning to chaff the fragile skin of her neck, but this only served to reassure her that the rope would do the trick. Once again the rooster began to crow, signaling to Bathsheba that it was now time to take the final step. For only a moment, she paused to close her eyes and envision the face of Jedson... the only man she'd ever truly loved, many, many years ago and whom she would soon be joining in death as she went to meet her God.

After taking a last quick breath, the old woman slightly bent her arthritic knees, then leapt forward from off of the wicker chair. The last thing Bathsheba Green heard was the crisp sound of her own neck snapping, like a dried corn stalk.

Sure enough, it was old Mr. Arnold who first made the gruesome discovery. Upon entering his barn shortly after sunrise, he had almost immediately noticed the faint glow of a lantern, which had been left burning within the front section of the barn. Wondering who could have been so utterly careless, Mr. Arnold stepped forward... then stopped when he spotted the overturned wicker chair lying in the center of the barn floor. Draped upon one of the legs of the overturned wicker chair was what appeared to be a small, white lady's bonnet.

It was then that Mr. Arnold glanced up and beheld the small, black clad lifeless form dangling from the center rafter just above him.

"What in the world?" he said to himself, momentarily wondering if someone had perpetrated some morbid joke by rigging up a scarecrow. But alas, a closer inspection revealed it was no rigged dummy or trick of the light. With a paralyzing shock, Mr. Arnold recognized the sightless eyes staring back at him as belonging to his neighbor's cantankerous wife, Bathsheba Green. "Oh my God," was all he could gasp, while weakly stepping backwards. "Oh my God…"

After recovering from the initial shock, Mr. Arnold quickly concluded that the "old witch" had simply tired of life and decided to end it on his property, a final act of retribution against him and his family. His mind now racing, Mr. Arnold desperately wondered what action to take next. How was he to avoid the scandal this would inevitably cause, once word spread within the community? Mr. Arnold decided that instead of immediately alerting the authorities, he'd first contact Bathsheba's husband, who lived only a short distance away on Collins Taft Road. After securely locking all of the barn doors, old Mr. Arnold then rushed back into his house, and quickly sent word to Mr. Green that he needed to see him right away on some urgent business.

Mr. Green arrived within the hour, and was privately ushered into the barn by Mr. Arnold himself. In a broken voice while staring up at the dangling corpse of his wife, Mr. Green absently commented, "I suspected that something might have happened, when I couldn't find her this morning. She… she hasn't been herself lately. More than once, I've found her wandering."

Shakily, Mr. Arnold told his neighbor, "You know that your wife has always hated my family, and that she's done this as her last act of vengeance against us." When Mr. Green remained silent, he added, "You also know that the scandal from this could very well ruin your reputation in this entire county, as well as mine."

"Let's first get her down, before discussing this any further," said Mr. Green.

Together, the two older gentlemen detached the rope from the overhead beam and lowered the woman's stout corpse to the floor of the barn. Mr. Green gingerly removed the makeshift noose from around his wife's neck. Indicating the twisted angle of her neck, he commented, "Looks like a clean break. A professional hangman couldn't have done it better."

"So, what do you suggest we do about this situation now?" Mr. Arnold asked his neighbor. "Should we risk involving the local constable?"

Mr. Green rose to a standing position and wiped a trembling hand across his brow. He then faced his neighbor squarely, and said, "No one has to know anything about this but us. Obviously, you and I both wish to avoid a scandal, so here's what we'll do. As for right now, we'll cover her over with a canvas sheet, and then you make damn sure no one comes in here. Give me about an hour, and I'll come back with a cart. Then we'll place her body on the cart. No one will ask any questions. Even if someone sees, they'll just assume we're conducting some routine farm business. Then later on this morning, I'll take her body into town, and say that I found her lying dead on the couch. Everyone knows that she hasn't been well for some time." After taking a deep breath, Mr. Green placed his hands on his hips and added, "Besides... Doc owes me a personal favor or two."

Equally desperate to avoid a scandal, Mr. Arnold readily agreed to comply with Mr. Green's plan.

A century passed.

It was the early 1970's, and my brother Carl and I were both 18 years of age. Both of us were also still members of the Parapsychology Investigation and Research Organization, affiliated with Rhode Island College. It was during the summer immediately following my high school graduation, in fact, that I took it upon myself to place a small notice in a local publication, advertising our free services to investigate alleged haunted locations. I figured what did I have to lose by doing so except for possible ridicule?

Somewhat to my surprise, I admit, the ad actually received a response less than a few weeks after it appeared. The individual who responded to the ad was a woman named Carolyn. She, along with her family, had been experiencing unexplained problems since they'd moved into their historic 18th Century farmhouse in Harrisville the previous year. She asked if we might be able to shed some possible light on what was happening to her and her family.

We readily agreed, and, following a telephone conversation arranged to meet with Carolyn later that very week. Our initial interview with her was held privately in a conference room at Rhode Island College. Present at the interview besides Carolyn and our Chairperson Donna, were members Jay, Billy, Michael, my brother Carl and myself. Upon first meeting Carolyn, she was a slim, attractive woman in her thirties… nicely dressed, with long dark hair and high cheekbones.

However, from the noticeable dark circles underneath her eyes, it seemed apparent that she'd recently been suffering from sleep deprivation, which she later confirmed. A pleasant, educated individual, Carolyn spoke very coherently as she related her story to us.

Several months earlier, she and her husband Roger had relocated from the mid-west to Rhode Island with their teenage daughter and three younger girls. The house they'd moved into, and in which they currently lived, was an historic, quaint looking farmhouse located on Round Top Road in the Harrisville section of Burrillville.

Built in the year 1768 and officially known as the 'Arnold-Richardson House,' it had eleven rooms, as well as a barn out in the back. Although the house itself was in relatively good condition, the most recent owner had neglected both the interior and exterior. However, Roger was very handy and was looking forward to taking care of most of the repairs himself. As for Carolyn, this antiquated farmhouse was the ideal kind of place she'd always dreamed of living in. In fact, she actually had the feeling that she'd been somehow guided to this very house. Seemingly as if to confirm this, on the day Carolyn first met the previous owner – a reclusive yet friendly older gentleman named Earl – he personally welcomed her with an air of familiarity. "My dear," he'd addressed her as if they were already close friends, "I just know that you and your lovely family were meant to live here in this house. I felt it the first moment we met. It's almost as though this house has been waiting for you, Carolyn."

Carolyn had replied with enthusiasm, "Well, Earl, that must be true, because I know I've had dreams of living in a farmhouse with a barn exactly like this, right down to every detail!"

It wasn't long after Carolyn and her family moved in, however, before the problems started. To begin with, whenever Roger would set about the renovations, something inexplicable always seemed to occur to hinder his progress. Either a tool would suddenly be missing from right where he knew he'd just left it, or he'd inevitably wind up cutting or injuring himself in some way. Roger was both annoyed and baffled at this, since he was skilled with home repair, and had never been so accident prone before.

Also, whenever Carolyn was alone inside the house, especially upstairs on the second floor where the children's bedrooms were, she often had the unnerving feeling that she was being watched. Sometimes she'd experience sudden cold spots in the upstairs area. At other times the air in certain rooms would suddenly become thick and nauseating, forcing her to retreat back downstairs.

On the first floor, the original wooden door leading to the cellar would seemingly open about half an inch by itself at certain times of the night, even after the family remembered locking it. One night Carolyn's husband Roger finally secured the cellar door by tying a knotted rope over the lock. However, at approximately 3:00 AM that night, a loud snapping sound from downstairs awakened the family. When they rushed into the kitchen area where the sound had seemed to come from, they found that the knotted rope now split apart with the ends frayed. Once again the door was opened about half an inch. From then on, they allowed the door to remain open just a crack overnight and only kept it completely shut during the day, which seemed to suffice.

One morning Carolyn was sorting clothes in an upstairs bedroom closet, when the by now familiar thick, uneasy feeling of being watched came over her. This time, instead of acknowledging it by rushing back downstairs, Carolyn was determined to first finish her chores. As she continued sorting the clothes, an empty coat hanger suddenly leapt off of the rack by itself, and began forcefully rapping her on top of her head as if wielded by an unseen hand. Carolyn raised her arms defensively to shield her head from the blows, which caused the coat hanger to clatter lifelessly to the floor. She then fled down the staircase, nearly losing her balance as she did so. Back downstairs in the kitchen, Carolyn was badly shaken, but otherwise unharmed. Glancing back at the staircase, which lead to the upstairs bedrooms, she hissed through her teeth, "You son-of-a-bitch! Leave me the hell alone!!"

Needless to say, Carolyn and her family soon came to the conclusion that something was definitely wrong with their newly purchased residence...VERY wrong! Upstairs two of her younger girls were starting to complain about hearing strange noises and of sometimes being touched and even shoved while they were in bed.

Carolyn's youngest daughter even claimed to have seen a man dressed in "old fashioned clothes" standing on the staircase early one evening. Concerned, Carolyn asked her, "Did he try to speak to you?" Her daughter replied, "No, he just kinda' stood there staring at me for awhile, without saying anything." After that, Roger and Carolyn allowed the youngest girls to sleep with them in their downstairs bedroom whenever they were feeling overly frightened.

The atmosphere in the dank smelling cellar felt even more oppressive than any of the upstairs rooms, so much so that even Roger felt uncomfortable when having to be down there for any extended period of time. Carolyn would only briefly venture into the cellar and that when absolutely necessary, to do the family laundry or to get supplies, and then she'd return upstairs as quickly as possible.

The bizarre activity wasn't just confined to the house itself. Within the first few months of Carolyn and her family taking up residence in Harrisville, at least two horrible vehicular accidents took place on Round Top Road right in front of their house. One of these accidents, involving a young motorcycle rider, had resulted in the young man's severed arm winding up on Carolyn's front lawn! Also, the barn out in back felt every bit as oppressive as the main house cellar, if not more so. In fact for some reason, the interior of the barn seemed to have a foreboding atmosphere all its own.

With all of this, Roger and Carolyn remained as upbeat as possible. They'd invested a great deal of money into their new home, practically their entire life savings excepting the children's college money, so they were determined to remain here as a family. As the weeks passed, Carolyn eventually developed a sense of humor regarding some of the mysterious activity surrounding her new home, especially regarding the animated coat hanger, which had suddenly sprung to life and attacked her. "Talk about your basic slap*stick!*" she privately said to Roger with a laugh.

Carolyn gradually began to make several friendly acquaintances within the community while she was out shopping or tending to other errands. She also toyed with the idea of hosting a housewarming party once more renovations had been done, and perhaps even publicly displaying some of her artwork in the community. One morning Carolyn unexpectedly made another new acquaintance, when an older gentleman knocked on the front door and politely introduced himself as one of her neighbors and an old friend of the previous owner Earl.

This older man explained to Carolyn that he and his family had lived in this area for generations, dating back to the time when the town was first founded. He also claimed to possess a wealth of knowledge about the history of the entire town, *including* her house, and that he'd be very willing to share it with her if she was interested. Since this somewhat eccentric older man seemed relatively harmless, Carolyn figured he was probably lonely and very eager for someone to chat with, especially since his long-time friend Earl had now moved away. Besides, if he really did know all about the history of her historic farmhouse, perhaps he could shed some light on the peculiar events which she and her family had recently been experiencing.

What the older man shared with Carolyn about the house both shocked and intrigued her. He explained that a long time ago, back in the mid-1800's, the grisly murder of a 12-year-old girl by the name of Prudence Arnold had taken place in this house. The poor girl's throat had been slashed by a straight razor. After committing this horrid crime, the murderer had attempted to cut his throat with the same razor, but found that it was now too dull to accomplish the task. This was coupled with the fact that he was also too drunk to find his own jugular vein. His only apparent motive in killing young Prudence was a mere $2.00. However, there were also rumors that this man, who was in his mid-twenties, had committed this savage act of murder, after 12-year-old Prudence refused to become his bride.

There was also a woman, rumored to have been a witch who used to live in this house around the time of the murder of young Prudence. Supposedly she killed a baby in the house while babysitting for it, because she was at odds with the Arnold family, to whom the baby belonged. But, they couldn't prove it, so she was never convicted. In her defense, this woman who'd had charge over the child, said that she'd momentarily laid the poor infant on a dressing table… and that when she'd done so, a sewing needle had accidentally been imbedded into the soft spot of the infant's skull. But it was quite possibly an act of retribution against the Arnold family, whom she intensely disliked. This same woman was rumored to also have drowned at least one of her own children in the basement well, although this particular story was never verified.

Carolyn anxiously pressed her new friend for more info about this alleged 'witch' who once lived in the same house she and her family now occupied. The older man said that she eventually married a local gentleman who was financially well off, and that she'd supposedly run their farm like a tyrant. She was said to have been very mean and cruel to the hired farm hands. In fact, they'd probably all celebrated when she'd met her fate. Carolyn then asked, "What did happen to this supposed 'witch' who lived here?"

The older man replied, "Oh, she hung herself in your barn out in back, when she was really old. Rumor was that her husband tried to cover up her suicide to avoid a scandal, but that some of the farmhands knew what really happened."

Carolyn asked her new friend if there was anything else he could tell her about the tragic history of her house. It was still sometime in the 1800's, he explained, that another member of the Arnold family living here in the Arnold-Richardson House committed suicide by drinking horse liniment. Also around the turn of the century, when Edwin Arnold owned the house, a man who was said to have been a lawyer was found frozen to death one winter morning inside of Edwin's shed. Not long after *this* incident, Edwin Arnold himself mysteriously disappeared one winter night. Edwin's frozen body was eventually discovered several weeks later in the woods of Harrisville, with no apparent signs of foul play.

Before her older neighbor left that day, Carolyn asked him if his friend Earl, the previous owner, ever mentioned having experienced anything unusual in this house. All he could tell her was that Earl was known to have always kept all of the lights on in the house overnight. Earl had never told him why, and he'd never bothered to ask.

Very soon after their elderly neighbor's visit, the activity in Roger's and Carolyn's house dramatically began to pick up, almost as if the spirits of the past had resented being talked about so graphically. The man dressed in the old-fashioned clothes which Carolyn's youngest daughter, Darlene had seen on the staircase was now reappearing to her. Only now the 'ghost-man' had given her a name, 'Eric.'

Also, the basement door would now sometimes immediately and forcefully reopen by itself at night, if anyone dared to shut it. Carolyn herself would no longer go down into the basement by herself after hearing her neighbor's story of a young child having possibly been drowned in the basement well. Besides, even with all of the overhead light bulbs on, the old dank basement still remained unnaturally dark and foreboding. On more than one occasion, Carolyn felt herself being touched on her left shoulder and her long dark hair being yanked while she was down in the basement.

Her husband Roger had now all but given up on the house renovations, due to repeated, unexplained mishaps. Although Roger had always prided himself on his logic and rationality, he finally told Carolyn in frustration, "Something here just does not want me to finish remodeling this damn house!"

Within the next couple of weeks, the activity both inside and outside of the Arnold-Richardson House began taking on a bizarre new twist. Not only did the door leading to the cellar stairs refuse to stay closed at night, but a heavy oak door leading from the cellar to the outside now refused to remain shut at night as well. Latching and locking it did not seem to matter at all. Both Carolyn and Roger were especially concerned about this, for fear of intruders out here in the darkened wooded area. Finally Roger not only secured the door with a heavy padlock, but also with a thick 2-by-4 inch wooden plank.

At about 2:00 AM that morning, what sounded like an explosion was heard form just outside, jolting the entire family from their sleep.

After immediately telephoning the local police, Roger and Carolyn ordered the younger girls to remain inside the house with their older sister while they went out to investigate. Unbelievably, they found that the outside door leading to the cellar, was not only open, but was now hanging partway off of its hinges! The police arrived within fifteen minutes and made a preliminary investigation, but could find no traces of a forced entry. In fact, one of the police officers mentioned to Roger that the door had been smashed off of its top hinges from the inside. Exasperated, Roger asked him, "Are you trying to tell me that someone was trying to bust OUT of my cellar?"

The patrolman replied, "Not at all, sir; just making an observation. All I'm saying is it doesn't appear to be a typical forced entry."

After conducting a thorough search of the cellar and the entire house, the police promised Roger and Carolyn that they would patrol the area of Round Top Road for the remainder of the night, and write up a report of the incident.

Roger did his best to repair the damaged door. Then a few mornings later, the family found one of the children's pet rabbits dead in the securely caged pen near the shed. Not only was the rabbit dead, but also its underside was horribly mutilated, as if it had been sliced open with a sharp instrument. But the strangest thing was, there were no signs at all that the wire cage surrounding the small pen had even been tampered with. Roger and Carolyn again called the Burrillville police. The police arrived and made a thorough search of the entire area surround the shed, but just as the last time, they could find no sign of an intruder.

As Carolyn was still attempting to console her youngest daughter Darlene, she asked one of the police officers how this could have possibly happened to one of their pet rabbits, especially since the protective wire surrounding the pen didn't even appear to have been disturbed. Somewhat embarrassed at not having a logical explanation, the young police officer merely shrugged and told her. "Strange things simply seem to happened in this area from time to time, Ma'am. Sorry."

By this time, Roger and Carolyn were beginning to fear that the police might be wondering if they were a couple of crackpots, or if they'd perhaps been perpetrating some of this activity themselves. After all, in both instances where the Burrillville police had been called out to their house to investigate, they'd found no evidence of any outside intruder having been responsible. All the police had to go on were the words of Roger and Carolyn themselves. They were now at their wit's end as to where they could turn for help. Although they'd considered asking for assistance from the local church, they were also concerned as to how their story might be received. After all, they were still relatively new to this town, and did not regularly attend worship services.

At Roger's place of employment, he'd mentioned to a few of his co-workers some of the details of what he and his family had been experiencing in their new home. No one there could really offer any practical advice either. Roger also feared the possibility of facing ridicule at the workplace, if he began confiding everything that was going on. After all, how would he have reacted only several months ago, if someone had told *him* this same story? Wouldn't he have begun to question their sanity?

As if to make matters worse, around mid-July, Roger and the two younger girls broke out with what appeared to be a case of hives, causing unsightly swellings to erupt on their faces and bodies. However, a trip to the doctor revealed that what they took to be hives was in reality a severe case of staff infection, requiring them to be placed on heavy doses of anti-biotic for an extended period.

Then one afternoon, Carolyn happened to be alone in the kitchen peeling an orange, when she suddenly became aware of what appeared to be blood trickling onto the kitchen floor. Assuming she'd accidentally cut herself, she instantly rushed over to the kitchen sink to wash to flow of blood and inspect the wound. However, unbelievable as it seemed, Carolyn could find no trace of a wound at all... the blood was actually oozing from the orange itself! "Am I outright loosing my mind?" she wondered aloud. And yet, there was no denying what she had just witnessed. Before her youngest daughter had the chance to wander into the room, Carolyn quickly washed the blood from the floor and the sink, and stuffed the bloody orange into the trash. Glancing up at the ceiling, Carolyn had then said to no one in particular, "Why are you doing this to us? Why?"

It was less than a week after this incident that Carolyn happened to notice my small add in a local publication advertising the services of our paranormal research organization. At this point, she figured she had nothing to lose, and had contacted us in the hope that we might be able to give at least some insight into her situation.

This was her story and after finishing her narrative, Carolyn paused and looked around at each of us who were seated with her at the conference room table and asked, "So... do you think I'm crazy, after telling you all of this?"

"Absolutely not," I assured her. "I want you to know that we understand, and that you're no longer alone in this."

For the first time since we'd met, Carolyn smiled. "Thank you, so much," she said with obvious relief. "I was so afraid that you might think I was nuts!"

"Not at all," said Carl. "Hey, some people would consider us nuts to be involved in the field of parapsychology."

Now much more at ease, Carolyn said, "Alright, my next question is, would you be willing to come out to my house in Harrisville to investigate my situation?"

"Absolutely," Carl and I both replied simultaneously.

Our chairperson Donna was also ready and willing. She then asked the other members if, after having now heard the details of the case, they were willing to participate in an on-site investigation at Carolyn's house. Jay, Billy and Michael were in agreement as well.

Donna then asked if any of us had any additional questions for Carolyn. Turning to Carolyn who was seated to my left, I asked, "Have you or any of you family members heard any poundings, scratching or unusual sounds in your house?"

Carolyn replied, "Yes, occasionally, now that you mention it. Once there was loud cracking sound, like lightening had struck the house, although there was no storm outside, and we couldn't find any signs of damage. But sometimes we do hear scratching and knocking in the walls at night."

"Is there ever any cadence or succession to these sounds, like a certain number of times in a row?" I asked.

"Usually there'll be three knocks in a row," said Carolyn. "Is that significant?"

"Well, it could be," I said. "There are certain types of entities which tend to follow specific patterns. And when you were touched down in the basement, you mentioned that it was on your left shoulder, correct?"

"Yes, on my left shoulder," said Carolyn.

Carl then asked, "Have you heard any talking or whispering going on in rooms, which you know for a fact isn't caused by family members?"

Carolyn replied, "I haven't, personally. But a few of the children have told me they've heard whispering coming from one of the empty upstairs rooms, although they couldn't quite make out what was being said. From what they told me, I guess it sounded more like gibberish."

Donna asked, "How about sudden, extreme changes in temperature, such as cold spots?"

"Not so much cold spots," said Carolyn. "Just that sudden very uncomfortable feeling of being watched, mostly in one of the upstairs rooms where the children heard the whispering, and in the cellar. Sometimes out in the barn, too."

"Have you or your family members ever experienced any unusual or unexplained odors anywhere in the house?" asked Donna.

"Just the musty smell which wafts up from the cellar when the doors opened, but I guess that would only be natural coming from an old, dank cellar," said Carolyn.

Before our meeting concluded, Carl asked, "Is there anything else you can think of, Carolyn, that you might like to add?"

"Nothing that I can think of, right now," she said. "But if I think of anything else, I'll be sure to give you people a call and let you know."

We then agreed to set the date of our investigation for the following Saturday evening. As we all rose to leave, Carolyn sincerely told us, "I really can't thank you people enough, for listening to me and for agreeing to come out to my house. You don't know how much better I feel already, knowing that you don't think me crazy after all I've told you."

Extending my hand to her, I said, "That's what we're here for. And please believe me when I say, that we'll do everything we can to help you. In the meantime, I'll be sure to keep you and your family in my prayers."

"Thank you, so very much," Carolyn said with a smile, placing her hand in mine. Although she spoke calmly enough, I noticed that Carolyn's slender fingers were slightly trembling.

That Saturday, I spent the daytime hours working at my part-time landscaping job. One advantage of this to me personally, was that I could at least pray and sing reassuring hymns out loud while mowing lawns, and no one would be able to overhear me. Our final assignment that afternoon was tending to the grounds of the Sprague Mansion in Cranston, itself a reputedly haunted location. Experiencing the dull yet perceptible psychic current emanating from the mansion actually helped to prepare me for the evening ahead.

As soon as I arrived back home in Scituate late that afternoon, my fellow P.I.R.O. members Carl, Donna, Jay, Michael and Billy were present and ready for us to be on our way. Although the others were freshly showered and dressed nicely, there was really no time for me to even throw on a quick change of clothes or to clean up at all. In fact, all I really had time to do was grab my Bible, trusting that our equipment was already packed, before we were out the door and on our way to Harrisville. Fortunately, this time I was not the one driving, which allowed me to read appropriate Scriptures and prayerfully meditate during the entire trip.

About an hour later the six of us arrived at the Arnold-Richardson House just off of Round Top Road, and were welcomed by Carolyn and her husband Roger. Roger himself was a good-looking gentleman who appeared to be in his mid-to-late-thirties, with curly brown hair and a neatly trimmed moustache. There was unfortunately a pronounced swelling on his left cheek, obviously lingering from his recent staph infection which Carolyn had told us about. Carolyn also introduced us to her three girls. The younger two had come rushing out to meet us, excitedly letting us know that they'd been waiting all day long for the 'ghost people' to arrive at their house!

The exterior of their antiquated farmhouse appeared to be in relatively good shape, with original pine clapboards still securely in place and a split rail fence cris-crossing along the front lawn. Since it was still early in the evening when we arrived with a good half-hour or so of daylight remaining Carolyn and Roger to give us a brief tour of the grounds. As they explained to us, the house was built on what had originally been a thousand-acre stretch of property. Now, however, only eight and a half acres remained with the house, the rest having either been sold off or assimilated by the state's Round Top Management Area.

The first place Carolyn and Roger took us to was the large barn out in back of their house. Upon entering it along with the rest of our group members, I instantly experienced an inclination that something was not right in here. It was the distinct feeling of being watched from the shadows of the barn's interior. Although at the time I refrained from mentioning this to the others, both Donna and Carl later reported having experienced the same foreboding sensation within the barn. Pointing to a low hanging overhead wooden beam near the center of the barn, Roger informed us, "This is supposedly the beam which the old woman hanged herself many years ago, at least according to what our neighbor told us. She's the one who was supposed to be a witch."

Observing the low level of the beam to the ground, I commented, "She must've been an extremely short woman, to have been able to suspend herself from here."

"Yes, she certainly must have been," Roger agreed.

As we were leaving the barn, Carl asked, "About this woman who was supposedly a practitioner of the black arts... did anyone ever find out what her name was, or why she hanged herself?"

Roger replied, "No, our neighbor never told us her name, or why she decided to end her life."

Carolyn added, "We'll ask our neighbor if he has any idea, next time he comes around. And like I said, we couldn't find any mention of her in the town records."

Continuing the tour, just outside of her house, Carolyn pointed out the door that had been partially torn off of its hinges, now temporarily nailed back together. This was also right beside the rabbit pen, where one of their pet rabbits had recently been found slashed and gutted.

When Carolyn took us into the house itself, it felt like stepping back in time to another era. Although much disarray and clutter was apparent, and the renovations were only in the beginning stages, the place gave off the feel of antiquity. Upon first entering the house, there was also an immediate sense of oppression... *not* overwhelming, but definitely noticeable. It was as if something just felt 'wrong' about the atmosphere within the house, seemingly as though prolonged exposure to this environment might result in illness. At least, that was my initial impression.

Carolyn then began leading us on a tour of her eleven-room house, beginning by showing us the inside cellar door that always remained open at least a crack at night. Along with the others, I followed Carolyn as we ventured downstairs to the dank basement. Carolyn had been right when she'd told us that there always seemed to be a certain ominous darkness to the cellar. In fact, all but a few of the overhead light bulbs were operational, and those that were functional did little to dispel the gloom.

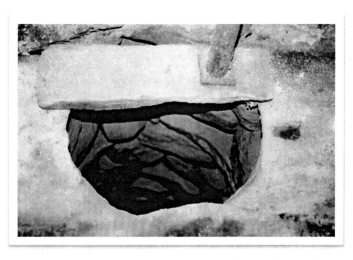

Basement well in which two children were allegedly drowned in Harrisville, R.I.

Carolyn reminded us that she did not like coming down here alone in the daytime, much less after dark. She also showed us the basement well, which was securely covered over with wooden planks. "This is where the supposed 'witch' was rumored to have drowned one or two of her children," she said, adding, "But of course, that may have been just fabricated. In fact, I pray that it is just a made up story." We were then glad to return upstairs, away from the musty-smelling air of the cellar, as well as the clumps of spider webs that we had to brush off of our clothing.

Once we were back upstairs, we tried experimenting with the cellar door a bit, by closing it and waiting to see whether it would open again while we watched. However, it seemed that the 'opening door' was just not going to perform on cue for us.

As soon as Carolyn had finished showing us the entire first floor, she led us up the rather narrow staircase leading to the upstairs bedrooms. She paused at one point to remind us that this was where her youngest daughter, Darlene, had more than once encountered the figure of a man named 'Eric' dressed in old fashioned clothes. Continuing on to the upstairs section, Carolyn also pointed out the closet from which the empty clothes hanger had 'attacked' her.

Once we were back downstairs, Carolyn politely offered us refreshments, while humorously assuring us: "I promise not to give you any 'bleeding oranges' if I can help it."

With a laugh, Carl told her, "Actually that might turn out to be a plus, since we could document that as evidence." The iced tea Carolyn served went down nicely, especially since I'd spent the entire day at my landscaping job. Carolyn's young daughters seemed to be particularly fond of me, even though I hadn't had a chance to change out of my landscaping clothes before rushing to leave. In fact, as it turned out, no one had even bothered packing what rudimentary equipment we possessed.

After refreshments, Carolyn's three youngest daughters ran into the room and began asking for me to accompany them outside before the sun had completely set. Apparently they were intent on giving me their own private tour *and* interview. Their mother apologized to me, saying, "They seem to have taken a liking to you, Keith, probably because you paid attention to them earlier. I hope they're not getting into your hair too much."

"No, not at all," I assured her. "They girls told me that I remind them of David Carridine, which I hope was a compliment."

Carolyn told me, "I think also like a young Danny Kaye, both you and your brother Carl."

Actually, I was able to glean some additional information from the children, from their own perspective. For one thing, I learned that not only had they experienced the 'ghost man' on the stairs – but they'd also glimpsed an older woman, and even a cat. I asked if they felt afraid of these ghosts. They replied that they weren't, of *these* particular ghosts. However, there was also a 'mean ghost' of which they were terrified, which would sometimes touch or pinch them while they were in bed at night. "Do any of you ever see this 'mean ghost'?" I asked them.

The second youngest girl replied, "I have, just a couple of times." When I asked her to describe it, she said that it really didn't have any face that she could see, but that it was more like a black shadow. Once she'd seen it standing in a corner of the bedroom she and her sister shared, and another time she'd awoken to see it standing right over her bed, looking straight down at her. She'd tried to scream, but couldn't, so instead she'd hid under the covers and prayed for it to go away. I asked, "And then did it go away when you prayed?"

"Yes, when I finally dared to look again, it was gone," she said, adding, "but I was underneath my covers almost the rest of the night."

"I can't blame you there," I said with a smile.

When I asked the eldest daughter, Andrea, what she'd experienced in the house, she explained, "Well, I haven't actually seen the ghost cat, or the young man and the older woman they were telling you about. I've been lightly touched a couple of times on the staircase by what I think was the spirit they call Eric, and that didn't really bother me. Especially since it happened in the daytime. But I can tell you, Keith, there is definitely something else here, and it's something that's not good. I've seen the shadow figure in the basement a couple of times, out of the corner of my eye."

"Has anything else happened to you in the basement?" I asked her.

"Once when I was alone down there, something which felt like a hand seemed to be pressing against my back, almost like it was about to shove me. That's all it took for me to high-tail it back upstairs!" Andrea then added, "And I think this shadow ghost, which seems to come up from the basement after sunset, is the one that always keeps the cellar door open just a crack at night. I feel that it's also the one that was responsible for the other cellar door being partially ripped off of its hinges, and for one of our rabbits being killed and mutilated."

The time was now approximately 8:00 PM. While doing a walk-through of the first floor bedrooms with the others, Carl suddenly glimpsed a flash of movement out of the right corner of his visual field. Turning, he saw what appeared to be a murky, semi-transparent mist slowly floating several feet in front of him. He was only able to observe this shadowy form for perhaps a few seconds, before it completely vanished.

Carl alerted Donna and the rest of us to what he'd just witnessed, causing Donna to gasp. He explained that the mist-like, indistinct form seemed to be gliding in the direction of Roger and Carolyn's downstairs bedroom just before it had dissipated. When the other investigators were asked if they'd experienced anything unusual on the first floor, both Jay and Michael reported having experienced a peculiar icy sensation in Roger and Carolyn's bedroom. As Jay explained it, "It was only for a brief moment, but in that moment, it felt like a prickly sensation on the back of my neck."

Carl, Jay and Michael then decided to venture down into the cellar and keep vigil there for the next half-hour or so. Donna, Billy and myself would remain upstairs with the family.

During this time, Carolyn's four children asked me to accompany them upstairs, where they personally were most terrified at night. Once upstairs, I asked them, "Where is it that you're most afraid to be up here?"

"Right in here," said Nancy, indicating the room we were in, which she shared with her two younger sisters. With tears now beginning to well up in her eyes, she said, "Sometimes people tell us there are no such things as ghosts. Some of our friends even call us crazy. But we know that these things do happen, especially at night and we're so afraid to be in here at night."

Andrea agreed, saying, "I'm afraid that's true."

Touched by the fact that this teenage girl and her three younger sisters were feeling so frightened in their own house, I asked them, "Listen, you do sometimes attend church together as a family, right? I remember your mom mentioning something about that to me."

Andrea answered, "Well, not every week, but sometimes we all go together as a family, yes."

"And you are believers?" I asked.

"Yes, we are," said Andrea. Her three younger sisters all nodded in agreement.

"Well, when you are feeling frightened," I told them, "try calling upon the name of Jesus-"

No sooner had I mentioned the name of Jesus, then the bedroom window to my immediate right, which had been opened halfway, suddenly slammed shut with tremendous force, causing the three girls to gasp in shock. At the same moment the air in the room instantly turned thick and somewhat nauseating. Nancy suddenly screamed in pain as her head tilted sharply, as though she'd just been struck on the left side of her head by an unseen hand. "Something just hit me!" she cried out in tears clutching her head with both hands.

Now angered that an invisible coward had struck one of these children, I told them, "Don't be afraid! Jesus is much more powerful, and it fears the very name of Jesus!"

In an instant the atmosphere in the bedroom changed back to normal, and a noticeable feeling of peace seemed to be surrounding us. Smiling, I said to them, "You see? It's gone from the room now, because it has to retreat in the name of Jesus. Just as it says in the Bible, *Jesus watches over his children, for of such is the Kingdom of God.*"

Wiping her eyes, Nancy said, "You're right, it's gone from the room. I can feel it!" She then smiled brightly and threw her arms around me, saying, "I'm not afraid now!" The two younger girls threw her arms around me as well, in one big hug.

With a laugh, Andrea told her younger sisters, "Don't strangle him now; at least let him breathe!"

As soon as the five of us returned back downstairs, Carolyn's three younger daughters excitedly ran into the parlor to tell their mother and father what had happened. "Mom, Dad, guess what *just* happened!" said Nancy. "We were all upstairs in my bedroom, when suddenly a window slammed shut real hard, and I got slapped on the head. But then, Keith said a prayer to Jesus, and the bad ghost left the room right away!"

"What?" asked Carolyn, as she and Roger looked at their daughters in surprise.

"It's true!" her two younger sisters said while jumping up and down in excitement.

Both Roger and Carolyn then glanced from me to Andrea. "Yes," said Andrea, "it's *all* true; that's exactly what happened." Roger and Carolyn both smiled, and expressed how relieved they were to see the girls elated instead of frightened.

Over the next hour, a strange tension among some of our investigators began building, as we sat there discussing our combined experiences in the house. A few of our team members even became a bit quarrelsome and ill feeling, until Michael and Billy expressed a desire to leave, claiming they were starting not to feel well. Smiling apologetically, Carolyn told them, "I'm afraid this house sometimes has that effect on people, especially at night."

Shortly before we left, Andrea approached me and asked if I would accompany her down into the cellar. She'd forgotten a few canned items from down there during the day. "Would you mind, Keith?" she asked. "Not that I'm a chicken, but…"

"I understand, there's safety in numbers," I said. For another thing, the cellar door leading from the kitchen had by now apparently opened on its own again, while no one was watching. While we were briefly down in the cellar, Andrea began trembling, but felt somewhat relieved when we said a quick prayer of protection together. We then hurried back upstairs.

Keith investigates the basement of the Harricville, R.I. residence.

"Whew!" said Andrea, wiping the cans off with a rag before setting them on the kitchen counter. "I'm glad that's over with. Thank you for coming with me."

"You're welcome," I said.

After checking to make certain that her younger siblings were nowhere nearby listening, Andrea asked me, "Keith, in your personal opinion, what do you think the evil presence in this house is? I don't mean Eric; I mean the malicious one."

"Well, in my personal opinion, I believe that it's a demonic entity, which may have been drawn in here by the woman who practiced witchcraft here all those years ago. It may even have enticed this woman into hanging herself."

Nodding, Andrea said, "I have to agree with you, Keith. That's exactly what I believe, too."

As we were leaving, Donna informed Roger and Carolyn, "Our next step will be to discuss our findings at our next group meeting, which will be early next week. Then I'll give you a call, and arrange with you for a follow-up visit, if that's alright with the both of you."

"Oh, yes, that would be most welcome," said Carolyn. "I just can't thank you people enough for coming all this way out here tonight, and for *not* thinking were crazy."

"Yes, thank you so much for all you've done," added Roger.

Carl assured them, "Believe me, after what we've experienced here tonight, we certainly don't consider you to be crazy."

"I'll say!" Donna agreed. "And don't worry, because like I said, we'll be following up on this."

"In the meantime," I said, "I'll be praying for your protection, and for the protection of your children. We're going to do all in our power to help you."

Once again, Roger and Carolyn sincerely expressed their gratitude to us. Carolyn added, "At least now we know that we're not alone in our situation, and that there's a light at the end of the tunnel."

The three younger girls then came running over to me, tugging on my sleeves and making me promise to come back and visit them again very soon. Nancy said, "Come back to see us again next Saturday, Keith, or even sooner!"

With a laugh, I told them, "Don't worry, I will."

Andrea then did her best to pull them away from me, while saying, "Thank you Keith. "I guess I'll see you when you come here again, hopefully next week."

As soon as we were back in our car with the engine started, Donna told us, "I don't know about you guys, but I don't think I'm gonna get much sleep for the rest of the week, especially not after tonight!"

Early on Tuesday evening, during our weekly meeting of P.I.R.O., we discussed our combined experiences during our visit at the Arnold-Richardson House in Harrisville. Unfortunately, because we'd brought no equipment with us, we'd been unable to capture any concrete photographic or audio evidence. But our personal observations had left us all with little doubt that something of a paranormal nature was making life uncomfortable for the family in that house.

When we began discussing what our next step should be in assisting the family with their situation, Carl reiterated that a return trip was definitely in order, preferably on the upcoming Saturday evening if not sooner. Our Chairperson Donna replied, "I totally agree that we should conduct a follow-up investigation, and the sooner the better. But speaking for myself, there's just no way that I'm setting foot in that house again after dark. I'm sorry, but I'm not up to another nighttime investigation."

Carl said, "We understand that, Donna, and we can try to work around that. The same goes for anyone who may feel uncomfortable about going back to the Harrisville house after dark or even going back there at all. No one here will hold it against you."

Michael interjected, "Actually, now that you mention it, I'm also feeling a little uncomfortable about going back there, at least so soon. I'm sorry."

Donna told him, "Nothing to be sorry about, Michael. We appreciate your honesty. Billy, how do you feel?"

Sounding somewhat relieved that Michael had spoken up Billy admitted that he too might feel a little uncomfortable about going back as well.

"Again, that's understandable," said Carl. "This case came upon us all pretty fast, and for being our first major investigation, we're having to deal with a very real and serious situation here. So, I assume that leaves just Donna, myself and Keith, correct?" Donna and I both nodded in agreement.

Turning to me, Donna asked, "Keith, is there anything you'd like to add at this time?"

"Actually, yes, I'd like to offer a suggestion," I said. "Like Carl said, we're involved in a rather heavy situation here, maybe it might be a good idea if we were to consult with Ed and Lorraine Warren on this. I mean, after all, they do have years of experience dealing with these types of situations. That way, we could at least gain some added insight."

The other members readily agreed with my suggestion. Donna said she would contact them on behalf of our organization.

When Donna asked if anyone else had any final comments, I said, "It's too bad that we don't have access to the Science Department. Think of the equipment we could be using on this case, to measure temperature changes and electrical fluctuations... even video, to monitor the two cellar doors in Carolyn's house."

"Yes, that *is* unfortunate," agreed Carl. "But, the lab equipment certainly isn't available to us now, this being summer vacation and all. All I can suggest, Keith, is that you try filming the cellar door with your Super 8 movie camera, although that would most likely prove to be an expensive waste of film."

Shortly after our meeting concluded a familiar figure from across the hall stopped by to greet us. This was Ron, who ran the only other 'rival' paranormal investigation group at Rhode Island College. "Hi, guys", he said. "Just thought I'd stop by and see what's up."

"Hi, Ron," Donna greeted him in return. "We're just finishing up our meeting."

"Yeah, we just finished ours, too," said Ron. Adjusting his glasses as he glanced around the room, he said, "I see you guys are having pizza."

Out of politeness I told him, "Come in and have a slice Ron."

"I don't want to intrude," he said.

Carl told him, "No, you're not intruding. Like Donna said, we just finished. C'mon in and join us."

"Well, okay, don't mind if I do. Thanks." Ron then walked in and eased his large, bulky frame into the chair beside me.

Pushing the pizza box towards him I said, "Help yourself."

"Thanks, Keith," he said, grabbing a slice.

"So, Ron, how many members are there in your group now?" I asked him.

In between munches, he replied, "Oh, it's still just the two of us, just me an' Dave."

"Well, it's good to keep small," I said. "Less confusing that way."

"Absolutely," agreed Ron, while reaching for another slice. He then took me a bit off guard by saying, "So, word's out that you guys are involved in a pretty interesting case somewhere. Is that true?"

Quickly I replied, "Well, I think all our cases are interesting, even if they don't always turn out to yield a lot of evidence."

"Yeah, but what's the case you're working on now?" Ron persisted. "You can tell me, investigator to investigator. I promise, it won't go any further than me."

"Yes, Ron, but still there's a matter of client confidentiality," I reminded him. Overhearing our conversation, Donna added, "That's right, Ron, we can't really divulge any details of what we're investigating, unless it's something like a field investigation." With a shrug, Ron ran a hand through his thick red hair and said, "Oh. Okay, that's cool, I understand." With that Ron said his goodnights to us and left.

Donna was successful in contacting the Warren's in Connecticut the very next day. After hearing the details of the case, Ed and Lorraine even volunteered to become personally involved. We arranged that they, along my brother Carl and Donna, would meet up together at the Arnold-Richardson House early on Saturday afternoon. Unfortunately I was scheduled to work my part-time landscaping job and was sorely disappointed at not being able to accompany Donna and Carl on the follow-up investigation in Harrisville.

Since Donna had requested that they not remain there after sunset, I would not even be able to meet them there later on. This being the case, I'd simply have to wait until after I returned home from a day of mowing lawns, for Carl to fill me in. Ironically, at the end of that workday, my supervisor called me into his office and informed me that work was becoming scarce, and he therefore had to let me go.

Back at home, I asked Carl how the follow-up investigation in Harrisville had gone. "It went extremely well," he replied. "We met up with Ed and Lorraine, who arrived almost the exact same time as we did. Of course, Roger's and Carolyn's kids were very disappointed that you weren't there. They kept asking, *Where's* Keith? *Where's* Keith?"

"Oh, I'm disappointed too," I said. "I hope you told the kids that I'll be there next time."

"Yes, I assured them you would be. Anyway, there have been a couple of new developments since we were there just a week ago. For one thing, Roger showed us a row of scratches he received on his left arm, from something unseen. Also, Carolyn looks very drawn and appears to be losing even more weight. She's been to their family doctor for a check up, but he just attributed it to stress. But, Roger and Carolyn were very grateful to have such two experienced investigators as the Warren's there."

"And did they find anything significant?" I asked.

Carl explained, "The two of them thoroughly interviewed Roger and Carolyn, and then did a complete walk-through of their house, during which Lorraine claimed to have sensed a malevolent presence in the cellar. I experienced a brief but intense cold spot in Carolyn's bedroom myself."

"So, what's our next step?" I asked.

"As it stands, we all plan to meet up again in Harrisville next Saturday afternoon. The Warren's even discussed the possibility of bringing in some Catholic clergy on this case. I hope you'll be able come this time, especially the way the children were asking for you today."

"Well, considering the fact that I just lost my job today, I'd say that I'll definitely be there."

"I'm sorry to hear that," said Carl. "But, at least now, we'll have another member of P.I.R.O. there beside Donna and myself."

A few mornings later Donna received a frantic phone call from Carolyn. In a trembling voice, Carolyn related the following events: The previous night, she and Roger had both gone to bed around 11:00 PM, as usual. It was not until several hours later, shortly before dawn in fact; a peculiar sort of hissing sound suddenly awakened Carolyn. Opening her eyes, she'd glanced over to where the sound seemed to be coming from, and saw what looked like an ignited fuse, or sparkler, going off on her dresser. It lasted only for perhaps a second or two, before fizzling out.

Wondering if she'd merely imagined this while emerging from a dream state, Carolyn blinked, and glanced around her bedroom as her vision adjusted to the semi darkness. It was then that she'd spotted a shadowy figure standing near the dresser, cloaked in what looked like a dark, hooded robe. Whoever or whatever this figure was, it actually seemed to somehow stand out from the semi darkness of the bedroom... and it appeared to be watching her. Instinctively, Carolyn realized that this specter was not a living human being. She instantly tried to scream to alert her sleeping husband but found herself completely paralyzed, unable to move or even make a sound.

As Carolyn watched helplessly, the figure slowly began gliding towards her. Although the facial features were hazy and indistinct, she could now see that this ghastly figure appeared to be that of a small, squat, older woman. Another curious thing that Carolyn noticed was that the old woman's head appeared to be lolling to one side, almost onto one shoulder, as if her neck might actually be broken. As the apparition came closer, a peculiar sounding chant, spoken in verse and sounding like an ominous warning began issuing from the indistinct mouth. Carolyn felt that she would literally die of fright, as the spectral woman ceased her maniacal chanting, hissed, and then came almost face to face with her. The last thing that Carolyn saw before the woman mercifully vanished was a leering, twisted smile within the grotesquely distorted facial features. And then the horrid apparition was gone, leaving a faint, lingering scent of decay in the bedroom.

When Carolyn finished her narrative, Donna gasped, "Oh, my God, Carolyn! What did you do then?"

Carolyn replied, "Well, as soon as I could move again, I grabbed onto Roger and began shaking him awake, then told him what had just happened. I was still practically in a panic, so he did his best to calm me down. The only proof I had of what I'd experienced was that there was still a lingering trace of decay, or of something sulfuric in the bedroom. But of course Roger believed me, when he saw how upset I was."

Donna then asked, "Carolyn, you mentioned that this apparition was speaking to you in some kind of chant. Do you recall exactly what it said?"

"Wait a second, what I could get I wrote down," said Carolyn. Donna could hear her fumbling for a piece of paper. She then apologized, "I-I'm sorry, my hands are shaking so much."

"That's alright, Carolyn, take your time," Donna told her.

"I didn't get all of it," said Carolyn, "but I remember it sounded like some sort of a witch's chant. Okay, here it is: 'I'll drive you mad with fiery brooms. I'll drive you mad with death and gloom. I'll drive you out, but it'll be too late, because you'll be dead!' That was the last thing it said to me before it vanished." Carolyn then began to break down in tears, as she asked, "Donna, why is this happening to us? Why does this 'thing' *whatever* it is, hate us so much? We didn't do anything to deserve this!"

"Of course you didn't," Donna assured her. "And please, try not to worry. I'm going to get in touch right now with the Warrens in Connecticut, and let them know what happened. And then I'll call an emergency meeting of P.I.R.O. to update the other members, so we can get back up there as soon as possible."

Sounding hopeful, Carolyn said, "Thank you, Donna. I want you to know that I appreciate everything you people are doing. It's such a relief just to know we have someone to turn to."

"It's no problem," said Donna. "Just like Keith told you, you're not alone in this. So, are you going to be alright until we get back there?"

With a sniffle, Carolyn said, "Yes, I think so. Roger called into his work this morning, and he's taking the rest of the week off. God bless you, Donna, and everyone else who's helping us."

"You too, Carolyn. Like I said, I'll be contacting everyone as soon as I'm off the phone with you. We'll get back there by this Saturday, or even sooner. In the meantime, if anything else happens, please promise that you'll call me right away, no matter what time it is."

"I will. And again, thank you, Donna."

At approximately 5:30 that afternoon, Carolyn and Roger and their children were clearing the table after suppertime, when a car was heard pulling into their driveway. Roger and Carolyn glanced at each other, wondering if it could be the two paranormal investigating teams returning to help them. Seconds later there was a knock on their front door. Both Roger and Carolyn anxiously rushed over to answer it. However, instead of the familiar faces they expected to see, they found two young male strangers standing upon their front doorstep. Roger asked them, "Yes? Can we help you?"

The taller of the two young men, a heavy set individual with thick red hair and glasses, asked, "This is 1677 Round Top Road? And you're Roger and Carolyn?"

Carolyn answered, "Yes, that' right. And who are you?"

Adjusting his glasses in a 'professional' manner, the young man replied, "We're affiliated with a paranormal investigation group from Rhode Island College. And we understand that you've been experiencing some psychic disturbances in your home; is that correct?"

Brightening, Carolyn said, "Oh, you're with P.I.R.O.! Did Carl and Donna ask you to stop by?"

After sharing a look with his companion, the taller of the two young men replied, "No, Ma'am. We both know Carl and Donna of P.I.R.O., but we're with another group at Rhode Island College. We do the same exact thing as they do, only *better*, and more professional."

The shorter individual added, "We hear that your house is seriously haunted, and that you're still having problems. You and your children are very frightened. But if you let us help you instead of P.I.R.O., we really believe that we can help you."

Nodding in agreement, the taller individual added, "He's right. Neither of us feels that you should have to put up with what you're going through any longer. Now, if you'll just give us a few moments of your time, I think we can convince you that we're the right people to investigate your haunting."

By now, Carolyn and Roger's three younger girls were curiously peering from behind their parents. "Hi there," said the taller man, smiling down at them.

With a shrug, Roger said, "Come on in for a few minutes, and we'll listen to what you have to say."

Seated at the kitchen table, the two men from Rhode Island College spent the next several minutes trying to convince Roger and Carolyn that they should allow them to take over their case completely. They also advised them that they should have nothing more to do either with P.I.R.O. or the psychic investigating team from Connecticut. While they were still speaking, 10-year-old Nancy asked, "When are Keith, Carl and Donna coming back?"

Peering at her through his glasses, the taller man said, "You don't need them, because we're better and more professional than they are. Trust me."

Rising from the table, Roger then said curtly, "Alright, we'll think it over, and if we decide we need you, we'll give you a call. Thank you for stopping by." He then walked them to the door.

As soon as they'd left, Roger turned to his wife and said, "Alright, that's it! I want no more college investigators setting foot in this house again, unless they're from one of the BIG colleges. The Warren's are welcome back here to help us, but no more teams from Rhode Island College." He then went outside

It was about twenty minutes later while Roger was outside adding more repairs to the cellar door, when Carolyn suddenly heard a cry of alarm coming from upstairs. She immediately recognized the cry as belonging to her youngest daughter Darlene. Carolyn rushed upstairs, to find her daughter standing just outside of one of the bedrooms, staring straight ahead. "Darlene – what is it, what's wrong?" she asked, placing her hand on her daughter's shoulders.

Teary-eyed, Darlene replied, "Mommy... I just came up here to see if any of the friendly ghosts wanted to play with me. But the mean ghost, the one that looks like a black shadow... she was standing in the bedroom doorway, and she scared me! She won't let the other ghosts come out and play."

Carolyn whisked the little girl downstairs, telling her, "Listen to Mommy, Darlene. From now on, I don't want any of you kids talking or playing with any of the ghosts in this house, whether they seem nice or not. Just like I've told you *never* to talk to strangers. Okay, honey?"

"Okay, Mommy," Darlene agreed. "I wanna go watch TV now."

As soon as Darlene was occupied in front of the TV set Carolyn determinedly returned back upstairs, and entered the first bedroom. Although the feeling was subtle, her maternal instincts told her that whatever appeared to her in her own bedroom in the wee hours of that morning was up here now. Carolyn quickly turned to make certain that none of her children were upstairs, before turning her attention back to the bedroom. For a moment, she could feel the air inside the bedroom beginning to thicken, accompanied by a prickly sensation on the back of her neck.

Her thin frame began trembling with a mixture of rage and apprehension. Without doubt, Carolyn knew that the malevolent presence was up here with her. She also began to feel lightheaded and slightly nauseous, but with an effort of will, she forced herself to maintain control of the situation. Knowing that she now had the thing's full attention, Carolyn verbally addressed it in a low voice: "Alright, you dirty, ugly old bitch, now it's your turn to listen to me! I don't care if you lived here once, or how long you've been here. This is *MY* house now, and until help gets here, you stay the hell away from my children! You understand me?"

Carolyn stood there waiting for several seconds, until the thickness of the air gradually began to dissipate. "Good," she said, when she felt the room was back to normal. "I'll take that as a 'yes'." She then strode out of the room and went back downstairs, holding tenaciously onto the railing for support.

The following morning Donna received another phone call from Carolyn, who explained to her about the visit they'd received from the rival psychic investigation team. She also regretfully informed Donna that her husband Roger had now adamantly decided against allowing P.I.R.O. any further involvement with their case. "I'm sorry, Donna," she tearfully apologized. "You've all been such good friends to me and my family. We wouldn't have received any help in the first place if it weren't for you. Believe me, Donna, if it were up to me, you'd still all be coming back here this Saturday. I'm so sorry about this!"

Donna told her, "Its not your fault, Carolyn. And I think I have a pretty good idea who these people are who tried to discredit us. Do you happen to remember you their names?"

Carolyn replied, "There were two of them, and I think one of them said his name was Ron. I don't remember the name of the other guy. But I could tell that they weren't really on the level, when they started saying they were more professional than your group."

With a sigh, Donna said, "Well, at least you still have Ed and Lorraine helping you out. And they're the most experienced people I know of in this field. In the meantime, I'll call Carl and Keith, and let them know that it's off for this Saturday. All I ask is that you stay in touch with us, and let us know what happens."

"Donna, I promise that I'll stay in touch," said Carolyn. "Again, thank you for all that you've done to help us. Please give my love to Carl and Keith, and to the other members of your team."

After getting off the phone with Carolyn, Donna called Carl and me, and informed us that P.I.R.O. would no longer be personally involved with the Harrisville case and the reasons why. During our next meeting of P.I.R.O. held at Rhode Island College, we discussed the particulars. "For those of you who are not already aware," said Donna, "Ron and his group apparently went in person to Harrisville, and tried to discredit us in front of Roger and Carolyn. They also made an attempt to convince them that they should take over the case, which didn't work. But unfortunately, as a result Roger will no longer allow any college investigation groups at his house, unless they're from one of the 'big' colleges. This is what Carolyn told me."

Carl added, "And apparently, Roger doesn't consider R.I.C. to be one of the 'big' colleges. So, I'm afraid that we're now officially off the case."

As expected, the other members of our team were aghast at hearing this news. "What!" exclaimed Jay. "So, that guy Ron and his group have gone and ruined it for everyone now?"

"Not quite everyone," said Carl. "The Warren's are still on the case, and will be assisting the family."

Throughout the next month, Donna kept in regular touch with Carolyn by phone. Carolyn informed her that the children were continuing to ask for their friend Keith to come visit them, but that her husband Roger remained adamant about not having any of us back there. Not only that, but the Warren's themselves were advising the Harrisville case was much too dangerous for us to be involved with.

Eventually, the Warren's were able to arrange for representatives from the Catholic Diocese to intervene on the family's behalf. Two Catholic priests arrived at the Arnold-Richardson House, along with Ed and Lorraine, to conduct a complete blessing of the house and of the barn. According to Carolyn, the blessing itself went without incident. There was, however, one moment while the two priests were upstairs, when Lorraine announced that she sensed a presence near the stairway. Ed immediately snapped a photo in the direction she'd indicated. When the photo was processed, there could clearly be seen a dark, shadowy human-like figure standing in a corner near the staircase.

The entire blessing took just under two hours. When it was completed, the two priests along with the Warren's sat down at the kitchen table to confer with the family. They explained that although the malevolent spirit that resided in the house was now rendered dormant as the result of the blessing, they were still there. It was actually Lorraine who was able to discern this. They also advised the family that as long as they maintained a positive, *loving* family environment, and refrain from any occult practices such as Tarot cards Ouija boards, the spirit which had been oppressing them should be kept at bay. Both Roger and Carolyn readily agreed that they'd do their part… anything to prevent a reoccurrence of the hell they'd been experiencing over the past several months. They then gratefully thanked the two priests and the Warren's for all they'd done, and said their good-byes to them.

Regarding our rival paranormal investigation group at Rhode Island College, they apparently disbanded soon after their attempt to 'case jump' the Harrisville case.

We soon lost touch with Carolyn, and never heard from her again. We later learned from the Warren's that although Carolyn would catch an occasional glimpse of the 'shadow figure' in the house, it never really bothered her to the extent it used to. She now felt comfortable in the house, and was never again assaulted in the way she'd previously been. The only area of the house Carolyn now tended to avoid was the cellar. She'd venture down there alone only when absolutely necessary, and spend as little time down there as possible. The feeling of being watched in the cellar was something that Carolyn could never completely adjust to though.

There was one incident that took place in the basement, reportedly experienced by the eldest daughter, Andrea, and some of her friends from Burrillville High School. Early one evening while entertaining a few friends, Andrea was giving them a brief tour of the house and led them into the cellar. Andrea was explaining to them about some of the haunting phenomena she and her family used to experience, especially the problems they'd have keeping the two cellar doors completely closed. Suddenly, while Andrea was speaking, the temperature within the cellar began to inexplicably rise to an uncomfortable level, and the cellar walls surrounding them took on an eerie reddish hue. One of her startled friends exclaimed, "Andrea, you weren't kidding, when you said this place was haunted!" Together, the frightened teenagers bolted back upstairs.

Years later, long after P.I.R.O. had dissolved as a group, I heard from a personal acquaintance who is a resident of Harrisville. Carolyn had become comfortable enough to host dinner parties and other social occasions within her house. Carolyn would often include a historic theme to these social events, even going so far as to dress up in colonial attire to entertain her guests.

Carolyn and her husband Roger were said to have eventually separated, after which Carolyn continued living in the Arnold-Richard House with her children until the early 1980's. When her children had all reached young adulthood and graduated from high school, Carolyn moved away, presumably relocating out of state.

The next people to move into the Arnold-Richardson House were a Protestant Minister and his family. They occupied the house for a number of years seemingly without interference from spirits, until one overcast afternoon when the pastor's 19-year-old son was returning home. Upon turning his car into the driveway, he spotted a short, somewhat stout elderly woman with long, gray disheveled hair standing in the front yard. Although he did not recognize this peculiar-looking woman, he wondered if she might be a parishioner who had stopped by to visit with his father.

However, he noticed no other cars in the driveway except those belonging to his family. She was also was attired rather oddly, wearing a long, old-fashioned gray dress, which looked as though it belonged to another century. Another oddity about this strange woman was that her neck seemed to be sharply tilted to one side. Despite this cervical deformation she kept a wary eye on him, turning to watch as he slowly pulled forward in the driveway. By now, the pastor's son began to wonder if this elderly woman might be suffering from some form of dementia, and may have wandered over here from a neighboring house.

After parking his car and getting out, he was about to ask the woman if he could help her... but the look of pure hatred on her wrinkled features as she continued to glare at him, caused the young man to refrain from addressing her. He also noticed that she kept her bony fingers in a clawed position, indicating that she might even be thinking of attacking him. Unnerved, the young man dashed inside the house to alert his family. When he glanced back, however, the strange woman in the long gray dress had vanished without a trace. According to the pastor's son, there was simply no possible way any living person could have run out of the yard that quickly, let alone a stout elderly woman with a twisted neck. Nevertheless, both the pastor and his son rushed outside and glanced up and down the street, but there was no trace of anyone.

In retrospect, the pastor's son described getting the distinct feeling from this woman's hateful stare, that she considered his family intruders on what was once her property, and that she wanted them out.

The minister and his family continued to live in the Arnold-Richardson House for another several years without further incident. After they moved away, the house remained vacant for approximately a year. During this time, one of the nearby neighbors who had gotten up in the middle of the night to let his dog outside, happened to see a glowing light floating from window to window inside of the supposedly locked and vacated Arnold-Richardson House.

In September of 1987, a sophisticated, world-traveled couple named Norma and Gerry bought the Arnold-Richardson House. They moved in the following month. Although the exterior of the house was in relatively good condition, the interior by now required extensive renovations. Norma and Gerry fell in love with the house, and immediately hired carpenters who specialized in the restoration of historic houses, to begin doing renovations. Norma, a licensed day-care provider with a master's degree in counseling, decided that her new home would be an ideal setting out of which to run her day-care business. Not only that, but also the large kitchen and dining areas, complete with an appropriately large cooking fireplace seemed perfectly suited for Norma's catering talents.

It wasn't long before Norma and Gerry heard the story of the hauntings regarding their new home. In fact, one of the nearby neighbors wasted little time in venturing over to introduce himself to Norma and Gerry. He launched into a complete haunted history of the house.

The neighbor began with the story of the nameless witch who killed at least two children in the house and then hung herself in the large barn out in back. He also told them all about the young family living in the house back in the 1970's, who'd been repeatedly terrorized by ghostly apparitions and a series of inexplicable mishaps. The neighbor concluded by telling them of the terrifying appearances outside the house of an elderly woman with a twisted wearing a long gray dress – obviously the ghost of the witch who'd hanged herself in the barn so many years ago. Before leaving, their neighbor once again welcomed Norma and Gerry to the neighborhood, and wished them good luck and happiness in their new home.

In time, Norma and Gerry also learned that at least two psychic investigation groups had come to the house when Carolyn and her family had lived there. They were also informed that a blessing by two Catholic priests had taken place in the house, which had succeeded in lessening the more bizarre ghostly activity.

Both Norma and Gerry were opened to the idea of the blessing having worked since they had so far experienced only very minor activity in the house. For example, their bed would sometimes suddenly begin shaking a bit in the middle of the night, arousing them from sleep. Strange lights would occasionally flash in certain rooms, although Gerry suspected that there may have merely been caused by the headlights of passing cars. Norma found being alone in the cellar slightly uncomfortable... but for the most part, things were relatively quiet and uneventful.

One afternoon, a few years after they'd moved in, Norma and Gerry returned home to find a strange car parked in their driveway with a Connecticut license plate. A man and a woman who appeared to be in their sixties got out of the car upon seeing them. They introduced themselves to Norma and Gerry as Ed and Lorraine Warren from Connecticut, and explained that they'd originally investigated the house back in the early 1970's. In fact, they'd been personally involved with the case when Roger and Carolyn had lived there, and had been responsible for arranging for the two Catholic priests to intervene on their behalf. Since the two investigators had driven there from out of state, Norma and Gerry politely invited them to come inside.

The Warren's highly complimented their hosts on the lovely job they'd done restoring the interior of the house. Taking in her surroundings, Lorraine smiled and told Norma, "The atmosphere in this house feels so much more comfortable and livable, than it did back then. I can tell that you're both very happy here." She went on to explain to Norma that she was highly sensitive on a psychic level, and was actually able to communicate with earthbound spirits.

However, there was one room in particular, which concerned Lorraine, and this was the room that had originally been Roger and Carolyn's bedroom, and which Gerry had now converted to his personal den. This was, of course, the room in which Carolyn had been confronted by the shadowy specter with the crooked neck.

With Norma and Gerry's permission, Lorraine entered the room and attempted to communicate with the presence she felt still lingered there. Seated in the middle of the room, she closed her eyes, and said softly, "There is a spirit of an older woman in this room, who is not at rest. She claims that she is still attached to this place, and that she does not want to leave. She's saying that people are always intruding in here, and disturbing her. I'm getting the impression that she died either in this house or somewhere very nearby. This person in life was a very mean-spirited individual… someone who was very accustomed to having her own way."

Moments later Lorraine had lost contact with the entity, and emerged from her light trance. She explained that although she'd attempted to convince this spirit to move on, this spirit adamantly refused to leave. In fact, it would take more than just a blessing to

coerce this particular entity to move on. She had ties with the demonic, and was not about to budge. However, due to the lingering effects
of the blessing performed by the two priests, her presence was not
currently a threat to the present occupants of the house.

Before leaving, Lorraine reiterated to Norma and Gerry that they
really had nothing to be concerned about regarding the spirits that
resided in their home. They thanked Norma and Gerry for their
hospitality, and promised to stay in touch.

Some time after hearing this story, a family friend of Norma
named Linda decided to conduct some extensive research at the
Burrillville Town Hall. She found that Noah Arnold, Jr. built the
house in the year 1768 for himself and his young bride, Anne Richardson. Over the years, the house passed from the Arnold's to the
Richardson's and to the Butterworth's, who were all part of the same
family. The name changes were the result of intermarriages.

There was also mention of the murder of a 12-year-old girl named
Prudence S. Arnold, which had been committed in the Arnold-
Richardson House on January 31 in the year 1849. An old newspaper
account described the girl's throat as having been "horribly cut, the
head being almost separated from the body." A man named William
Knowlton had been implicated in the crime. The article also mentioned Knowlton's blotched suicide attempt, along with the fact that a
mere $2.00 had been taken by Knowlton at the crime scene.

Reading on, Linda came across the brief mention of a 7-day-old
male child who had died in the house on March 18, 1866. The parents
of this child were listed as George and Jane Arnold. However, no
name or cause of death for this child was given. Linda wondered if
this could have been the poor child, who had supposedly died as the
result of a needle piercing its skull?

In December of 1883, John Arnold died at the age of 57 after drinking horse liniment. Also, in 1903 a man named Jarvis Smith, reputedly
a lawyer, was found frozen to death inside the shed near the road.
Edwin Arnold owned the Arnold-Richardson House at this time. Late
in the year 1903, Edwin Arnold was still residing at the house when
he disappeared for several weeks. A hunter finally discovered him in
the surrounding woods. Edwin had been coming back from Slaters-

ville, and had stopped off for a drink or two at the Western Hotel. After taking the trolley back to Harrisville he'd set out on foot to return home... but had apparently somehow become helplessly lost and disoriented along the way.

There was also mention of a woman named Bathsheba Green, who died on May 25, 1885 at the age of 71 years, 2 months and 15 days. She was born in Burrillville in a house near 'Witches Hollow' on March 10, 1814 and was the daughter of Epharim Thayer. She died in Burrillville and was married at the time of her death. Her cause of death was listed as 'paralysis.'

Bathsheba was originally married to Jedson Sherman, and although she was remarried to a man named Green after Jedson's death in 1881, she was buried next to Jedson along with their three children in the small cemetery across from the Harrisville Fire Station. Linda took it upon herself to visit this historical cemetery. She quickly found the graves of Judson and Bathsheba Sherman. Although her married name was Green at the time of her death, the name on her stone was Bathsheba Sherman. Her headstone was badly damaged, nearly broken in half. Judson's headstone bore a curious inscription: *"Mark the upright, the end of man is peace."* Linda also noticed that the headstones of their three young children all had religious verses on them, which did not seem to fit in with their mother having been a 'witch.'

While standing there reading the various inscriptions, Linda was moved to say a brief prayer for the souls of these three children who'd died so young. Suddenly and inexplicably, she was overcome with a feeling of dread. Although this was a clear, reasonably warm afternoon, Linda suddenly felt chilled to the bone. Not only that, she felt personally threatened as well. Linda immediately said a quick prayer of protection for herself, then hastily fled the cemetery.

It was more than thirty years following my *original* visit to the Arnold-Richardson House, that I contacted Norma, the current resident of that house. She proved to be a delightful individual, and once I'd explained to her who I was, she readily extended an invitation to investigate her home. Previously, I'd written the story of our original investigation in Harrisville and had posted it on the TAPS web site, which had first brought me to Norma's attention.

Just recently, several TAPS members as well as John Zaffis had investigated her house for an episode of "Ghost Hunters." While they'd been there, one member of the camera crew had been touched on the shoulder by something unseen, while John Zaffis had momentarily experienced vibrations while seated in a chair in the study. Also, one of the latched doors in an upstairs bedroom had been videotaped opening on its own.

Thus it was on a warm August evening, Sandra, Carl and I, along with three other members of New England Anomalies Research, set out from Warwick to the town of Harrisville. Upon our arrival at the Arnold-Richardson House on Round Top Road, Carl and I found the exterior of the house to look very much as it had during the 1970's, when we'd conducted our original investigation of the place. After being welcomed in by Norma, we discovered the interior to have been greatly improved. Stepping into the kitchen area was almost like stepping into a colonial museum, with the rich display of antiques and antiquated household items, framed photographs, prints and oil paintings adorning nearly every available space. Also, there was no longer the sense of foreboding or oppression that I'd felt upon entering this house those thirty-plus years before. Combined with the down-to-earth personalities of both Norma and Gerry, the atmosphere inside the house actually seemed quite charming.

Gerry proved to be a very relaxed, soft-spoken, cerebral gentleman, who seemed very much at home with the exhaustive collection of books that comprised his personal library. Norma, on the other hand, was very much the extrovert of the two. She was a gracious hostess who was willing to speak as much about the haunted history of her house as she was her world travels and favorite recipes. Somehow, their contrasting personalities managed to complement each other, making them a delightful couple.

When asked whether she had experienced anything in the house that might be considered paranormal, Norma replied, "Every once in awhile, I'll feel a slight vibration while either lying in bed or sitting in one of the chairs. And there are times when I get the distinct impression that I'm not alone, enough to make me turn around and look. This is especially true when I'm down in the basement. But I wouldn't say that I've ever experienced anything that was actually disturbing in this house." Norma also added, "There was one time when I came home to find three latched doors wide open, which I know I'd left closed. My first reaction was that there might be an intruder in the house but after we did a thorough search we found that both the front and back doors were still securely locked. Of course, we have 'door issues' anyway."

Gerry basically felt very comfortable in the house. The only thing unusual he'd experienced was a strange vibration while seated in his favorite chair in the study, which he assumed was a truck going by the house. Upon checking, though, there never was any large vehicle going by the house. Gerry had also seen what appeared to be bluish orbs floating in some of the rooms. One time, both he and Norma felt the front door rattling almost as if an earth tremor was taking place. However, this rattling subsided after only a moment and the door could be opened as if nothing had happened.

We also asked Norma if anyone else had experienced anything in the house, since they'd been living there. Norma answered, "Well, of course there was the time that Mrs. Warren claimed to have been in communication with Bathsheba Green, while she was in Gerry's study. And as you know, that's the same room that was formerly the downstairs bedroom, where Carolyn saw that spirit manifestation back in the 1970's. Other than that, we once hired a young woman who's also a friend of ours, to housesit for us while Gerry and I were away traveling for a week. She was going to staying here along with her boyfriend. Well, when we got back, we found that the young woman was still there, but that her boyfriend had left after the first night, and that he refused to step into the house again. He simply felt too uncomfortable in the house, for whatever reason."

Norma also mentioned that a couple of guests at her house had mentioned seeing a young man and an older woman, both dressed in old fashioned attire from perhaps the turn of the 20th Century, standing in Gerry's study. Neither of the spirits would ever say anything, but would instead simply stare. Of course, Norma never had any such individuals visiting with her in the house that fit this depiction. However, the description of this man and this woman did seem to match the two ghosts that Carolyn's daughter had reported seeing when they'd lived in the house.

Another time a female guest was visiting Norma; she had never heard anything relating to the house being haunted. For some reason this woman refused to enter the den where Roger and Carolyn's bedroom had once been. As she stood in the doorway, Norma'a guest suddenly said, "I can't go in this room. I just felt something walk right through me."

Throughout our investigation that evening, both Norma and Gerry continued to be gracious hosts, allowing us to set up our equipment throughout their house. In an upstairs bedroom, Sandra captured a peculiar double-image with her digital camera. The photo seemed to show the hazy images of various items that were not in the room at the time, such as eyeglasses, a throw rug, and Venetian blinds. Of course, this in no way indicates that anything of a paranormal nature was the cause of the images. But because the photo was taken with a digital camera, a double exposure *could* be ruled out.

Down in the cellar, Norma showed us the well where two children had allegedly been drowned, explaining to us, "Of course, there's no verification at all that this actually happened. This is just the legend as I was told it, and as it was told to Carolyn and her husband years before."

Although our thermocouple did register some mild temperature fluctuations in the musty cellar air, these could easily be attributed to natural drafts. All in all, we were unable to obtain any definitive evidence of paranormal activity in the cellar.

Back upstairs in the kitchen area, Sandra and I conducted an EVP session, which did yield some results. During this session we mentioned several of names of people who'd been or were now associated with the house. When we played back the audio recording of me mentioning the name of Lorraine Warren, a barely perceptible, whispering male voice repeated the name back to me, followed by "...*yeah.*" When I randomly mentioned the name "Rebecca" the same hushed male voice whispered "*Yeah.*"

Sandra also snapped a couple of photos while we were still recording in the kitchen area. Both times she announced "Flash" to warn me before taking the picture. Apparently whatever unseen entity was in the room with us did not like the idea of the flash going off, because one time Sandra said, "Flash" on the audio recording, the male voice softly whispered *"No."*

Shortly after our EVP session, we concluded our investigation for the evening and packed up our equipment. Before we left, however, Norma further entertained us all by relating the story of the time she's nearly been attacked by killer bees, while on safari in Africa!

Naturally, I saw no need to employ religious provocation during this investigation of the Arnold-Richardson House. The situation there was almost entirely different than it was back during the 1970's, when Carl and I had originally visited the house. Certain entities, even those that are malevolent in nature, will tend to prey upon certain families and individuals more than others, for any variety of reasons. In the case of the Arnold-Richardson House in Harrisville, members of the Catholic clergy had also blessed the house at one time. While this may not have totally alleviated all paranormal activity within the house, it did seem to have had a very positive effect.

When leaving the premises that night, I of course led the other members of our investigation team in a prayer of protection, asking that nothing unholy be allowed to follow us. Yet, as mentioned, there was no ominous feeling of oppression about the house or the property. Norma and Gerry continue to live there unmolested by unseen guests, and experience only a brief vibration or the sound a random knock now and then. Hopefully, the spirits within the house will continue to remain inactive, at least for the most part.

CHAPTER 12

The Possession of Lucas

T HE FOLLOWING EVENTS took place during the winter months of the year 1980. At the time, Carl and I were affiliated with Monitor East, a paranormal investigation group based in Providence, Rhode Island. During this time the story of Lucas was brought to the attention of Carl and myself. Lucas was a slender, fourteen-year-old boy of Puerto Rican heritage. Actually, both Carl and I had been friends with Lucas and his family for several years, and we'd always known him to be a mild-mannered boy, with a pleasant, friendly disposition. Lately, however, Lucas had been exhibiting sudden and inexplicable changes in his personality, along with episodes of bizarre and often violent behavior.

During these episodes, Lucas would often thrash about as if in a frenzy. In this state he'd emit a series of high-pitched screams, and curses at those around him in a harsh, guttural tone of voice which did not resemble his own. Having heard stories from the family regarding what this boy had gone through, Carl at first suspected the cause of these problems stemmed from his own psychology. However, Carl was subsequently invited to spend a night as a guest in the house where Lucas and his family resided, which was located in Providence. The family hoped that Carl would have the opportunity to witness for himself some of the strange behavior, which fourteen-year-old Lucas had been exhibiting.

At about 1:00 AM that *very* night, Carl and the other family members were suddenly awakened by blood-curdling screams coming from Lucas' bedroom, sounding as if the boy was being murdered. Rushing to the bedroom along with his Uncle Antonio, Carl switched on the overhead light. Immediately, Lucas shot passed them out of the bedroom, his body whirling in an impossibly fast, circular motion! As Carl later described it, the young teenager was spinning "like a dreidel, in a way his body couldn't possibly have done, even *with* accelerated motor function."

Both Carl and Antonio watched helplessly as Lucas went spinning into the adjoining parlor, banging and careening into the walls as he did so. Lucas then whirled back into his bedroom, jumped up on his bed, and began bellowing out a deep, demonic sounding laughter. Several minutes passed in this manner before the episode finally subsided. Lucas suddenly collapsed onto his bed, awakening in an apparent state of dazed bewilderment, with no perceptible recollection of what had just taken place.

Since the family members were aware of both Carl's and my own combined experience as paranormal researchers, they asked if we would look into their situation. We readily agreed. Thus, throughout the next few weeks, Carl and I were both present to witness some of these "fits" which Lucas was experiencing. During these episodes, not only did Lucas exhibit bizarre physical and emotional behavior; the atmosphere in whatever room he was in at the time would also noticeably change. It was a sensation, which I had personally experienced before when dealing with a demonic presence, which I can best describe as "oppressive."

In fact, it actually felt as though energy was being drained out of each and every one of us who happened to be in the same room as Lucas. That sensation was accompanied by an almost tangible sense of foreboding that permeated the immediate area. This oppressive feeling within the room would also *instantly* dissipate, the moment Lucas came out of his frenzy and returned to his normal self.

One evening, shortly after Lucas had recovered from one of his episodes, I accompanied him to his room, and asked him if he had any idea why this might be happening to him. Up until this time, none of us had interviewed Lucas in-depth. He felt somewhat uncomfortable discussing his situation to a group, and people also tended to be a little apprehensive about being in the same room alone with him.

Lucas explained to me that when he was a young boy of perhaps six years old, he'd been walking through a cemetery one afternoon with family members. During the walk he'd noticed a single, discarded glove that happened to be lying upon the ground. Out of normal childhood curiosity, he'd reached down and picked the glove up. At that *very* moment, an odd sensation came over him. "It's hard to explain," said Lucas, "but it felt as if something had suddenly 'attached' itself to me. It was like something I couldn't see was now with me. I know that sounds silly."

"No, it doesn't," I said. "Perhaps the glove had been used or worn by someone in some sort of occult ceremony or profane worship there in the cemetery. Anyway, please, go on."

Lucas continued: "That night, shortly after I'd gone to bed alone in my room, a crazy looking old man suddenly appeared right at the foot of my bed. And he began telling me that I belonged to *HIM* now, and no one else!"

"You must have been terrified," I said. "What happened then? Did the crazy-looking old man say or do anything else?"

"He came back the next night, and told me the same thing," said Lucas. "And he came back a lot of nights after that, always reminding me that I belonged to him."

"Did you tell your family about this?" I asked.

"Well, I tried to tell my parents a couple of times, but they said that I was probably just having nightmares. And also, the crazy old man threatened that he would really hurt me, if I kept trying to tell people."

"I see. And how long did this crazy old man continue to visit you at night?"

"It went on for about a year, and then he suddenly stopped show-ing up," explained Lucas.

"You certainly must've been relieved," I said.

"Yeah, I'll say I was!" Lucas agreed.

"Perhaps after a year had passed, you reached the age where you were no longer vulnerable to him," I suggested. "And did he ever come back to you again? I mean, in a way that you could still see or hear him."

"No, he never did again. But now, these attacks are suddenly happening to me. And I feel so terrible afterwards, because people tell me what I've said and done, but I don't remember *any* of it," Lucas explained with his eyes now filling with tears.

Patting his shoulder, I assured him, "This isn't your fault, Lucas. I don't blame you, and you shouldn't blame yourself. We'll do every-thing that we possibly can to help you. In the meantime, I'll certainly keep you in my prayers."

Appearing somewhat relieved, Lucas smiled, and thanked me for understanding, instead of judging him.

Joining my brother Carl who was in the parlor, I sat down with some of the other family members and began discussing Lucas' situation. His parents informed us that they'd repeatedly taken Lucas to doctors, who could find no definitive organic cause for the teenage boy's condition. Although a psychiatric counselor had placed Lucas on a prescribed medication for hypertension, all medical tests for any sign of possible psychosis had proven to be negative. Ultimately, no explanation for the frenetic episodes he'd experienced could be found.

Carl asked, "Have any of the doctors you've taken Lucas to ac-tually witnessed any of his fits, while he was experiencing one?"

"No, it's only what we have told to them," Lucas' mother replied. "They tell us that our son is just going through some sort of 'identity crises', and is a little withdrawn."

His father added, "They say that Lucas will just grow out of it in time and otherwise he is a normal teenage boy."

Carl then said, "Now let me ask you, since you're his family, and you know him best… what do you personally feel is causing Lucas to experience these episodes?"

Without hesitation, Lucas' mother replied, "I feel that this is an evil spirit which has been troubling him for years, and now is sometimes entering him, and taking over him completely."

"You mean, as in "possession?" Carl asked.

"Si," she replied. She then pulled out a tissue, and began dabbing her eyes. "I'm so sorry," she apologized.

"No, that's quite alright," Carl assured her. Turning to Lucas' father, he asked, "Do you feel the same way?"

"Si. I do," he replied, nodding affirmatively.

Addressing Lucas' cousin Maria and his Uncle Antonio, who were also in the room, Carl asked for their opinion as well. Both of them adamantly agreed that an evil spirit was possessing Lucas. A spirit, which was often invading him and completely taking over his personality.

It was I who then said, "If I may ask, what is your family religion?"

"We are Catholic," Lucas' father replied.

"Practicing?" I asked.

Everyone responded that although they did not regularly attend church services, they were all believers in the faith.

"Good," I said. "Now, have you consulted your parish priest about your situation?"

Lucas' mother explained that a priest had recently been called in and had performed a blessing in their apartment, using holy water. However, the blessing had done nothing to alleviate her adolescent son's situation. In fact, if anything, Lucas' condition had grown even worse since the priest had visited their house, with the frequency of his fits having increased.

"I see," said Carl. "Well, Keith and I both understand your situation, as you've explained it to us. Now, I have to ask, in what way would you like for us to help you?"

Lucas' family told us that we already had helped quite a bit, by observing their situation first hand, and by not judging them to be crazy, which they greatly appreciated. Also, they did intend to arrange for further religious intervention. Because of our experience in such matters, and due to the fact that Carl and I were friends with the family they requested that we be active participants in this religious intervention. In other words, they were talking about us assisting in an exorcism, to free Lucas from his spiritual affliction.

During the drive back home from Providence that night, Carl and I discussed the details of the case, along with our possible involvement in Lucas' deliverance session. We both agreed that Lucas did appear to be suffering from legitimate spiritual possession. Seated behind the wheel of the driver's seat, I asked Carl, "Do you feel these people are on the level? Lucas' family members, I'm referring to."

In the passenger's seat, Carl replied, "Well, they certainly seem sincere, and their concern over Lucas is obvious. His parents have had him undergo legitimate medical testing. But from what they said, Lucas' doctors have basically been attributing his problems to no more than teenage angst; something he'll simply grow out of in time. So, perhaps an exorcism *is* in order."

"You're right," I agreed. "At this point, I certainly don't think that it would make his condition any worse. Besides, they're of the Catholic faith, and they did mention something about having a member of the clergy involved, didn't they?"

"Yes, they did mention that a priest or someone of the faith would be presiding over the exorcism. And would you agree to participate in the ritual, as the family requested?"

"Yes, most definitely; I'd very much like to assist in whatever way I can."

"Good," said Carl. "Then I'll let the family know, that we're both willing to be present and to participate in the exorcism."

Thus the exorcism was scheduled for a Saturday evening in February. The family made arrangements for the actual ceremony to be held in the same apartment building in which Lucas resided with his parents and siblings. Days before the exorcism was to take place, Carl again visited with Lucas' Uncle Antonio to discuss some of the particulars we could expect regarding the upcoming ceremony. However, Carl returned that evening with some rather surprising info, which I had certainly not been anticipating.

Although Lucas' family had claimed to be of the Roman Catholic faith when we'd interviewed them, their primary faith was actually

"Santeria." Santeria, Spanish for "The Way of the Saints" is an old-world religious practice, which in many aspects resembles the religion of Voodoo. The official name of this religion is Regla de Ocha or *The Rule of Orisha*, although Santeria is the name by which it is more popularly known.

Also during our interview with Lucas' family, they had assured us that a member the clergy would be present at the exorcism. When they'd said this, I'd naturally assumed they were referring to a Catholic priest. However, Carl now informed me: "Based upon what Antonio says, they apparently feel totally competent and capable of dealing with the situation themselves. So in their opinion, having a Catholic priest present *won't* be necessary."

"But, didn't they specifically tell us that an ordained member of the clergy would be present at the exorcism?" I asked.

"Oh, there will be a member of the clergy presiding over the exorcism on Saturday night," Carl explained. "Except it will be a member of their own family. It seems that Lucas' Aunt Lucia happens to be a "Santera', or priestess, in their religion. According to what Antonio told me, this position has been handed down through that line of the family for generations. Apparently Lucia's mother is a recognized Santera in Puerto Rico, as was her mother before her. In fact, Lucia's grandfather was a renowned 'Babalocha', which is quite an esteemed position to hold in Santeria."

"But didn't they specifically tell us that a *Catholic* priest had been to their house, and that he'd used holy water?"

"Apparently it was actually Aunt Lucia, and not a priest."

"So, am I given to understand that Lucas' Aunt Lucia will be presiding over the ceremony on Saturday night?"

"Yes, it seems as though Aunt Lucia will be the main individual in charge. And as I explained, Antonio says that they're sure they can handle the situation themselves."

"Well, do they even still want us to be there to participate?" I asked.

"Oh yes, they still want our assistance during the exorcism," Carl assured me. "They seem to value our experience in these matters as well as our familiarity with *this* case."

"So, who else will be participating in this exorcism, besides us?" I wanted to know.

Carl replied, "From what Antonio tells me, Lucas' sister and two of his cousins will be there, assisting in the ceremony. They're the ones who we gave a ride home to with Antonio the other week."

"Oh yes," I said. "I remember that whenever we drove past that large cemetery off Broad Street, they'd place their hands over the tops of their heads, to prevent wandering spirits from entering them. One of them even placed her hand over my head too as we drove past the cemetery. Which shows that they're certainly strong believers in spirit possession."

"Yes, spirit possession plays a significant role in the belief system of Santeria," said Carl.

"But, from what I understand, the family also follows the basic teachings of the Catholic faith. I mean, don't they believe in the power of Jesus Christ, to free people from demonic oppression?" I asked.

"Yes, they do incorporate the basic belief systems of Catholicism into their faith," said Carl. "However, they also seem to firmly believe that the Santero... or in this case, the Santera... has specifically inherited the God-given power to personally cast out evil spirits."

"Well, as long as they gather together in the name of Jesus Christ, I really don't see any major contradiction," I said.

It was on a chilly February evening that Carl and I arrived at the apartment on Hanover Street in Providence for the intended exorcism. After being greeted and welcomed in by the family, we were ushered into the parlor, which was dimly illuminated by candlelight, the electric lights having been extinguished.

We noticed that against one wall a table had been set up to serve as an altar, upon which rested several lit candlesticks surrounding a punch bowl filled with what resembled fruit punch. In reality, the punch bowl contained a pulpy-looking "holy water" to which slices of various herbs, spices and fruits had been added. This mixture was to be utilized in the ceremony that was about to take place.

Carl and I were then asked to join four members of the family, who were seated in a semi-circle in the parlor. Among those family members were Uncle Antonio, as well as Lucas' sister Maria and two young female cousins. Carl was seated in a chair to my left. In front of us was placed a single, small foldout chair, presumably where Lucas would be seated. Lucas' mother and father would be waiting in the adjoining room, and would not be actively participating in the ceremony.

Lucas' Aunt Lucia – a short, stocky, smiling woman in her mid-forties, whom Carl and I had met several times before – entered the parlor and pleasantly announced that she was ready to begin the ceremony. Aunt Lucia was attired in a brightly colored evening dress, and not in a flowing white robe as I might have anticipated. Nonetheless she exuded an air of quiet authority in her position as Santera, as well as exorcist. Aunt Lucia then instructed her 14-year-old nephew to take his seat in front of our semi-circle, facing us.

We respectfully took our seats in the candlelit parlor as Lucia began reciting an invocation in her native Spanish, followed by some prayers. For my own part, I opened up the Holy Bible, which I'd brought along with me, and silently began reading Scripture. At first, Lucas merely sat there slouched in his seat, obviously feeling somewhat awkward and self-conscious as he shyly glanced around at us.

Suddenly, the atmosphere within the parlor became noticeably oppressive, seemingly as a "warning sign," indicating to us that something of a paranormal nature was about to take place. This was followed seconds later by a low, rumbling vibration, which was both heard and felt by everyone in the room as it traveled along the wooden floor directly underneath our feet. Although at first I assumed that a large truck was driving by causing this vibration, it could distinctly be felt traveling along the floor in the direction to where we were seated in a semi circle. As the vibration reached us, we all watched as the chair which my brother Carl was seated in, suddenly began being pulled backwards by some unseen force. "Oh, Dios mio!" said one of the cousins with a gasp, pointing to what was happening. The chair moved backwards about three feet, before coming to a stop. Glancing about, Carl appeared more startled than actually frightened.

As Lucas sat there facing us, a wild, unearthly look suddenly came into his eyes… the same frenzied look that always distorted his youthful features whenever he was overtaken by one of his fits. Lucas then slid off of his chair and onto the floor, while defensively backing away from his Aunt Lucia's rapidly spoken incantations. The teenage boy then bolted up into a kneeling position, with both arms firmly positioned at his sides, and began swaying back and forth in the fashion of a cobra. While Lucas' Aunt Lucia continued her rapid-fire chanting, Lucas began emitting a series of piercing screeches, as he repeatedly leapt up and down throwing himself onto the hard wooden floor, apparently somehow without seriously injuring himself. Although I say that he threw himself, at the time it appeared more as if Lucas was actually being picked up and dashed down repeatedly by unseen hands!

All pandemonium then broke loose, as Lucas suddenly raced over to the makeshift altar and began knocking over the candlesticks and spilling the contents of the punch bowl. *"I HATE CANDLES!"* he shouted in a harsh, guttural tone that was totally unlike his normal speaking voice. It all happened so fast that no one had much of an opportunity to intervene. Meanwhile, the continuous chants of his Aunt Lucia, the Santera, only seemed to further infuriate Lucas.

As Lucas began to run about the darkened room in a frenzy, overturning furniture and such, Carl reached out and intercepted him. Carl tackled him about the waste, as I grabbed onto his legs. Antonio also jumped over to assist us, and together, the three of us managed to tackle him to the floor. As thin as Lucas was, it took the combined strength of all three of us to keep him restrained. Lucas cursed and screamed at us as he struggled violently to free himself from our grip. *"I HATE YOU!"* he cried out fiercely with that same harsh, unearthly voice. *"GODDAMN YOU ALL! I HAAAAATE YOOOOOU!"*

Lucas eventually began to relent a little in his thrashings. As he darted, his glazed, hate-filled stare was over each one of us who pinned to the floor. Looking down at him, his Uncle Antonio asked, "Who are you? Tell us your name!"

In response, Lucas spat full in Antonio's face, and glared at him with defiance.

Looking into those wide, hate-filled eyes, I then addressed the invading spirit directly: "In the name of Jesus Christ, you know that you are going to have to leave this boy!"

98

To my surprise, I received an immediate reprimand from Antonio. "No, no, don't tell him that! "We don't want this spirit to leave; we want it to stay, so we can talk to it!"

"But, I thought our purpose here was to cast it out, in the name of Jesus?" I protested.

"Not until we talk to it first, and find out information," Antonio clarified.

Suddenly, the strong scent of cigar smoke began wafting around us. Glancing up, I observed that Lucas' sister and two young cousins were leaning over us, rapidly puffing upon thin cigars as a means of protection against the evil spirit. It was obvious that they, too, were intent upon conversing with the evil spirit, which had taken possession of Lucas. Meanwhile, Aunt Lucia had ceased her frenetic chanting, and was apparently anticipating some spirit communication. "Alright," I relented, realizing we'd probably get on with the actual expulsion part of the ceremony once the interrogation session was done.

"What's your name, and where do you come from?" Antonio asked the possessing entity. Lucas merely growled in response.

Before I had the chance to ask the same question by the shed blood of Jesus Christ, Lucas suddenly closed his eyes, and his body went completely limp. Antonio shouted his name a couple of times, but the boy did not respond.

"What happened?" asked Aunt Lucia, quickly stepping over to us.

"Not sure," I replied. "Lucas either just passed out, or he's pretending to be passed out. It happened very sudden."

Antonio said, "He seems to be at peace now. He is resting." Antonio glanced up at Lucia, who gave him a nod of agreement.

As soon as the three of us began to release our grip, Lucas instantly began thrashing and jerking underneath us once again. A moment later he'd managed to work himself free and sprung up once again, easily eluding our attempts to grab onto him. *"HAW-HAW-HAW-HAAAAW!"* he laughed at us derisively.

The Santera resumed chanting rapidly *and* loudly in Spanish, while Lucas raced around the room upsetting furniture and causing mayhem. Aunt Lucia's epithets eventually seemed to have some effect, for Lucas gradually slowed, became lethargic, and slumped back onto his chair. Lucia then instructed us to resume our seats. As Lucas sat there, his normal personality began to emerge.

No sooner had Lucas begun to recover, then the young woman who was seated directly to the left of my brother Carl grabbed the back of her neck, and let out a cry of alarm. "*It* touched me!" she screamed, leaping up from her chair. "Oh Dios mio, oh Dios mio!" She then fled from the room, sobbing hysterically. Seconds later Maria, who was seated to my immediate right, also reacted as if she'd just been touched on the nape of her neck.

While Aunt Lucia and some of the other women attempted to console the terrified girl, Carl and I discussed what had just transpired. Carl explained that immediately after the young woman seated to his left had screamed that she was being touched, he had also experienced a tingling sensation of being touched on the back of his neck. This sensation had been combined with an increasing amount of pressure, giving him the impression that something was attempting to get inside of him. Fortunately, he'd managed to fight it off by sheer will power.

Also, Carl had experienced this sensation immediately before Maria, seated to my right, had reacted to being touched on the back of *her* neck. This would seem to indicate that an unseen entity – perhaps temporarily absent from Lucas – had been systematically "probing" each person who was seated in the semi-circle, perhaps even testing for weaknesses. The nape of the neck is sometimes believed to be a point of access for invasive spirits. This invisible force was also traveling along the semi-circle in a left-to-right direction, which is typical of a demonic spirit. Interestingly, since I happened to have my open Bible resting on my lap, the entity apparently had passed by me altogether.

Carl and I momentarily turned our attention to Lucas, who remained slouched in his foldout aluminum chair. "How are you holding up there, buddy?" I asked, approaching him and placing a hand on his shoulder.

"Alright, I guess," he replied, smiling at me. "And a little tired. I also feel kinda' embarrassed, especially since I don't really remember what I was doing just a little while ago."

"The usual stuff," Carl told him in a casual tone. "It took three of us to hold you down at one point, so at least we got our exercise in for the night. And we found out that you definitely don't like candlelight when you've gone under."

"Really?" asked Lucas, sounding interested. "Wow... that's weird!"

"Just remember," I said, "none of this is your fault, my friend."

"Thank you," said Lucas, smiling up at me. For the next several minutes, Carl and I continued to chat with Lucas and to put him more at ease.

Lucas' Aunt Lucia then reentered the parlor, and announced that the exorcism ceremony would now recommence. She instructed Lucas to rise from his seat, and to stand facing her. Once he'd done so, Lucia asked Lucas if he was ready. "Yes. I think so," he quietly replied.

"Muy bien," said Lucia. She then firmly took hold of her nephew's hands and began forcefully shaking his arms in a circular motion. "Presentado ahora!" or "come forward, now!" she commanded the oppressing entity. When the first attempt failed to produce results, Lucia paused to catch her breath before repeating the process. "Presentado!" she commanded more firmly, while again aggressively shaking Lucas' arms. "Ahora!"

This time, Lucas visibly reacted to Lucia's provocation. His eyelids fluttered, and he began to collapse. Still holding onto him, Lucia helped ease Lucas down onto the floor.

"What is happenin'?" asked Antonio. "Is he gonna be alright?"

Aunt Lucia did not reply, but instead kept her attention focused upon her nephew, who lay sprawled upon the floor. Within seconds, Lucas' eyelids fluttered open, to reveal the same wild, glazed look as before. In the next instant he'd leapt up from off the floor, and was once again racing around the room, screaming and causing complete pandemonium. *"I HATE ALL OF YOU!"* he bellowed at us. *"I HATE YOU, I HATE YOU, I HATE YOU!"*

After Lucas had managed to knock over the remaining candles from the makeshift altar, he made another grab for the punch bowl, which contained the pulpy holy water. Fortunately, Carl, Antonio and I were able to intercept him in time to grapple him about the waist, and pull him away from the table. With a considerable effort, the three of us once again managed to tackle him to the floor. Lucas cursed, struggled and violently thrashed underneath us, while we were *barely* able to restrain him. Gasping to catch my breath, I said, "In the name of Jesus Christ... you will stop this... and be still!"

Gradually, Lucas began to cease his struggling, and became somewhat lethargic once again. He eventually even seemed to be going into some sort of a trance. A dazed, clouded look came into his eyes as he lay on the floor, no longer making eye contact with any of us. "Lucas?" Carl asked, waving a hand in front of the boy's eyes. "Lucas, are you alright? Are you with us?" But Lucas did not respond. As we released our grip, he merely lay there staring vacantly into space.

Our attention was suddenly diverted away from Lucas, as one of Lucas' cousins shouted out: "Mira! La Santera!"

We all turned to look in the direction to which the young Puerto Rican woman was pointing. In front of the altar, Lucia was standing with her eyes closed, as if she also had suddenly gone into some sort of a trance. Her stout body appeared to have become completely rigid and her hands now balled into tight fists.

Before anyone could intervene, Lucia fell straight backwards. Her stout frame went crashing down upon the altar with full force, totally collapsing it. "Lucia! Lucia!" her family members began crying out as we all rushed over to her assistance. Looking closely at her, we saw that her eyes had rolled back into their sockets, exposing the whites, and she seemed to be convulsing in what appeared to be a gran mal seizure. Although the area around her looked like a disaster, the glass punch bowl had not been shattered. Looking around at the others, I asked, "Should we call for medical assistance?"

"No," Antonio replied. "Let's see what happens first." Glancing behind us, I ascertained that Lucas was now reclining listlessly against a wall on the other side of the parlor. Surprisingly, Aunt Lucia soon seemed to have recovered, apparently without injury, and allowed herself to be assisted into a sitting position. However, there was now something noticeably different about Lucia's physiognomy and her general demeanor. Her eyes had become darkened and narrowed, resembling black slits, and the corners of her mouth were drawn up into an eerie, mask-like grin. In fact, her face had actually now taken on the resemblance of a theatrical "comic mask." Her plump torso was also rhythmically swaying back and forth. In general, she now appeared quite jolly.

"Lucia?" Carl called out. "Are you al-"

"Do not attempt to speak to her!" Antonio quickly cautioned him.

Lucia then began waving her arms, and in a shrill, high-pitched tone, which did not resemble her normal speaking voice, she announced in Spanish that she wished to smoke. Obediently, one of the young Puerto Rican women passed a lit cigar over to her. Lucia then motioned for everyone in the room to gather around her.

"What's going on?" Carl whispered to Lucas' sister Maria.

Maria pointed to a small, black-painted Buddha statue resting in a nearby corner of the parlor... almost right next to the spot where Lucia now sat. Maria explained to both Carl and I that La Santera's "spirit guide" normally resided inside that small statue. However, it had now temporarily left the statue and had taken over La Santera to communicate with everyone.

"Do you mean to say, that La Santera is now under possession by her familiar spirit?" I asked.

"Si!" Maria whispered, nodding excitedly. "That is her spirit guide, speaking to us through her right now!" She then rushed over to join the others who were huddled around Lucia. As it turned out, the spirit channeling through Lucia was now supposedly telling fortunes for everyone. Almost maniacally, Lucia continued swaying and speaking rapidly in that sickening-sweet, shrill voice in between puffs of her cigar, as most of the others sat together on the floor in front of her, eager to have their fortunes told. Meanwhile, I returned my attention to Lucas, who was now seated in a nearby parlor chair. "How're you feeling now, Lucas?" I whispered to him. But he did not respond, seeming to be in a daze.

103

Suddenly, Antonio began calling me over to where Lucia and the others were gathered together. "Keith! Come over here; she wants to talk to both you and Carl!"

As Carl and I knelt down among the others who were huddled on the floor, Lucia, the stout woman motioned for us to come closer. With her torso gyrating back and forth, Lucia spoke to us in Spanish in between puffs of the cigar she held, while Antonio translated for her. Aunt Lucia – *or* rather the "guardian spirit" which was speaking through her – told Carl and I that because we were twins, we shared an extremely close bond. She also predicted that there would soon be an illness within our immediate family and when this took place, we were to call upon her for a healing, and then we would know that she "has the power!" Not unexpectedly, there were gasps of astonishment from the others that were huddled together. As a precaution, I silently said a prayer of protection on behalf of my family members, in the name of Jesus Christ.

It also dawned on me that while the "spirit guide" was boasting of its power in that high-pitched whiney voice, everyone's attention was being diverted away from Lucas. After all it was originally for his sake that we'd all assembled here in the first place. At this point, however, Carl and I felt helpless to do anything more for Lucas, except to offer him our verbal encouragement.

Eventually Aunt Lucia came out of her trance and announced to everyone that her guardian spirit was back resting comfortably inside of the little black Buddha statue. Carl and I stepped back over to Lucas and asked him whether he felt comfortable enough to continue with the deliverance session. "Yes… I think so," he told us. From his manner, I sensed that he wanted to get it over with, once and for all.

"Don't worry, Lucas," I said to him. "By the power of Jesus Christ, you will be freed from this unholy spirit which has been afflicting you."

Aunt Lucia, now completely back to her normal personality, asked for Lucas to approach her. After gazing intently into his eyes she declared that through her gift of discernment, she could sense that the spirit which had been possessing Lucas was now gone. With authority, Lucia announced that the exorcism was now successfully completed and pronounced Lucas to be completely freed! She then warmly embraced her nephew.

Lucas' mother, along with the other family members who were gathered there tearfully expressed their gratitude to Lucia, for her miraculous intervention on behalf of her nephew that evening. "Aaaaahhhhh! Gracious, La Santera! Gracious, gracious!"

Glancing at Carl, I whispered, "That's it? It's over?"

"Apparently so," said Carl. "After all, Aunt Lucia is 'La Santera' here, and she has the final say. Hopefully we can trust her ability to discern that the spirit has truly been cast out from Lucas."

Privately, I also asked Antonio if he thought we should perhaps test Lucas once more or at least have him seen by a priest *just* to make certain. But Antonio was adamant that there was no further need for intervention, confidently assuring me that "Lucia is *never* wrong. No need to see a priest."

The family also gratefully thanked both Carl and I for venturing out on such a cold night and for our participation in the ceremony. Lucas also personally thanked us for our efforts on his behalf and again apologized for his behavior that evening. Placing a hand on his shoulder, I assured him, "Hey, like we said, there's no need to apologize."

Carl added, "Trust me, Lucas… not only did we get our exercise for the night, but on top of that, it was *quite* an enlightening experience!"

Although he still seemed rather fatigued, Lucas brightened and managed a relieved smile.

"Get some rest tonight kid," I told him with a wink.

It was after midnight when Carl and I rushed through the frigid night air to our waiting car parked on Hanover Street, our breath issuing in thick puffs of vapor. During the drive back to North Scituate we discussed the events, which we had experienced that evening. "What's your take on the exorcism ceremony we just saw take place?" I asked Carl, while turning the heater up another notch.

"Not quite what I was expecting," Carl replied. "Like you, I was actually expecting it to be more of a Catholic deliverance session. And Aunt Lucia becoming possessed herself and telling fortunes really took me off guard! I mean, that's not exactly what we came to Providence for, was it?"

"No, it wasn't. And in my opinion, that may have been an example of spirit entities working in conjunction with each other to intentionally create a distraction."

"Well, if that was the case, then it certainly seems to have succeeded," said Carl. "However, when Lucia came out of her spate of possession, she did declare that Lucas was now completely freed from his own affliction."

"So... in your opinion, you feel that the exorcism actually did take effect?" I asked.

With a sigh, Carl replied, "At this point only time will tell. All we can do now is to keep in touch with the family and see what transpires."

Throughout the week following the exorcism of Lucas, the family kept in almost daily contact with us, reporting that Lucas had suffered no further episodes of spirit possession. Carl and I were naturally pleased with the good news. When I suggested to his family that Lucas receive some follow-up spiritual counseling from a priest, they assured me that this would certainly not be necessary. Then, a few days later, during a telephone conversation with Carl, Lucas' Uncle Antonio informed us that his nephew had suffered an episode of possession while the family was driving past a church. However, Antonio and the rest of the family were reportedly not overly concerned by this incident, since the possession had just as quickly subsided after they'd driven around a corner past this particular church.

At the conclusion of the telephone conversation with Antonio, I asked Carl, "Well, doesn't that indicate that Lucas might possible still be under the possession of this spirit, since it afflicts him when he goes past a particular church?"

Carl said, "Well, Antonio said that Aunt Lucia merely attributed it to Lucas experiencing lingering after-effects, and that he couldn't possible still be possessed... not after the Santeria exorcism which took place."

Throughout the next year, Lucas remained free of any "lingering effects" of spirit possession, as long as he avoided the vicinity of certain Christian churches. Since his family members were not practicing Catholics, and only attended Catholic worship services on special occasions, Lucas also easily avoided having to actually enter a church. It seemed to his entire family that his Aunt Lucia, the Santera, had truly performed a miraculous cure by ridding her nephew of his terrible affliction.

Unfortunately, less than a year after the exorcism ceremony had taken place, Lucia herself experienced a family tragedy. Her lovely nineteen-year-old daughter, who was at the time living with a boyfriend, suddenly stopped answering telephone calls. After a few days her family grew concerned, and went to her apartment to investigate. When no one answered the door, they summoned the landlord and the police. The landlord unlocked the door for the Providence police officers when they arrived. Together, the landlord and the police discovered the mutilated and partially decomposed body of Lucia's daughter, who'd apparently been murdered by her insanely jealous boyfriend, who'd subsequently skipped town. My brother Carl later demonstrated his support to the family by attending the funeral.

As the years passed, Lucas' parents moved out of their apartment on Hanover Street. Carl and I eventually lost touch altogether with Lucas and his family. We can only pray that today, Lucas remains freed from his spiritual affliction.

CHAPTER 13

Mary Eliza

THE FOLLOWING STORY took place during the mid-1980's, before I was married and at a time when I was not associated with any particular paranormal investigation organization. My close friend Peggy, who was in her mid twenties at this time, shared a mutual interest with me in both historical and paranormal research.

"Here we are," I announced to Peggy – an attractive, red haired young woman, stylishly attired in a long black dress – as we pulled up just outside of the small historical cemetery located in North Scituate, RI. "This is the burial place of Mary Eliza, who is rumored to sometimes make her presence known to people who come here. I know you've been anxious to visit this cemetery for awhile now."

"Oh, yes. I'm really looking forward to meeting her," said Peggy.

After shutting off the car engine, I walked over to the other side and opened the passenger door for Peggy. She swung her long legs out of the car and together we made our way up the slight incline to enter the small cemetery.

For some months, I'd been researching information on a local girl named Mary Eliza Brownell, who had died of "consumption" (tuberculosis) on March 22, 1841. Mary Eliza was buried in this particular cemetery. Peggy had recently taken an interest in my research and her assistance during this project soon proved invaluable. As we continued gathering information on this young girl, we learned that she was apparently quite beautiful, and very much loved by the members of the community in which she lived...the entire town went into mourning for her when she died.

Having entered the cemetery on an overcast Sunday afternoon, I escorted Peggy over to Mary Eliza's grave. Inclining forward to get a closer look at the headstone, Peggy read aloud: "Mary Eliza...daughter of Col. George and Ann Brownell. Died March 22, 1841, age 17 years and 11 months."

"As you know," I said, "the Brownell's were prominent members of the community and were considered 'pillars' of the church they attended. Mary Eliza was especially loved by all those who knew her, it's no wonder the entire town of Scituate was said to have gone into mourning at her passing."

Glancing over at my friend Peggy, I was surprised to notice that her long, dark eyelashes had now become moistened. Peggy then suddenly burst into tears and said, "Ohhh...she was so young!"

Touched by my friend's compassion and sensitivity for this girl who had died so many years ago, I placed a comforting arm around her and said, "You're right, Peggy, that was a very untimely age for young Mary Eliza to be taken. But tuberculosis was rampant during that era. Medical science, as it were, could offer no cure and many families lost young children to the disease."

After Peggy had composed herself and dabbed her eyes, I asked her if she'd prefer to leave. "No...I'd like to stay just a little while longer," she said. "I'm picking up the impression that she's still here and that she's calling out to us."

"Others seem to have sensed that when visiting this cemetery, according to the woman who owns this property," I said. "But to my knowledge no one's ever reported being overly disturbed by this presence, or been frightened out of here."

"That's comforting to know," said Peggy. She then asked me, "Do you feel that Mary Eliza ever made her presence known to you while you visited this cemetery?"

"Well, I wouldn't say that I've ever specifically been aware of her presence per se, I have felt drawn over to her grave, as have other people," I explained.

"What about that illustration which you recently did of her? Do you think it's possible that Mary Eliza may have inspired you from the spirit world?"

"Well, that was simply my impression of what she may have looked like in life, since no contemporary portraits of Mary Eliza seem to exist. At least not to my knowledge."

Peggy then pointed out the fact that during her own historical research, she'd come across photos of family members which did coincidentally bear some slight resemblance to the illustration which I'd done. "I mean, it's true that they're mostly photos of old men," said Peggy. "But they were members of the Brownell family who were alive at the same time as Mary Eliza. I'll have to show you when we get back to my house."

"Yes, I'm very much looking forward to seeing those photos," I said. "But before we start heading back, would you like to take a closer look at the house where Mary Eliza and her family actually lived?"

"I'd love to!" Peggy said with enthusiasm.

After leaving the small cemetery, Peggy and I walked a short distance, about 1/8th of a mile along Rocky Hill Road, passing by the section of the road, which overlooked Hunting House Brook. We soon stood in front of the two story colonial house that the Brownell family once called home. "Oh, it's lovely!" Peggy said in admiration. "What I'd give to live in an historic house such as this."

"The family who owns this house now has really done a wonderful job renovating the place. Surprisingly, the house was rather dilapidated looking for years, back when I was a kid."

"You're kidding!" said Peggy.

"Although you'd never know it now," I said. "Back when our elementary school bus used to drive by this place, we actually used to refer to it as 'the haunted house.' Supposedly, an eccentric old lady used to live there all by herself...and it was always a thrill when we'd catch a brief glimpse of her, watching out of the window. It was not

Keith Johnson

until years later, that I began thinking about how lonely that poor old woman must've been."

"That *is* sad," Peggy agreed. "Hopefully she at least had family who came to visit her. But anyway, the house looks absolutely charming now; it's hard to picture it in a state of disrepair. I'd love to meet the people who currently own it."

"They've probably already left by now to go back to Connecticut," I said. "But they're usually here during the weekends, fixing up the interior. Someday we'll stop by and I'll introduce you to them."

"I'm really looking forward to it," said Peggy with a knowing smile. She then suggested that we make the trip back to her house, where her mom would be happy to serve us some desert.

Back at Peggy's house her mother graciously served us some coffee and delicious homemade apple pie, while Peggy leafed through the thick book of historic records that she'd recently borrowed from the Providence Public Library. "Here they are," she said, indicating the sepia tone photos of several distinguished-looking older men. "These are the members of the Brownell family I was telling you about. As you can see, they all share a certain family resemblance...the high forehead, and the arched eyebrows. The same as you've given Mary Eliza in your illustration of her." She then placed a small snapshot of my illustration next to the page for comparison.

After taking a closer look, I had to agree. "You're right, the young girl in my illustration *does* appear as if she could be a niece or a granddaughter of some of these men." After washing down another bite of apple pie with hot coffee, I added, "Of course, each of these aging gents in the pictures also bears an uncanny resemblance to John Quincy Adams, what with their balding pates and heavy white side whiskers."

"Yes, you're right, they do," Peggy agreed with a laugh.

Just then, Peggy's mother came back into the kitchen, holding an old photo. Here's that snapshot from the 'fifties I wanted to show Keith; I just came across it in one of the old photo albums."

"Oh, yes," Peggy told me as her mother handed me the photo. "You should find this quite interesting."

112

At first, it merely looked like a black and white photo from the mid-1950's of two smiling women wearing overcoats, standing outside in front of someone's garage. Peggy explained, "Those are two of my aunts, in Pawtucket, back in 1957. But, look closely at the upper left corner of the picture, near the top of the garage."

As I did so, I suddenly became aware of something very peculiar in the photo, which I had failed to notice at first glance. Directly in front of the upper section of the garage roof, suspended in mid air, was the small but clear image of a headless woman wearing a dark overcoat. The headless woman's arms were slightly held out at her sides, with the fingers of her hands curled into a claw-like position, giving the impression that she might be ready to strike out.

Peggy's mother explained, "We've had that photo in our album for years and we have no idea why that image is in it. As far as we know those women were never involved in any sort of a haunting. At least they never mentioned it."

Peggy asked me, "So, what's your opinion of the image in the photo?"

"Well," I replied, "I'd certainly say it's an excellent example of psychic photography. And totally by accident, too, I assume."

Peggy's mom said, "My brother was the one who took that picture and he sure wasn't expecting anything like that to appear in it. In fact, I don't think he ever even noticed the image."

Peggy added, "However, the women in our family seem to some-how attract spirits; at least I believe we do."

When I asked if they could relate an example of this, Peggy' mom told me, "There's the 'spectral nun' which several women in our family have seen...always just before a family member dies. She appears as a shadow figure wearing a nun's habit...you can't see any facial features, just a shadow."

"Have you ever seen her?" I asked.

"Once I did, when I was a teenager," said Peggy's mom. "I was in my bedroom getting ready for bed one night, when I happened to look up...and there she was, peeking around the door at me. The next day, we received word that one of my uncles had died."

Intrigued, I asked, "Have you ever seen the nun again after that night?"

"No, it was just that one time," said Peggy's mom. "But, she doesn't seem to be a frightening or malicious spirit at all. I just think of the nun as a spiritual messenger."

Turning to Peggy, I asked if she's ever witness an appearance of the nun. "No, I haven't," she replied. "But, I do sometimes get premonitions about things and people, which often turn out to be true. And I have the ability to sense when a spirit presence is nearby, just like I sensed that Mary Eliza was there today in the cemetery with us. As Mom said, this type of sensitivity seems to be inherited among the women on her side of the family."

Several minutes later, Peggy's mother went into the adjoining room and began playing the piano. While we were alone in the kitchen, Peggy suddenly surprised me by suggesting that we should attempt to contact Mary Eliza's spirit. In a hushed tone, she told me, "I really feel that Mary Elisa's spiritual essence is near to us. Perhaps we should make an attempt to contact her, especially since she seems to be a kindred spirit to us. That's the impression I received from her while we were in the cemetery."

"Yes, but I'm sure you understand, Peggy, that there are inherent dangers in attempting spirit communication," I reminded her. "To begin with, we'd have to examine our motivations for doing so. I mean, it would be different if her spirit was actually haunting us, or haunting someone else. But this just isn't the case here."

"But Mary Eliza is probably so very lonely after all these years," Peggy persisted. "She'd probably be happy to know that there are people who still care about her!"

"There are also deceptive spirits which play on people's sympathies by pretending to be the souls of the departed…when in fact they are not. In fact, they may never even have walked the earth in human form," I explained.

"Yes, but I sensed the presence of a benign spirit in the cemetery. When we first arrived I was also momentarily overcome by a feeling of intense sadness."

Picking up the black and white snapshot from the kitchen table and handing it to Peggy, I said, "As you know, the female apparition floating above the two ladies in this photo is headless. Now, when a spirit manifests itself with a body part missing, that can sometimes be an indication of the demonic. In fact, it's almost as if the demonic spirit has to follow a sort of cosmic law, indicating that it's not of human origin. Who knows, but *this* spirit might still be lingering somewhere nearby to your family? After all, you and your mom do share a certain sensitivity to spirits."

"Well, that's why I'll be attempting to contact Mary Eliza under controlled conditions," Peggy assured me. "And I'll make certain that I'm psychically protected beforehand. I can understand if you feel hesitant in participating, Keith. But, I might ask my college friend Debbie to assist me. She's also somewhat sensitive…and knowledge-able about incantations as well."

"All I can say is, please be careful, and make sure you know what you're doing," I advised her.

Peggy once again assured me that there was no need for me to worry.

A few evenings later, with her mother out visiting relatives for the evening, Peggy made a quick call to her college friend Debbie, who lived a short distance away. Together, they'd decided to attempt to contact the spirit of Mary Eliza Brownell.

Inside the parlor of Peggy's apartment, they placed two candles in front of my small, framed photo of the likeness of Mary Eliza and began calling out her name. When they asked her to give them a sign of her presence an eerie thing happened. As Peggy later explained it to me: "The eyes of the portrait just suddenly started to glow…I mean, *REALLY* glow! Debbie and I both saw it happen."

Next, they both distinctly heard heavy boot steps just outside one of the parlor windows, accompanied by what sounded like heavy breathing, or growling…but when the two terrified young ladies glanced outside, there was no sign of anyone out there! They then quickly snuffed out the candles and ended their ceremony.

A short time later when Peggy was walking Debbie out to her car, they did indeed notice there were some footprints underneath the parlor window…some of which were still forming, right below them as they watched! After the two rushed back inside the apartment, Peggy quickly re-lit the candles, and prayerfully asked whatever spirit was manifesting, to please depart in peace. Fortunately, they experienced no further incidents that night.

The following day, when Peggy related the incident to me, she concluded by saying, "Whatever spirit we succeeded in summoning last night it definitely wasn't Mary Eliza! Debbie was half scared out of her wits and I have to admit that I was, too."

"Well, the important thing is that you're both alright, and that you seem to have successfully banished this entity from your apartment," I told her, adding, "I definitely agree that it wasn't the spirit of Mary Eliza."

On the afternoon following my conversation with Peggy, I paid another visit to the small cemetery known as the Brownell Lot located along Rocky Hill Road in Scituate. Standing alone in the middle of the cemetery, I recited a brief, simple prayer: "Merciful Jesus, who takes away the sins of the world, grant them rest. Merciful Jesus, who takes away the sins of the world, grant them rest. Lamb of God, who takes away the sins of the world, grant them rest eternal. Amen."

Before leaving the Brownell Lot, I paused to place a small bouquet of hand picked wild flowers upon Mary Eliza's grave. A warm breeze momentarily picked up accompanied by what to me felt like an undeniable sense of peace and tranquility.

CHAPTER 14

The Atlantic Paranormal Society

MY INITIAL involvement with The Atlantic Paranormal Society actually began one afternoon while I was doing an Internet search for local paranormal investigation groups. It was the late 1990's, and for the most part during this time I was limited to doing local on-site investigations, as well as an occasional radio interview. Requests for investigations of private homes were few and far between. And so, with this in mind, I'd been toying with the idea of either organizing my own investigative group or hopefully finding a local group with which I could become actively involved.

Thus it was that I felt delighted, when I unexpectedly came across the small, modest website of a local paranormal organization known as The Atlantic Paranormal Society, founded by Jason Hawes. In fact, not only was this group local, but the founder apparently lived right in Warwick, Rhode Island, the same exact city in which I lived! It had been in existence under its current name for less than two years. Although the website was comprised of only a couple of pages containing mostly general info on the paranormal, I appreciated the fact that they did not charge for their investigations. They also seemed to take a sincere approach, looking for a rational explanation instead of automatically assuming that every situation was haunted. Thus I decided to contact founder Jason Hawes within the week.

It was early on a Tuesday evening that Jason Hawes and I met for the first time at a local coffee shop in Warwick. Jason instantly recognized me as I entered, having first a met with Carl earlier that week. "Keith," he said affably, coming over and shaking my hand. "I knew who you were tight away from your resemblance to Carl."

I had also recognized Jason from Carl's description of him. He was tall with a husky build, with gray-blue eyes and a shaven head, which gave him a somewhat more physically mature appearance than his actual age; he was in his mid-twenties at the time. Jason treated me to a coffee and sat down with me at a nearby table.

Over the next hour and a half we discussed our various experiences involving the paranormal. Jason was very impressed with the fact that Carl and I not only had quite a few years of experience in paranormal research, but also that we specialized in non-human types of hauntings. He was also impressed with the fact that Carl and I were long-time acquaintances of Ed and Lorraine Warren, and Ed's nephew John Zaffis. Jason informed me that he was also a personal friend of the Warren's and John Zaffis and that he'd worked with them on several cases.

During our conversation, Jason explained to me that while growing up, he'd never had anything more than a casual interest in anything having to do with the supernatural. However, about five years ago he'd had a personal experience, which had forced him to reexamine the possibility of paranormal phenomena in his own life. And it was this search for answers that had eventually brought Jason into contact with Johns Zaffis, as well as Ed and Lorraine Warren.

He'd consulted with the Warren's and John Zaffis, who'd been instrumental in helping him understand and cope with his own personal situation. Afterwards, both the Warren's and John Zaffis had offered Jason the opportunity to work closely with them on some cases, through which he'd gained some valuable experience. However, since they were all located in Connecticut, John eventually encouraged Jason to consider forming his own group right in Rhode Island, once he felt confident enough to do so.

Jason explained to me, "So, it was about a year later after I'd been working with the Warren's and with John, that I decided to found

Rhode Island Paranormal. I only had a couple of other members at first, but shortly after I put my site up on line, I began getting requests from all over New England. And so another paranormal researcher in Connecticut named Andy Thompson and I founded the Atlantic Paranormal Society. So including myself, we had seven full-time members."

Jason also explained that because Andy Thompson now had various personal obligations that were interfering with his duties as co-founder, he'd recently more or less had to step away from the field of paranormal investigation. But fortunately, Jason's close friend and fellow TAPS member Grant Wilson had volunteered to step up to the plate, and officially assumed the duties of co-founder. "Grant's a great guy, and I know you'll get along very well with him," said Jason. "In fact, you two actually have a lot in common. He also comes from Scituate, and attended Scituate High School just like you and your brother Carl did."

"Oh, really? Well, I look forward to meeting him" I said. I was also interested to learn that Grant also had his own private, personal experiences, which had sparked his interest in exploring the paranormal.

As mentioned another thing that interested Jason about Carl and myself, was the fact that we had experience dealing with inhuman spirits. The reason that Jason was particularly interested in this was because he had been involved in such rare but extreme cases... not only with the Warren's and john Zaffis, but also with TAPS.

I asked Jason if he could share an example with me. "Absolutely," he said. "Awhile back, some of us were involved in an investigation in New Jersey. Come to find out, there was some occult activity in the home. But we were unaware of that fact when we'd first been contacted, because the person renting the home had just moved in. Anyway, we didn't realize it was cult activity until we found pentagrams and other things downstairs. One of our original members named Jim was with us. He was out from Connecticut. As it turned out, Jim was more sensitive than even he himself realized and as a result he kept on experiencing feelings that he wasn't used to."

"Bad combination in a situation where inhuman spirits are involved," I said.

"Yes, *so* we found out," Jason said with a laugh. "Of course, when we first arrived at the place Jim seemed perfectly normal. But then all of a sudden he just snapped. He started swearing at the rest of us and then he even began physically attacking us. So to prevent Jim from possibly being injured or hurting others I grabbed his foot as he was trying to get up. He then became even more violent and tried kicking me away. So I ducked, and slid his legs down the stairs. He then started thrashing about so violently and became *so* completely out of control that I finally had to hit him. And when I did, his head hit the stairs, pretty much knocking him out. And after that, we quickly got him out of the house and to the vehicle."

"Jeez!" I said. "I've seen people who are sensitive suddenly become overwhelmed but it sounds like Jim was completely taken over. So, how did that investigation wind up?"

Jason replied, "Oh, once we got him out, Jim recovered completely in a matter of minutes, with absolutely no recollection of what had just happened. We eventually called in clergy and they blessed the whole home. We never heard back from the tenants because they moved out shortly after that. But, as far as we knew, they hadn't had problems after the home was blessed."

"Well, hopefully Jim learned form his experience," I said. "It's vitally important, especially for someone who's sensitive, to properly ground himself or herself prior to entering a situation like that."

Jason agreed. He then asked me, "Keith, how would feel about performing religious cleansings, in a situation such as that? I know you've had a lot of experience with these types of situations and that you also have strong religious convictions."

I explained to Jason that I had church approval to perform religious cleansing through prayer and intercession. Not only that, but for years I'd felt that I'd been called for this work. Jason nodded in approval. He also asked if I was currently affiliated with any other paranormal groups. I informed him that I'd been involved with an organization located elsewhere in New England. However, in the nearly two years in which I'd belonged to this organization, I had not even so much as had the opportunity to meet together with other members, let alone been invited to actively participate in any of the group's investigations.

"So I've simply been mailing in my annual dues and keeping in contact by phone with the founders, hoping for an opportunity to at least do something with other team members," I said.

Jason said, "It sounds as though your years of experience haven't really been appreciated in this other groups."

I told Jason, "Well, as I'm sure Carl mentioned to you, he and I have been seriously considering forming a group of our own. Either that or we've been hoping to join a group that's closer to our vicinity and in which we'd actually be allowed to actively participate in paranormal investigations. That's why I've been scanning the Internet and how I came across your organization."

"Are you currently involved with any investigations on your own now?" asked Jason.

I replied, "Well, I've recently been investigating a historical cemetery located in Coventry, which has been the scene of some serious cult activity and vandalism. But nothing other than that right now."

Jason smiled and said, "Well, Keith, I'd like to officially welcome both you and your brother Carl, as prospective members of The Atlantic Paranormal Society."

"Thanks, Jason," I said, shaking hands with him. "I was hoping you'd say that."

Keith and Carl Johnson on the job in TAPS uniforms.

121

A few evenings later, both Carl and I arrived back at the same local coffee shop to again meet with Jason and to be introduced to some of the other members of TAPS. Although Grant Wilson was not present this evening, Jason promised us we'd be meeting him soon. Like Jason, some of the members were also Warwick residents and most of them were in their early-to-mid twenties. They were all very anxious to meet Carl and myself, having been prepped by Jason beforehand about our years of experience. And each of them courteously welcomed us into the group.

Besides Jason, Carl and myself, there were four other members present. Jason first introduced us to Valerie Southwick, a petite young woman who had an avid interest in the paranormal and who was searching for answers. We were next introduced to Andrew Graham, a college student, who had a very compact build and, like Jason also had a background in marital arts. Andrew was also searching for answers and had done extensive research on his own prior to meeting Jason and joining TAPS.

Richard Einig was in his mid-twenties and soft-spoken, with long, straight medium brown hair tied back into a ponytail. He held the position of being the main technical specialist of TAPS. Rich also happened to be somewhat sensitive to his surroundings on a psychic level, although he preferred to concentrate mainly on the scientific approach to paranormal investigation.

Brian Harnois, from Woonsocket, had been in the process of organizing his own small paranormal group after four years in the Air Force, but had instead decided to join up with TAPS. Brian was tall, of somewhat slim build, with short dark hair and sideburns. He seemed to exude nervous energy and enthusiasm regarding anything to do with the paranormal and he was *very* eager to share with Carl and I his own personal experience.

"I remember it as if it was yesterday," said Brian. "It was back when I was eleven years old and I was staying overnight at my friend Josh's house. We were in his bedroom and we were fully awake talking, when all of a sudden a full-bodied apparition walked right through the bedroom wall! We both watched in amazement as it walked right through another wall on the opposite side. We slept on the floor in his parent's bedroom for the rest of the night. Come to find out later on, someone who was a Vietnam vet had actually hung himself in that house years before. Needless to say, that's what first started my interest in ghosts and hauntings."

I told Brian, "So, you've been into the paranormal ever since before your teen years."

"Oh, yeah," said Brian. "All throughout high school, I was made fun of for studying anything to do with the paranormal. Even before you could go online to do research, I used to take out books from the library, and photocopy pages and pages. After graduating high school, I served four years in the Air Force and after returning to civilian life I decided to seriously start investigating the paranormal."

Shaking his hand, I said, "Well Brian, I certainly look forward to working with you on investigations."

"Oh, definitely!" Brian said with enthusiasm. "And I'm also looking forward to getting to learn more about demonology, from you and Carl. I've always been fascinated to learn more about angels and demons."

"In that case, I'll be glad to share with you what I know," I said.

The following week Carl and I attended our second TAPS meeting, during which we had the opportunity to meet Grant Wilson. We found him to be the perfect counterpart to Jason, with his easy-going manner and affable sense of humor. Physically he was slim, with thick, short dark hair, and an ever-ready smile. Although outwardly he took a more casual approach in helping to supervise the group than Jason did, he also took the reality of the spirit world quite seriously.

Grant was also a devoutly spiritual person and I was pleased to learn that he and I shared some beliefs. Like Jason, Grant also had some personal experiences, both in his hometown of Scituate and overseas in Europe which led to his interest in perusing paranormal research. And, because of his personal faith *and* his experiences, he also felt led to help other people who were going through situations that were not easily explainable by natural means.

Carl, Grant and I spent some time catching up on people and places we were both familiar with in Scituate. Since all three of us had attended Scituate High School, Carl was especially interested to know what teachers were still there while Grant was a student. Grant was pleased to learn that we all shared some mutual friends and acquaintances, and that I still attended worship services there in Scituate.

Before the meeting at our familiar coffee shop concluded, Carl and I were personally invited by Jason and Grant to attend our first official investigation with other members of TAPS. Jason explained, "This will just be a local cemetery investigation, it's located in Apponaug. The name of it is Brayton Cemetery."

"Oh yes, I'm familiar with that cemetery," I said. "As a matter of fact, my brother-in-law and his wife once had a sighting of some kind of winged specter while driving by there in the middle of the night. It sounds like an excellent place to investigate."

"No kiddin'?" said Brian, obviously intrigued. "Well, let's get going, Dude!"

The investigation of Brayton Cemetery, with group members Jason, Grant, Valerie, Brian Rich, Andrew, Carl and myself was an extremely enjoyable experience. And although we did not come away with a great deal of paranormal evidence, it felt great to be investigating as part of a team once again! I was also impressed with the fact that not every situation we encountered was automatically presumed to be paranormal in nature. In fact, a healthy dose of open-minded skepticism was welcomed on investigations and even encouraged.

Both Jason and Grant's basic approach was, if natural explanations could first be ruled out, or "debunked," then what remained might *possibly* be considered as paranormal. I personally found this approach rather appealing, because it seemed somewhat "Sherlock Homles-ian" to me.

Our next investigation with TAPS tool place at the Joseph P. Ladd Center in Exeter, R.I., which was also known as the Ladd School. The Ladd Center was a very familiar Rhode Island mental health institution for many years, until closing in 1982. Since being shut down it was *also* very well known locally for its reputation of being haunted. At this location we were able to obtain some possible evidence of paranormal activity, especially disembodied footsteps, which we were able to record audibly. We also recorded some examples of

Electronic Voice Phenomena in the form of what sounded like muffled conversation within some of the empty rooms.

After leaving the Ladd Center, we also visited the Exeter Cemetery beside the Chestnut Hill Baptist Church. Here the graves of two sisters and their mother had been violated in 1892, during the last of the infamous "vampire" scares in Rhode Island. It was for this reason that the Exeter Cemetery had a reputation for being haunted. And although we encountered no paranormal activity there that night, there was some excitement when we spotted some lone individual crouching atop of an above ground tomb, apparently observing us. Since there were no other vehicles parked in the cemetery other than ours, this was most probably someone who was local to the area. When Brian shone his flashlight in the direction of the tomb, the person instantly scurried off. Brian cried out, "Did you see that guy up there? It's a freak, it's a crazy freak, up there watching us!"

As I was to discover, it would never be a dull investigation whenever Brian Harnois was included.

Chapter 15

Vengeful Spirits in Skowhegan

(The names of the family involved have been changed to protect their identities.)

THE WALL CLOCK had just chimed 1:00 AM on a Thursday night and in the parlor of their 19th Century farmhouse, George and Mandy Kingston once more began discussing the unexplained occurrences that they and their four children had been experiencing. As usual, a disagreement soon arose between them as to how their situation should be handled. "You know, we can't go on living like this," Mandy told her husband. "The kids are terrified and we are all losing sleep every night. We simply have to have outside help with this."

"Yeah? From whom?" George asked, somewhat gruffly. "We've already tried that route, remember? That priest wound up turnin' his back on us, just because he was too scared to set foot in here again. An,' then there was that ghost huntin' group that was here. They didn't prove nothin' either."

In a hoarse whisper so as not to wake up her children upstairs, Mandy said, "We're just lucky that the leader of their group wasn't seriously injured while he was here! What about when he was out in the garage and those boards started falling down from the rafters? He was standing right underneath them, and if he hadn't moved in time... well, I don't wanna think about what might've happened."

"That still don't prove nothin'," said George. He then reached for the can of beer beside his easy chair, took a swallow and reached for the TV remote ending the conversation.

But Mandy was not done yet. "Besides," she said, "they said that it might be more that just ghosts we have here. Bill said it might even be something 'inhuman.' And they recommended that other group from Rhode Island, called TAPS. The Atlantic Paranormal Society."

"Yeah, I seen that you've been checkin' them out on the computer."

"Bill said that TAPS has people in their group who specialize in dealing with inhuman spirits, whereas a lot of other groups refuse to even deal with these types of situations."

Slamming down the TV remote on the armrest of his chair, George shouted, "Aw, how the *hell* are they gonna deal with it if even a Catholic priest can't? Or won't?"

"SHHHH!" Mandy shushed her husband. "You'll wake the kids, an' Michelle has school tomorrow."

But it was too late. From one of the upstairs bedrooms, they heard a soft moaning coming from one of their daughters. "There, y'see?" Mandy said accusingly.

With an obvious twinge of guilt, George spoke in a subdued voice. "Sorry. But she'll go back to sleep."

Another quiet moan sounded from one of the upstairs bedrooms. Michelle, the eldest of the three girls, then sleepily called out, "Mom? Dad?"

George pulled a cigarette from the pocket of his red flannel shirt, popped it into his mouth and called back, "Go back to sleep Michelle." He then reached for his lighter.

From the nearby kitchen, their 4-year-old African gray parrot Skippy began squawking: "The bitch is home! The bitch is home!"

"Alright, you. That's enough," George said in the direction of the large parrot cage. Fortunately, the cage was covered over with a dark sheet as it always was at night, which meant that Skippy would most likely go back to sleep.

Mandy whispered, "So, I was thinking of contacting the two guys who run TAPS tomorrow. Their names are Jason and Grant."

Instead of verbally replying, George lit his cigarette, inhaled deeply and then slowly exhaled the smoke.

George seemed to be thinking it over.

Mandy had just opened her mouth to speak again, when from upstairs; a high-pitched female scream could suddenly be heard. George and Mandy glanced at each other. The two of them bolted out of their seats and rushed upstairs, with George in the lead.

They found 16-year-old Michelle, along with her two older sisters, Megan age 19, and Melissa age 21, standing in their sleepwear just outside the doorway of Michelle's second floor bedroom. All three girls were wide-eyed and visibly trembling. "Girls, are you alright?" asked their mother. "What just happened?"

Glancing at her parents, Michelle replied, "Mom... Dad... it was the Indian again! I woke up and he was standing over my bed!"

"What?" their father asked. "You're not 'seein' the Indian' stuff again?" Nonetheless, he knew that it was his duty to survey not only the girls' bedrooms, but also the entire upstairs area for intruders, while their mother tried to comfort the girls.

A few minutes later, George returned and told his wife and two daughters, "Nothin', just as I expected. Same as last time, there's no sign of anyone else upstairs. Michael, Crystal and the baby are sound asleep."

Now teary-eyed and trembling Michelle said, "I swear, I saw him! It was the tall man, dressed like an Indian, wearing the same turquoise medallion around his neck."

Turning to Megan and Melissa, Mandy asked, "Did *you* seem him?"

"No," not this time," said Megan. "We just woke up when I heard Michelle scream."

Mandy turned to her husband and asked, "Was everything in their bedrooms in place?"

Reluctantly, George said, "Everything's in place except that Grandma's picture is on the floor again... face down, of course."

All three daughters gasped and huddled closely to their mother. Their parents finally agreed that the girls could leave their overhead bedroom lights on throughout the remainder of the night, provided that they tried to go back to sleep instead of talking with each other.

The three girls agreed and returned to their rooms. "Remember Michelle, you have school tomorrow," Mandy said over her shoulder.

Before George and Mandy made it to the staircase they found their 18-year-old son Michael and his girlfriend Crystal standing at the other end of the hallway. They'd just emerged from the "in-laws room" they now shared. They also appeared to be visibly shaken. "Aw, cripes," said George. "Now the whole household is awake. Just go back to bed Mike, everything's under control. Your sister just had another bad dream, that's all."

Concerned Mandy asked, "Is the baby okay?"

"Yeah, still sleeping," Crystal said quietly.

In a much more understanding tone of voice than George's, Mandy told her son and his girlfriend, "I'm sorry if the noise woke you two up. But like Dad said Michelle just had a bad dream."

"No... it's not that," said Michael as he and Crystal stepped forward. "Something was in the room with us, just now. And it wasn't my imagination."

In the dim light of the hallway, George and Mandy could see that both their son and his girlfriend truly appeared to be terrified. George suggested, "Maybe you just had a bad dream too, Mike. I think you should just go back to bed."

Crystal protested, "No, we both experienced it. Something was right there in the room with us moving around."

In a patronizing tone, George asked, "Alright then Mike, what did it look like? Was it the Indian?"

From downstairs, Skippy the parrot began squawking once again. "Hi Mike! Hi Mike! Hi-"

"Shaddap, ya stupid bird!" George called back.

Michael replied, "I-I couldn't really see it... the room was too dark. But we could both feel it."

Crystal added, "And it just attacked Mike! Go ahead, Mike, show them."

Michael then pulled up his tee shirt to reveal several fresh-looking scratches across his chest that appeared to be claw marks. Although superficial the scratches were slightly bleeding.

"Oh my God!" Mandy gasped, placing a hand over her mouth. "Are you sure the baby's okay?"

Michael replied, "Yeah Mom, he's fine. We both checked to make sure."

Mandy then stepped closer and examined the wounds. "Oh, honey, we've got to put something on those!"

Michael informed them that there were also some scratches on both of his upper thighs.

George also stepped forward to get a closer look at the scratches. "Mike… you think that maybe you or Crystal could've accidentally done this in your sleep?" he asked.

Michael again insisted, "No Dad, I was fully awake when it happened!" When his father instinctively glanced over at Crystal Michael quickly added, "She didn't have anything to do with *it* either. Why won't you believe us?"

"We do believe you honey," said Mandy, placing a comforting arm around her son's neck. Turning to her husband she hissed, "George, the kids are starting to be attacked now. Things are just getting worse and we can't keep putting up with this."

George had opened his mouth to protest when suddenly, three loud, resounding thuds could be heard against the side of the house just outside. The family's hound dog Blue, began loudly barking. Mandy shrieked and clutched tightly to her son. "Ow!" Michael winced, as his mother's body made contact with his painful scratches.

"Oh I'm so sorry honey!" Mandy tearfully apologized to Michael.

"What the hell is it now?" said George instantly heading back towards the stairs. The rest of the family followed close behind.

Back downstairs, George rushed over to the nearest window and pulled back the curtain. But all he could see was darkness beyond the frosted window. Next, he bounded over to the side door and flung it open, while switching on the outside light. A rush of frigid air assaulted his exposed face and hands. Squinting while peering past the swirling snowflakes, all George could see outside was the thick, unbroken blanket of snow covering his back yard, illuminated by the back porch light. No trace of any footprints were visible in the freshly fallen snow... and certainly, no one could have slammed three times on the side of his house and then run through the snow completely out of sight within less than fifteen seconds!

Cursing under his breath, George forcefully shoved the side door shut and re-locked it. Trudging back into the parlor, George faced the five terrified others who now stood there huddled together. He could see the faint bloodstains on his wife's blouse from when she'd pressed against Michael. There were also smears of blood on Crystal's night-shirt. "No sign of anyone out there," he told them. "No trace of any footprints in the snow, either... just like the last time."

Glaring at her husband accusingly with tear-stained eyes, Mandy said, "George you have to admit, we do need help with this!"

George allowed himself to collapse back down into his easy chair. He pulled out another cigarette from his shirt pocket. With a weary sigh, he then grudgingly admitted, "Christ... maybe this TAPS can help us, after all."

It was early on a January evening in 2001 that a 'high-priority' meeting of The Atlantic Paranormal Society was called together. As founder Jason Hawes, co-founder Grant Wilson and Case Manager Brian Harnois informed us they'd recently received a call from a woman in northern Maine named Mandy Kingston, who was franti-cally requesting help from us.

She claimed that the founders of the Maine Paranormal Research Association, who'd recently visited with her and her family, had referred us. According to Mandy, just several months earlier, she, her husband George and their four children had relocated from Massa-chusetts, to an antiquated two-story farmhouse in the rural town of Skowhegan, Maine. The original section of this farmhouse had been built in the year 1826, with succeeding generations living in the house and making additions to it of their own. The most recent addition was a guestroom or "in-laws room," which had been added onto the second floor sometime during the 1930's.

At first it seemed like they'd found the ideal setting. They were now living in an historic farmstead in a fairly isolated community, where they could keep horses and other livestock, far removed from the stresses of living in a city. Sure, there was some bizarre looking graffiti on two of the upstairs bedroom walls, which looked as though it might be occult related. But George and Mandy attributed this to the work of bored teenagers who'd simply been expressing their artistic bent. However, it soon became apparent that all was not as it had at first seemed in their new home. Within a few weeks after moving in, they began experiencing some rather strange rapping sounds throughout the house. There would also be sudden cold spots in certain rooms, sometimes accompanied by disgusting odors, which would suddenly permeate the entire room and then vanish just as quickly.

At first, the family attributed the knockings and the sudden cold spots to living in an old house that admittedly needed some repairs. Things like this were expected in an old house. As for the unpleasant smells, they assumed that a small animal, perhaps a mouse or some other rodent, had simply died somewhere underneath the floorboards.

As the weeks and months progressed, unusual activity within the house gradually began to increase. Mandy herself never really felt comfortable being alone in *any* of the rooms, especially the cellar. She often had the eerie sensation that unseen eyes were watching her. As if to confirm that she was not alone, Mandy sometimes even began to be poked or to have her hair tugged by invisible fingers. The Kingston's family hound dog, Blue, would suddenly become agitated and begin barking and howling at certain areas in the house for no apparent reason. Although George remained somewhat skeptical, Mandy eventually reached the conclusion that they might be sharing their 19th Century farmhouse with a ghost.

Upstairs in the bedrooms, as well as the in-laws room, an old black and white photo of their grandmother, who had died two years before rarely seemed to stay put. Before even unpacking the photo when they'd first moved in, they'd found it out of the box and lying in the middle of the floor, face down. Although they always made sure to leave the photo placed carefully in a small frame and resting upon a shelf, the family would always return to find it face down, no matter where they left it.

Soon afterwards, photos all over the house would sometimes be found face down, especially if they were photos of people who were deceased. The two teenaged girls, Michelle and Megan, then began seeing what appeared to be the spirit of an Indian in their bedroom in the middle of the night. Often they would awake to see him standing next to their beds, peering down at them. From what Michelle and Megan could make out this spirit seemed to be dressed in buckskin and wearing some sort of pendant or medallion around his neck. Then one evening shortly before bedtime, Michelle and Megan entered their bedroom they shared to find that Megan's plastic toothbrush had somehow been impaled straight through her thick oak bedpost, without breaking!

Nor was the activity confined just to the house itself. Michelle, Megan, Melissa and even Michael claimed that the barn out in back was also haunted. While doing chores or simply hanging out inside the barn, they reported glimpsing strange lights, as well as shadowy figures inside the dark recesses of the barn's interior. And then, Michelle would often find herself locked in her bedroom, even though she always made a point of never locking her bedroom door.

The family, being of the Catholic faith, had eventually called in their parish priest to come and bless their house. Upon his arrival, the priest seemed strangely reserved and even reluctant to be there. Apparently, he'd also heard rumors of this farmhouse having a reputation for being haunted, years before the Kingston family had taken up residence there. The priest hastily performed his duties by standing in the middle of the parlor, rapidly reciting some prayers and spraying holy water in all four corners of that room only. He then went upstairs and repeated the process in one room only and hurriedly left.

Megan had spoken up, by asking, "But Father, aren't you going to bless the rest of the house? We've been experiencing some very strange things here and we feel this house and the barn outside might be haunted."

Michelle added, "And what if there are spirits here other than just ghosts? What if there are demons or something in this house?"

While quickly packing up his accoutrements the good father had suggested that they were probably letting their imaginations get the better of them. He'd then made a hasty departure, explaining to them that he had another appointment elsewhere.

Although George Kingston had up until now remained skeptical of the activity, refusing to admit to the possibility that his house might be haunted, an event soon happened which was to change his mind. One evening, while the family was preparing for bed, a tremendous crash was heard from outside of the house. It sounded almost like an explosion. Rushing outside to find out what had happened, George discovered that the large door leading to the cellar had literally been torn off its hinges, seemingly from the inside!

The very next morning, George had telephoned their parish priest again, informing him that they were now in an emergency situation and that they desperately needed him to return. The priest refused, suggesting that perhaps "watching too many horror movies" had caused their imaginations to run away with them. At this, George had become infuriated and accused the priest of having angered the spirits in his house, instead of driving them our. He even swore at the priest over the phone. Having finally gained control over his temper, George then apologized to the priest for his outburst. The priest accepted George's apology but still refused to have anything further to do with blessing their house.

Mandy Kingston had then done an Internet search on local paranormal investigation groups who might be able to help her and her family. She was successful in contacting the founders of Maine Paranormal Research Association. Members of Maine Paranormal *did* conduct a thorough investigation of the Kingston residence and verified that paranormal activity was indeed taking place both in the house and in the barn out in back. However, because there was also the possibility that inhuman entities might be involved, the founders had recommended that TAPS be consulted on this case as well.

Not long after Maine Paranormal had visited their house, the activity increased, almost as if the entities that were haunting their house were seeking retribution, for Mandy having called in a paranormal investigation team. Sightings of the full-bodied apparition in the girls' room became more frequent at night. Recently Michael had moved out of his downstairs bedroom, because of the disturbing feeling he was getting while in there. His parents had allowed him to move into the second floor section of the house known as the in-laws section, with his 18-year-old girlfriend Crystal, who had recently given birth to Michael's baby.

One night, Michael and Crystal were in bed upstairs with the baby asleep in a crib nearby, when Michael suddenly felt a searing pain across his chest and legs as if something had just attacked him. They turned on the overhead light and were both shocked to see bleeding scratches had been inflicted upon Michael's chest and legs.

Jason and Grant agreed to accept the case. Jason especially requested that I be included in this investigation because of the possible demonic implications. Due to prior commitments, both Grant and my brother Carl would not be able to accompany us on this investigation. Other members of the TAPS team to be included would be Brian Harnois, Richard Einig, Valerie Southwick and Andrew Graham.

By special arrangement and with the permission of the Kingston family it was also agreed that on the second night of our weekend investigation, we would be joined at the Kingston residence by novelist Jodi Picoult. Jodi happened to be researching various aspects of real-life paranormal investigation for an upcoming novel, and as part of her research had asked to accompany TAPS on some of our investigations. Also meeting us there in Maine would be freelance photographer Eric Falk, who had previously worked with Jason.

Thus it was that on a cold January morning in 2001, our team of six TAPS members set out in a rented van from Warwick, Rhode Island to make the estimated five-hour trip to Skowhegan, Maine. Jason would be the driver while Valerie rode "shotgun" in the front seat beside him and the rest of us in the comfortable back seats. From the seat directly behind Jason, I commented, "We few. We happy few."

"I hear ya, buddy," Jason replied. "Let's just hope the weather holds out for us along the way."

The trip to Skowhegan began as an enjoyable event, with everyone sharing light-hearted conversation and laughs. Of course, there would be no way of knowing exactly what we were up against until we were actually at our destination. But because we were all aware of the fact that we were going into a situation, which possibly involved inhuman spirits, it was especially important for us to maintain a positive and upbeat frame of mind.

Also, for Jason and myself, the situation possessed an added element of emotional stress, since we were the only two who had to leave behind families of our own for this weekend trip. It was for this reason that Jason had burned a CD especially for this excursion. The CD contained spiritual, family related songs that he knew would be significant and comforting for the two of us.

It was not until shortly after we crossed the border of New Hampshire and entered the state of Maine that the weather abruptly changed. A snowfall began and by the time we were nearing Skowhegan, the driving conditions were nothing short of treacherous. The roads had not yet been sanded and were therefore incredibly slick and the heavy snowfall was severely reducing driving visibility.

During the last hour of our journey, we passed by no less than five major roadway accidents, each progressively worse than the last. In fact the very last accident we came across involved a van that had slid off the highway and down an embankment, tipping over into its side. This van happened to be an exact replica of the one we were in! Fortunately, Jason had developed considerable driving skills after years of driving in all sorts of New England weather conditions, and maintained complete control at all times. I was praying continually for our safety and by the grace of God we arrived at our destination in Skowhegan without mishap, having been delayed only about an hour and a half. Just down the street we met up with photographer Eric Falk, who thankfully had also made it there safely.

It was after dark when Jason pulled the van onto the snow-covered driveway of the 19th Century farmhouse. George Kingston, dressed in a heavy winter parka came outside to welcome us and to guide Jason forward to park beside his pickup truck.

Once inside, George introduced Jason to the rest of the Kingston family, which included George's wife Mandy and their four children, Michael, Michelle, Megan and Melissa. They certainly presented the appearance of a typical northern New England family. While George was dark haired with somewhat rugged features, Mandy was blonde with a round face and large expressive grayish blue eyes. Both Michelle and Megan were pretty teenagers with red hair and some freckles, who shared an upstairs room. 21-year-old Melissa was a slightly older version of her two younger sisters. Michael was a good-looking lad of 18 with boyish features and dusky blonde hair. Michael's girlfriend Crystal and their infant son would be away from the house for the entire weekend, staying with Crystal's mother.

Mandy immediately expressed her gratitude for our having driven all this way in such treacherous weather conditions. "Thank you so much for coming, I'm so glad you're here!"

Jason told her, "The important thing is that we all made it here in one piece. The snow came upon us quite suddenly and it got even worse during the last couple of hours of our trip." He then informed George and Mandy about the five accidents we'd seen along the way.

"Oh, my God!" said Mandy. "Well again, bless you for coming all this way to help us."

George said, "Yeah, we really do appreciate you guys making the trip here. As my wife's told you, we've had some mighty strange things going on in this house, both inside and outside."

Jason then introduced the rest of us. "These are five of our main investigators, Valerie, Andrew and Keith, Brian and Rich. And this is freelance photographer Eric Falk, who you've been expecting as well. Eric will be documenting the investigation."

As we all greeted the family, Mandy smiled and commented, "Yes, I recognize all of you from your pictures on the TAPS website."

"I guess you've really done your homework," Jason told her with a smile. He then explained to her, "Mandy, you mentioned that after we've concluded our investigation you'd like to have your house blessed by a member of our team. This is what Keith specializes in. He'll be performing a blessing of your entire house as well as the outbuildings. And for safety reasons at least one other team member will be accompanying Keith at all times during the blessing."

"Yes, that's a good thing," said Mandy. "And again, I want to thank all of you so much for coming out here to help us. And especially for not thinking that we're crazy, or just imagining it all."

Her husband George added, "Yeah, just like that priest we had here, who told us that it probably all just in our minds!" He then chuckled while shaking his head.

Stepping forward, I said, "Yes, I heard about that. But didn't this priest also already know that this house is supposedly haunted?"

Mandy said, "Oh yes, he did, which is why I think he was so uncomfortable about being here and was in such a hurry to leave after performing the blessing."

Her daughter Melissa confirmed, "That's right, it was like the priest couldn't wait to get out of here. He just stood here right in the middle of the parlor and quickly shook holy water at the four corners of this room only, and one room upstairs and then said he was done. *And* he refused to come back even after my dad called him and told him that things were still going on here, even worse than before."

George said, "After our cellar door outside exploded off its hinges, I called the priest up and told him we needed him to come back and finish the job. But he told me we'd probably just been watching too many horror movies. So that's when I lost my temper and swore at him. Of course, I apologized to him later, before getting off the phone."

With a shrug, I said, "It sounds to me as if maybe the priest was the one who'd seen too many horror movies."

"Yeah, you got that right," said George.

Mandy then took our overcoats and told us to make ourselves at home. She even insisted on fixing dinner for us. "It's the least I can do for you brave souls," she told us. "Now I understand that your author friend, Jodi Picoult will also be joining you here tomorrow night, is that correct?"

"Yes, with your permission," said Jason. "She really wants to follow us step by step for the research she's doing for her newest book. She's also hoping to actually experience some genuine paranormal activity."

Mandy said, "Well, chances are that she will here. I'm looking forward to meeting her, too."

Before settling in, Jason and I of course telephoned our families to let them know that we'd arrived safely, and that everything was in order. At Mandy's insistence, we then sat down to a delicious home-cooked meal with her and her family. The Kingston's were quite interested to hear all about the history of TAPS and about some our experiences with investigating the realm of the supernatural. All through our lively dinner conversation the family's African gray parrot Skippy repeatedly squawked and added his own comments. With a laugh, Mandy said, "I'm sorry but Skippy's just so excited with all this company over. He probably thinks you've come here just to visit with him."

Valerie said, "Oh no, don't apologize. That certainly is a beautiful bird! How old is he?"

"Four years old," said Mandy. "I've actually had him since he was little more than a hatchling without even any feathers at all. He was just covered with feathery down. His mother abandoned him so I used to feed him by hand with a medicine dropper."

Andrew commented, "I've heard that parrots can sometimes live as long as people or even longer."

"That's true," said Mandy. "Skippy could very likely outlive me."

Brian said, "I'm impressed. He sure seems to know a lot of words."

Mandy agreed. "Oh yes, he has quite a vocabulary and he's learning more all the time. Isn't that right, Skip?"

Skippy suddenly began squawking, "The bitch is home! The bitch is home!"

Everyone laughed as Mandy explained, "Skippy's just mimicking my husband's sense of humor. That's what George says sometimes if I happen to get home from work after he does."

"Yeah!" said George, smiling and nodding in agreement. "You gotta be very careful what you say around here, 'cause trust me, it'll wind up getting repeated."

Brian then inclined his chair closer to the large parrot cage, and said, "Skippy… can you say, 'Hi, Brian?' C'mon, Skippy. 'Hi, Brian. Hi, Brian.'"

From his perch, Skippy the parrot merely eyed Brian as if he thought he was crazy. Valerie said, "I don't think he's going to say it for you, Brian."

Immediately after supper we commenced setting up our equipment in various rooms of the house and began our separate interviews with each member of the family. Before we had the chance to interview George Kingston he received an emergency telephone call from the road service that he worked for, telling him he was needed to go out to plow. "Well, it looks like I probably won't be back until well after midnight," he announced to us with a sigh, while pulling on his heavy winter parka. "My wife will have to fill you in on my part of the story. I'll see you guys when I get back."

After George had left, Mandy reiterated to Jason and me about the cellar door had seemingly been "exploded" off of its hinges. "It just scared the hell out of us all when it happened," she said. "And it actually sounded to us sort of like an explosion. Have any of you ever known something like that to happen?"

"Actually, yes, I have," I said. "It was during a case which my brother and I were both involved in quite a few years ago, when we were still teenagers. So, yes, I know that things of this magnitude sometimes do occur."

Mandy explained to us how their hound dog, Blue, would often begin growling and barking at certain areas in the house, although he'd never been known to behave this way before. And the dog usually refused to go anywhere near the barn out in back. Mandy also called her son Michael over and mentioned about the scratches that recently appeared on his chest. "They weren't deep," said Mandy. "But they were bleeding a little bit." She then asked Michael to unbutton his shirt and show us where the scratches had been. Sure enough, there were still the lingering traces of several thin scratches, although they were fairly well healed by now.

"Were they painful when they were first inflicted?" I asked.

"Yeah, they sure were," said Michael. "It kinda' felt like I'd just been scraped while going through a briar patch, y'know?"

"Yes," I said. "And tell me, Michael, did anything happen just before you received the scratches, like any sort of warning? Or did you just wake up with them?"

Michael replied, "I was in bed, and the lights were off, but my girlfriend Crystal and I were wide awake when it happened. Our baby was still sound asleep in his crib. I remember all of a sudden there was a terrible odor in our bedroom and we had the strange feeling that something was in the room with us. It was then that I was scratched."

Jason asked, "Could you describe this odor for us?"

"It was a rotten smell, like something dead," Michael explained.

Jason asked, "And did you *or* your girlfriend actually see anything in your bedroom with you when you were scratched?"

"No, it was too dark," said Michael. "But when I used to have my bedroom downstairs, I sometimes used to see what looked like a shadow figure moving around. But I've never been able to get a good look at it. I just used to see it more out of the corner of my eye, y'know? And sometimes I used to smell that terrible odor in my downstairs bedroom, too. It was like the smell of something rotting."

"Did you feel threatened at all by this presence in your downstairs bedroom?" I asked.

"Oh, yeah," Michael emphatically replied. "In fact, that's the reason I moved upstairs into the in-laws section upstairs. It was to get away from whatever was in there, because I couldn't take it anymore. And since there was a lot of room up there in the in-laws section, that was when my girlfriend Crystal moved in, with my parents' permission. That was right before she had the baby." Michael added, "Things were alright for awhile after I moved up there, so I was hoping at first that it hadn't followed me. But I guess now it has."

While Michael was speaking Mandy went to get a snapshot, which she handed to Jason. "Please, both of you take a look at this and tell me what you think," she said. It was a photo of her daughter's solid oak bedpost, with an unbroken plastic toothbrush driven straight through it. When all had taken a look, Mandy asked us, "Can any of you explain how that could've happened, especially without the toothbrush breaking?" We admitted that we had no immediate explanation.

Jason thanked Mandy and Michael for the interview and asked if there was anything else which they could think of to add. Mandy thought for a moment before telling us, "Well, there was one thing in particular which happened while the group from Maine Paranormal was here. The leader of their group, Bill, was out in the barn with his wife Nancy and some of the other members of their group. I guess they were making recordings with some of their equipment. Bill was standing there near the center of the barn and he'd just asked if there were any spirits in there which would like to communicate. All of a sudden one of the long wooden boards that are hung up near the ceiling slid off and almost hit him! Bill was just barely able to jump out of the way with it missing him by inches! He'd would have been seriously injured if his wife hadn't screamed for him to get out of the way."

"Him... interesting," said Jason. I could tell that he was intentionally hiding the concern in his voice.

Next, while Jason, Brian and Eric remained downstairs, Rich, Valerie, Andrew and I went upstairs to interview the two youngest daughters, Michelle and Megan. They of course immediately showed us the hole bored through the oak bedpost of Megan's bed, which was where Megan claimed to have found her unbroken plastic toothbrush. Megan momentarily excused herself to run downstairs and came back with the same snapshot their mother had shown Jason and me of the toothbrush impaled through the bedpost. The wood surround the hole was splintered on one side.

"That's pretty amazing," Andrew commented.

The two girls then led us into the next bedroom where their older sister Melissa now slept and showed us the two walls, which had "occult related" graffiti on them, left over from the previous tenants. Upon one wall, scribbled in black ink, were a number of unfamiliar letters and symbols along with a pentagram. To the right of these symbols was a small, crudely illustrated cartoon of a lion head with human-like features. On another wall of the bedroom, there was a cartoon caricature of Mark Twain. While examining and photographing the graffiti, I asked the girls, "What do you know about the people who lived here before you?"

"Not much," Megan replied. "Just that they were some young guys who were into some sort of black magic. You'll have to ask my mom more about that."

Both Megan and Michelle then provided us with greater details about the "Indian" spirit they were occasionally seeing in their bedroom. When Valerie asked the girls to describe this spirit Michelle said, " I really think it's the spirit of an American Indian, because from what I've seen of him he has long dark hair, even though his face looked a lot like my dad. In fact, I thought it was dad at first until I saw his long hair and he wouldn't answer me when I talked to him. He also seems to be dressed in buckskin like an Indian. And whenever I see him, he's also wearing some sort of medallion." Megan agreed with her sister's description of the Indian spirit in every detail.

Rich asked, "Could you describe this medallion to us?"

Michelle replied, "Well, I couldn't really see a lot of detail of it in the dark. But I could definitely see that it had a turquoise stone set into it and it even looked very similar to a medallion that my dad used to have."

Megan said, "Yes, I noticed the medallion the Indian was wearing too and it did look like the one our father used to own."

"And does your dad still have this medallion?" asked Rich.

Megan replied, "No, Dad said that he lost it over a year ago. We even asked him about it and told him that the Indian we saw was wearing what looked like the same one he used to have."

"And what was his reaction when you told him?" asked Rich.

"Well," said Megan, "at first he didn't really believe either of us. He told us that it was probably just our imagination or that we were both dreaming it all up, y'know, about the Indian spirit. But then after so many other things started happening in this house, he did finally start to believe what we were saying."

Valerie then asked them, "Do either of you feel threatened by this Indian spirit?"

"No," both girls said together. Michelle said, "We actually feel that he may be some sort of guardian spirit who's watching over us and maybe even protecting us."

"So you don't get an uncomfortable feeling from this Indian spirit at all?" I asked them.

"No, not at all," said Michelle. "It just used to scare us sometimes when we'd wake up and see him standing there. But I don't think he really means us harm."

"Besides," Megan added, "the psychic that was here said the Indian is a friendly spirit."

"You had a 'psychic' here?" I asked.

Megan replied, "Oh, yeah, he was a friend of our dad's who was studying to be a priest before. He was staying here for awhile."

Andrew asked, "Why was he staying here?"

Melissa explained to us, "Well, he was an alcoholic and I guess he had some other emotional issues. He was studying to be a priest but then he got sent to Vietnam and when he came back he was an alcoholic. So because he was a friend, my dad let him stay here for a while. But he was a very spiritual person, and he could sense whether spirits were good or bad."

I asked her, "So, he had the spiritual gift of discernment?"

"Yeah, I guess that's what you'd call it. He seemed to be real sensitive," said Melissa.

The two girls also informed us that this psychic friend of their dad's was picking up on the number four... and that there was an entity present who wanted to completely take at least one of them over.

"When he said, 'take one of you over,' did he mean as in 'possession'?" I asked.

"Yes, that's what he meant," said Megan.

Andrew asked, "Now when he mentioned the number four, was he referring to there being four children?"

"Yeah, I guess, "said Megan. "He never really explained."

Rich asked, "Where is this psychic friend now?"

Megan said, "We don't know for sure where he is now... just that he told my dad he's afraid to come back here."

Before we concluded our interview with Megan and Michelle, they gave us a tour of the rest of the second floor. Further down the hall was a sparsely furnished spare bedroom. They explained that this used to belong to their older sister Melissa, until she recently moved into the bedroom next to theirs to be closer to them. A little further down the hallway, just outside of what was known as the "in-laws room," the girls pointed to the ceiling and indicated a small opening, which led into the attic. Megan emphasized, "We've never been all the way up there, because my dad says it's unsafe. Besides, I just looked up there once and it gave me the creeps, it's so dark and cruddy." There was also a modern bathroom at the end of the hallway and to the right.

Megan and Michelle then took us into the in-law's room, which was located at the very end of the hallway and which was slightly larger than the other rooms. Michelle said, "This is where my brother, Crystal and the baby sleep, as you can tell."

Indeed this room, which now substituted as a bedroom, was somewhat more cluttered than the other bedroom. But it was spacious, with a lengthy counter, cabinets and even its own tiny bathroom at the far back end of the room. There was even an old but comfortable looking loveseat near the center of the room. On the floor in front of the counter were a few opened cardboard boxes containing various unpacked household items. Beside one of these boxes was a small, framed photo of an older woman. Megan explained to us, "This is the picture of my grandmother who has passed away. Shortly after we moved in we found it taken out of the box and lying face down on the floor. We know that none of us did it. And no matter how often we put it back up on the counter here, or anywhere else, sooner or later we find it lying face down on the floor again."

Michelle added, "It's the same with other pictures all over the house, especially if it's a picture of someone who's died."

When we asked Megan and Michelle if they had anything else they'd like to add, both girls once again stressed to us that even though they believed the Indian spirit meant them no harm, they still felt very threatened by some unseen force within the house. They especially believed there was some malicious entity in the upstairs area, which did intend to harm them and the rest of their family.

Back downstairs I asked Mandy what she knew about the previous tenants who had moved out shortly before she and her family had moved in. Mandy replied, "From what I was told by the owner of this house, they were just a bunch of young guys who lived here for only about a year or less, and that they liked to party a lot. I guess they were into the whole sex, drugs and rock n' roll scene. But later on I heard from some neighbors that they used to dress in black all the time and that they were Satanists. They supposedly used to hold satanic rituals in the cellar, and maybe even performed animal sacrifices down there."

"*Charming,*" I said. "And was the priest who came here to bless your house aware of this?"

"I imagine he's heard about it, yes," said Mandy. "Which was probably part of the reason why he was in such a hurry to get out of here and why he refused to come back when we asked him to."

Shortly after 9:30 PM we officially began our investigation of the Kingston residence. Because of the heavy snowfall outside which was still accumulating, we decided to hold off our investigation of the barn out in back, although we certainly planned to get out there tomorrow. For now, we'd confine our investigation to the main house alone. We divided ourselves into three groups, with Jason and Brian investigating the basement, Andrew, Valerie and Eric going through the first floor and Rich and I taking care of the upper rooms.

Rich and I began by using an Electromagnetic Field Detector and a digital thermometer as we moved through the second floor bedrooms. These bedrooms of course included the one with the graffiti on the walls, now used by the older sibling Melissa and the bedroom that both Megan and Michelle shared. Aside from some high readings near the electrical outlets these rooms showed nothing significant. Moving onto the now unused bedroom, we again found nothing unusual. While in Megan and Michelle's room, I pointed out the hole in the bedpost through which the toothbrush had been impaled. "What do you make of this, Rich?" I asked.

"It's hard to tell," he said, taking a closer inspection. "I mean, I suppose it could just as easily have been drilled through, although it doesn't really look that clean. For now, I guess we'll just have to take their word for it."

We then tried opening and closing the door to their bedroom several times to see if it would lock or even catch by itself, however, the doorknob seemed perfectly functional.

Moving on to the bedroom, which was formerly Melissa's, in which the only furnishings were a bed without covers plus a wooden chair, our readings indicated nothing out of the ordinary. Melissa had

147

moved out of this room because she felt uncomfortable with the appearance of the "Indian" spirit, she also wanted to be closer to her two younger sisters. Rich asked me, "Keith, what do you make of this 'Indian' spirit that they keep seeing?"

I replied, "Well, aside from startling the girls, it hasn't done them any harm. They describe it as resembling their father and wearing the same exact kind of medallion that he used to have. Assuming they are actually seeing this manifestation, perhaps it is a guardian angel. Or maybe they're seeing it in their mind's eye, because it's a comforting familiar figure."

Smiling, Rich said, "Unless of course it really is their father, dressed up like an Indian and wearing a long black wig."

We then continued on into what was known as the in-laws room. This was the room that Michael Kingston shared with his girlfriend Crystal and their infant son and in which Michael had allegedly been attacked. While scanning the room, we again picked up some high EMF readings from the electrical outlets near the bed and in front of a closet. Because of the reported attack, as well as the spaciousness of the room, Rich decided that later on he'd like to set up his new video camera in this room "If possible, I'd even like to leave it running in here overnight," he said.

"That might not be a bad idea," I agreed. "We can even set Grandma's picture back on the counter and see it if falls off by itself."

Rich then suggested that we take a moment to check in with our other team members. Using one of the small two-way radios that each team carried, Rich first signaled Andrew and Valerie, who were downstairs on the first floor with the family. "Hi guys," he said. "This is Rich calling from upstairs. Anything going on down there?"

Valerie's static-sounding voice replied, "Nothing unusual to report down here. Andrew and I have been doing a sweep of each of the downstairs rooms, but we haven't really found anything yet. Eric's been busy clicking away with his camera." With a chuckle, Valerie added, "I think that Skippy the parrot likes me, because every time I walk by him, he gives me a little suggestive whistle."

"Nice," Rich said with a laugh.

Valerie asked, "How about you guys? Anything exciting going on up there?"

Rich said, "Keith and I have been getting some rather high readings on the EMF in the bedrooms up here but only near the electrical outlets. We also just got a temperature spike right outside of the bathroom that's next to the in-laws room."

Speaking into the radio I asked, "Did either of you get any unusual readings or feelings inside of Michael's downstairs bedroom?"

"Nothing significant," Valerie replied. "But, we can always check his room again later."

Rich said, "Okay then, I'm gonna check in with Jason and Brian now. You guys are certainly welcome to join us up here. Over n' out."

"We'll take you up on that," said Valerie. "Over n' out."

Next, Rich signaled Jason and Brian who were down in the cellar. Brian's distorted sounding voice came over the radio. "Yo, what's up?"

"Hi, it's Rich, just checking in to see if you guys have come across anything unusual down there. Keith and I are up here on the third floor."

Brian said, "I'll tell ya, this place is giving me the creeps down here! In fact, there's like a tunnel leading between the two main sections down here."

"Really?" asked Rich. "Anything else?"

Brian said, "There's also a few crosses on the walls, which I guess the family put up. It's really damp and cold down here, so I don't think we're gonna stay down here much longer."

We suddenly heard Brian let out an expletive. Rich asked, "Brian? Are you guys okay down there? Did something happen?"

The two-way radio on the other end momentarily shut off. When it came back on again, there was a fumbling sound as if Brian had dropped his radio. We overheard the voices of Brian and Jason rapidly conversing with each other. Brian then replied, "Yeah, sorry about that. I almost tripped over a friggin' dead deer's head!" Brian's radio then began crackling.

"What?" asked Rich. "Brian, did you just say something about a dead deer's head?"

Brian replied, "Yeah, I sure did. It's right here on the floor, staring up at me with no eyes! But I'm all right. It just gave me the heebie-jeebies, since I wasn't expecting it."

Jason took over the radio for a moment. "Hi guys. We just had a couple of spikes down here on the EMF, but we've been able to trace the source to some old electrical wiring within the cellar. We're heading back upstairs soon anyway." There was then more static and crackling over the radio.

"Hello?" asked Rich. "Jason, Brian, you're really breaking up, I think we're losing you."

Brian's voice again came over the static. "Yeah it's really poor reception down here."

Rich said, "Okay. Andrew and Val are on their way up here to join me and Keith."

We could just about hear Brian saying, "Okay, guys. Ten-four."

Andrew, Valerie and Eric then joined Rich and myself up on the second floor. Rich and Valerie confirmed that there did not seem to be anything out of the ordinary with the first two bedrooms. Turning to Eric, Andrew gave a slight laugh and said, "I hope you're not getting too board, Eric, just because we haven't gotten any activity as of yet."

"No, quite the contrary, I find his all *quite* fascinating," said Eric. "In fact, I'm quite intrigued with this writing on the wall here. What do you think it means?"

I said, "It could be occult related although I'm totally unfamiliar with this form of inscription. But I think the other cartoon illustrations are just from someone doodling on the wall."

Eric took several photographs of the writing and the cartoon illustrations, before we moved down the hallway into the next room.

Inside of Melissa's former bedroom, we did another sweep of the room with EMF. As expected our readings again proved to be normal. Andrew, Rich, Valerie and I decided to conduct a brief EVP session, asking general questions such as "Is there anyone in this room that would like to communicate?" etc. When we were done, Andrew explained to Eric, "So far, this is very typical of an investigation. We often don't find any evidence until we review our collected data."

"I totally understand, you have to have a lot of patience in this work" said Eric.

We then moved on into the in-laws room at the end of the hallway. Andrew again commenced with an EMF sweep in this room. As he continued slowly moving about, Rich asked, "Getting anything?"

Andrew replied, "No, nothing at all. Excuse the pun, but it seems to be pretty dead in here right now." Andrew suddenly stopped in his tracks and exclaimed, "Whoa!"

"What is it?" asked Rich.

Andrew said, "I just got an energy spike of one-point-two, as if something just passed right in front of me! It was right here where I'm standing, in between the bed and the doorway, but it's not there now."

"Try tracking it!" Rich said anxiously.

Instantly following Rich's suggestion, Andrew began wildly sweeping the air with the EMF detector he held in left hand. "Nothing... I'm not getting anything. Wait—here, by the doorway!" Andrew did his best to "track" whatever was causing the energy spike, by quickly stepping out of the bedroom doorway and into the hallway. Rich and Valerie and I followed close behind.

Andrew stopped less than several feet from the bedroom doorway. "Ah... I'm afraid I've lost it," he told us, glancing at the meter in disappointment. "It was *right* here and then it seems to have gotten away from me."

Indicating the ceiling, Valerie asked, "You don't suppose whatever it was could have gone up into the attic, do you?"

"Anything's possible," Andrew said with a shrug. "That's assuming that it was anything paranormal in the first place. But if it was something, paranormal or not, it's gone now."

"Anyway," I said, "the in-laws room over here seems to definitely be one of the major 'hot-spots' for activity in this house."

"You're absolutely right, Keith," Rich agreed. "So, I think that later on I'll set my video camera up in this room and leave it running for at least a few hours. That is, if Mike will agree to other sleeping arrangements tonight."

"I think he will, especially since his girlfriend or the baby aren't here with him tonight," I said. "After all, he and his family know that we're here to help, and to try to offer an explanation – and hopefully a solution – to what they've been going through."

Our three teams met up again downstairs and began discussing our game plan for the remainder of the evening with the Kingston family. Fortunately, Michael readily consented to allow Rich to set up his video camera upstairs on the in-laws room. As Michael told us, "I guess since it's been following me around anyway, it won't hurt to sleep downstairs for a night." Both Rich and I thanked Michael and assured him that it would only be for that one night.

After our stationary equipment was set up in various rooms throughout the house the seven of us gathered with the Kingston's in their downstairs parlor. Since the family members were wound up because of the stress they'd been going though, and excited to have us investigating their situation, we decided to stay up with them and share conversation while waiting for George Kingston to arrive back home. Rich and I spent some time reviewing the audio recordings that had been made so far, but could find no conclusive trace of Electronic Voice Phenomena.

At about 12:30 A.M, Jason decided it was time for us to do a quick walk-through of the rooms and check on our equipment. With the exception of one audio recorder in which the fresh batteries had already been drained, everything else appeared to be in order. Rich ascertained that his video camera was still properly recording inside the in-laws room, while I checked to see if any of the framed pictures upstairs had fallen over. So far, everything was still in place. Andrew replaced the batteries in the audio recorder with another fresh set and we all returned downstairs to rejoin the family in the parlor.

Everything remained basically quiet for the next couple of hours. As Mandy explained to us, the activity usually did not start picking up until between 1:30 and 3:30 AM.

We were still sitting the parlor chatting with the family, when, sometime after 2:00 AM, what sounded like the loud slamming of a door was heard from somewhere upstairs. Startled, Mandy and her three daughters all reflexively jumped in their seats. Brian asked, "What the hell was that?"

With a wide-eyed expression, Mandy told us, "My husband's not home, so no one's in the house but us!"

Michael said, "It sounded like it came from the second floor, up in the in-laws room."

Rich reminded us, "I've got my video camera set up in there. It should still be taping."

"Let's go check it out," said Jason, quickly rising from his seat. "But I also need at least two people to stay down here with the family."

As Mandy glanced at us with concern on her face, Valerie said, "I'll stay down here."

"I'll stay too," I also volunteered.

"Good," said Jason. "We should be right back." Jason then quickly began making his way upstairs, accompanied by Brian, Rich, Andrew and Eric.

The five of them returned back downstairs several minutes later. Anxiously, Mandy asked, "Did you guys find anything?"

With a shrug Jason replied, "To be honest, we didn't find anything unusual *or* out of place. No doors are shut that were opened before."

Andrew added, "Even the picture of your grandmother is still in place where we left it as well as all the other pictures."

"Maybe the slamming sound we heard was merely a 'projected' sound," I suggested.

"That's one possibility," Andrew agreed.

Resuming his seat, Rich told us, "At least my video camera is still set on the tripod upstairs in the in-laws room, still recording. And as Michael pointed out that's where the sound seemed to come from." With a yawn, he added, "We'll just have to review the tape tomorrow to see if the sound was picked up."

"Good enough," said Jason. Turning to Mandy, he then said, "Well, I think all of us are pretty beat right about now. I suggest we all try to get at least a few hours of shut-eye. We'll of course leave some of our recording devices running in some of the rooms and as

Rich said, we'll go over our evidence tomorrow, and see if we've picked up anything."

"Yes, I think that's a good idea," said Mandy. "And you know, I actually feel a lot safer with you people here in the house."

"Not a problem," Jason said with a tired smile. "In the meantime, if anything else at all happens tonight, we'll be right there in a flash to check it out."

"Thank you all, so much," said Mandy.

"Yes, thank you," said Melissa.

An exhausted George Kingston returned home less than a half-hour later and told us just how terrible the road conditions were. We in turn filled him in on what had taken place during his absence. Like the rest of his family, George also seemed to be somewhat comforted by the knowledge that the TAPS team was there to immediately assist, should anything else out of the ordinary take place that night. Stretching, George said, "Well, it's after 3:00 AM now, so after a whole night of plowing, I'm ready to hit the hay. It's nice knowin' that you people are here to help out, so I can at least get a few hours of sleep. I'll see you all tomorrow."

As we were getting ready to retire, Jason privately said to me, "Keith, I especially want you to get some rest. I know I don't have to tell you, you'll definitely need it for tomorrow night."

Fortunately, there were enough unoccupied rooms in the house to accommodate us and we did get to sleep somewhat late into the morning. After we'd all risen and come downstairs, Mandy served us a delicious breakfast of bacon and eggs with toast, along with some much needed coffee. Skippy the African gray parrot was obviously excited to have us all there in "his" kitchen and he began joining in on our breakfast conversation as much as possible. Skippy seemed especially delighted with Valerie's company, which was evident from his suggestive whistle whenever she rose from her seat.

In the early afternoon we began reviewing some of our data collected from the night before. Another fortunate thing for us was the Kingston's had a large screen TV in their parlor, which proved ideal for our viewing of Rich's video footage. We were comfortably seated in the parlor with Mandy, Michelle, Megan, Melissa and Michael, reviewing the footage from the third floor in-laws room. As Jason explained to Mandy and her family, "This is one of the aspects of paranormal investigation, where a great deal of patience is required. You could be watching footage of an empty room, waiting for something to happen and more often than not nothing does."

Melissa said, "Oh, I find this part exciting even if nothing happens!"

"Yeah me to," said Eric.

With a laugh, Brian said, "Trust me, you won't after a couple of hours of just sitting and watching."

Megan asked, "Why does the picture look that way, like glow-in-the-dark?"

Rich explained, "Because the camera was set to night shot, so what it's actually picking up is infrared. It's the same thing as night vision goggles, which are used in the military. This way we're hoping to catch something that may not be visible to the naked eye. Or, in this case, we're hoping to catch something that may not be picked up on regular video."

Jason added, "Also, when we want to videotape a supposedly haunted room or other location at night we do so without lighting. Because you figure that if you shine a flashlight in daylight or in a room with electrical lighting the flashlight beam is going to be cancelled out. In the same way, if something of a paranormal nature were to manifest, say as in the form of an apparition, it might not be perceived in natural or artificial lighting."

"Oh, now I understand," said Megan. "Thanks for explaining that to me."

After viewing several more minutes of footage, displaying the eerily illuminated room with no apparent activity taking place, Rich asked, "By the way, did anyone happen to note the time when we heard that sound of a door slamming upstairs?"

"Yes, it was just before 2: 30 AM," I replied.

Jason said, "Well, let's fast forward to that time to see if anything was picked up. We can always go over the rest of the footage later."

In excited anticipation, both Megan and Michelle scooted over on the sofa and huddled together with their mother, while Rich began fast-forwarding the video. "You say in was around 2:30 AM that we heard the sound of the door slamming, Keith?" Rich asked me.

"Yes, I believe it was just before 2:30 AM," I replied.

When the video time counter on the screen arrived at 2:22 AM, Rich slowed the tape back to normal playing speed, saying, "Alright, let's try it from here. If we don't find anything after 2:35 AM or so, then I'll rewind it further back to see if we've missed anything."

We did not have to wait long. When the counter on the video indicated 2:26 AM, the distinct sound of a door slamming was heard, which caused Mandy and her two daughters to gasp and huddle even closer to each other. Michael and Michelle remained seated at the other end of the sofa. Brian exclaimed, "Alright! We caught it!"

Rich commented, "That's strange, though. It kind of sounds like a metal locker door slamming shut, doesn't it? But when we first heard it last night, it sounded more like a regular bedroom door slamming."

"You're right," Andrew agreed. "But, at least the sound was picked up."

While continuing to listen, I suddenly detected a faint whispering sound on the audio track. "Wait a minute," I said to Rich. "I just thought I heard something else on the tape, right after the sound of the door slamming. Could you please go back just a bit?"

"Sure," said Rich. He then rewound the video to just before the slam, adjusted the volume to a higher level and began replaying it at normal speed.

We again heard the metallic slamming sound... and then, about three seconds later, we also heard what sounded like the voice of a little girl, whispering: *"They're coming."*

Mandy placed a hand over her mouth as her three daughters all loudly gasped in astonishment. The rest of us glanced at each other, before turning our attention back to the wide TV screen. On the video, we could then hear the footsteps of the four TAPS members in the background as they began ascending the stairs... along with what now sounded like a low male voice. "There's something more!" said Brian. "I just heard another voice right afterwards."

Jason said, "Rich, let's listen to this section again, starting with the door slam, this time with the volume turned all the way up."

Rich again rewound the tape back to 2:26 AM and began replaying it, this time at maximum volume. There was the loud, metallic "locker door" slamming sound, followed seconds later by what could now clearly be heard as the child-like girl's voice, with an almost teasing quality, saying, *"They're coming."* There was also the expected sound of approaching footsteps on the stairs.

However, about three seconds before the TAPS members and Eric entered the room, a low, ominous sounding male voice could be heard saying: *"They're here."* We then saw Jason; illuminated by the infrared, enter the in-laws room, followed close behind by Rich, Brian and Andrew. Guided by a flashlight, they searched the room and the entire third floor area, before leaving to go back downstairs. As soon as their footsteps had trailed off, a clearly audible tapping sound could be heard in the once again vacated room. It actually sounded like two drumsticks being tapped together. After four unevenly spaced taps, a small cluster of what appeared to be globules began shooting throughout the room. Everything in the room then became completely still and silent once again.

Still huddled together on the sofa, Mandy, Megan and Michelle were now all wide-eyed with amazement. Megan commented, "I knew we weren't just imagining all of this! Now if only the priest could see and hear this, then he'd finally believe us!"

"I think he already does," I said.

Later that afternoon, Jason, Brian, Rich, Valerie, Andrew and I ventured outside to investigate the barn, with Megan and Melissa volunteering to lead us. We found ourselves having to wade through three-foot high snowdrifts as we made our way. The Kingston's friendly, droopy hound dog Blue was happy to have our company with him outside. Because the drifts were a little too much for his short legs to maneuver, Blue was confined to a small path in the snow leading from his doghouse, but he seemed quite content to enjoy our company from a distance. And from what the Kingston's had told us, Blue was also usually reluctant to approach the barn itself.

The interior of the barn was just as it had been described to us, with a dozen or more extremely long, loose boards supported by the ceiling beams hanging directly overheard. Although these boards appeared to be securely in place, they no doubt would do serious damage if they were to fall on someone. Turning to Melissa I asked, "So, one of the boards from up there fell almost hitting Bill of Maine Paranormal when he was here?"

Melissa replied, "Yes, and it just missed him by inches! In fact, he was standing exactly where you are right now."

As I quickly stepped away from directly underneath the boards, Megan said, "We don't know how it happened, but none of those boards has fallen before or since and we've been in here a lot."

Elsewhere in the barn, there were the remnants of two older model cars, both Volkswagens, which perhaps either George or one of the previous occupants was planning on restoring someday. There was also a great deal of debris and clutter strewn about most of the floor, which was typical of an old country barn that was not in regular use. It was actually difficult to maneuver over the floor, even in daylight. At one point Andrew stumbled over a loose board lying on the floor, nearly loosing his balance. Both Meagan and Melissa gasped, while Brian asked, "You okay over there, dude?"

"Yeah, I'm okay," said Andrew with a laugh. "I just almost went head long, is all, and I almost managed to twist my ankle in the process."

Concerned, Valerie asked, "Are you sure you're alright, Andrew?"

"Yeah. Just have to watch where I step in here, but I'm fine."

Jason switched on his flashlight and said, "Let's watch where we step in here. Besides, it's freezing. It actually seems colder in here than outside. Let's not stay in here too much longer, guys."

What was primarily noticeable about the large interior of the barn was the uncomfortable sensation of being watched and feeling unwelcome there. Both Valerie and Rich seemed to be affected in particular. This combined with the frigid temperature made us decide not to prolong our stay in the barn any than twenty minutes.

CHAPTER 16

Vengeful Spirits in Skowhegan
The Deliverance

THE SUN WAS already lowering on this January afternoon, when I readied myself to begin the blessing of the exterior buildings on the Kingston's property. These structures would of course include the barn, as well as the smaller chicken coop out in the back. Since I happened to be mentoring Brian in demonology, he readily agreed to assist me outside.

After we'd once again bundled up for the frigid temperature, we first ventured out to the barn. The blessing of the barn itself did not take long. However, while we were in there, Brian reported glimpsing a shadowy figure darting by over in one of the far corners. "Right over there, I just saw it out of the corner of my eye," he alerted me, his breath coming out in large puffs of vapor. "It was only there for a spit second, but I know I saw it." Although Brian and I used our flashlights to search the interior of the barn as thoroughly as we were able, we could find no natural explanation for the shadow figure he had seen.

As soon as we'd concluded our blessing of the barn, Brian and I moved onto the much smaller chicken coop. The structure itself was quite dilapidated, obviously having been allowed to fall into disrepair. The Kingston's claimed to have never used it. There were actually two small sections within the coop, with drifts of snow scattering the floor in spots, from where it had fallen through holes in the low roof overhead. When I'd finished blessing the first section, Brian stepped through the low doorway and shined his flashlight inside. He suddenly called over his shoulder to me, "Dude! Check this out!"

"What is it?" I asked, stepping forward.

"You gotta see this to believe it," Brian replied. As I stepped over beside him, Brian slowly swept the beam of his flashlight over the floor, revealing several chicken carcasses in various stages of decay. Although some of them were merely bones sparsely covered with feathers, a few of them appeared perfectly preserved, half buried in snow and frozen solid in standing positions, almost as if they were still roosting. Brian commented, "Some of them look as though they'd been freeze-dried." He then asked, "You don't think these could've been used as occult sacrifices, do you?"

"Doesn't really look it," I replied. "It looks more like they were just neglected and left to die out here."

"Yeah, I guess you're right," Brian agreed. Wiping his nose with his sleeve, he said, "Pre-frozen and ready for packing. Anyway, we better hurry up and get this over with. The holy water is starting to freeze up right inside the container."

Brian and I returned to the main house to find every else already seated down to a supper of homemade pasta and meatballs. Upon seeing us, Mandy said, "Oh, you poor guys look half-frozen! I'm so sorry we didn't wait for you, but please come in and join us." Both Brian and I took off our overcoats and readily accepted Mandy's invitation.

The two of us had scarcely warmed up before it was time to continue. One thing that would present a problem with the entire blessing of the main house was the attic. As Mandy had informed us, the floor of the attic was probably not sturdy enough to hold the weight of an adult even someone as petite as Valerie. However, on the north side of the house there was a small ventilation window leading into the attic, just above the third floor. After conferring with Jason, as a team we decided to try spraying some holy water into the attic through this shaft.

Thus it was that after borrowing an aluminum ladder from the Kingston's, we ventured outside once again as a group, with Eric accompanying us to record the event on film. It took quite a bit of maneuvering to correctly position the ladder against the house while trudging through the three-foot snowdrifts, but with a concerted group effort we somehow managed.

Jason volunteered to take a turn at the blessing and climbed the ladder himself. Fortunately, he made it safely to the small ventilation window and successfully sprayed as much of the blessed water into opening as he was able to. He then carefully made his way back down, as both Rich and I tightly held onto the aluminum ladder from below. We then retracted the aluminum ladder and allowed it to drop into the three-foot snowdrifts, as Jason commented, "I don't think they'll really be needing it until the spring thaw."

Back inside, we warmed ourselves with hot chocolate provided and rested up a bit for the long night ahead of us. Shortly after 6:00 PM Jodi Picoult arrived as expected. Her complexion was flushed from the biting wind which had picked up outside and she was still catching her breath as Mandy and George Kingston welcomed her inside. "So nice to meet you, Jodi!" said Mandy enthusiastically. "Glad you made it here from New Hampshire. Come on in and make yourself at home."

"Oh, thank you," said Jodi, stepping inside and brushing back her long wavy strawberry-blonde hair, which had fallen over her face when she removed her wool hat. "So nice to meet you! This is a beautiful house you have here and you're out in such a secluded area."

Mandy said, "Thank you, so much, Jodi! It's so exciting to have such a well-known author like you visiting with us."

George added, "Nice to meet you, Jodi. Please, take your coat off and relax. You've got a bunch of your friends already here waiting for you."

Jodi was thrilled to see Jason and threw her arms around him as soon as he came over to greet her. "Glad you made it here in one piece, Jodi," Jason told her.

"Believe me, Jason, it's already been a full day, since I participated in a hiking excursion in New Hampshire this afternoon!" she said.

Jodi was pleased to see the rest of the TAPS team again, since she'd had the opportunity to work with us just two weeks earlier. We also introduced her to Valerie and Eric whom she had not met before tonight. Jodi then assured us, "Now, I certainly don't intend to get in everyone's way tonight. I'm just fine with being a casual observer in the background."

With a wry smile, Jason told Jodi, "You just may find yourself in the center of the action. We really don't know exactly what to expect tonight, so be ready for anything."

Jodi appeared to be filled with excitement as well as an understandable amount of trepidation.

Before commencing with the blessing of the interior of the house we sat down to another delicious meal with the Kingston's. We all shared lively dinner conversation, discussing some of Jodi's recently published works. Mandy asked, "So, Jodi, what's the title of the book you're doing research for with TAPS?"

Jodi replied, "Well, it's still in the beginning stages of a work-in-progress, of course. But as of now, I've pretty much decided on 'Second Glance' for a title."

We all agreed that 'Second Glance' was an excellent title for a book about a family having to deal with the paranormal. Melissa commented "This must be really exciting for you Jodi, getting some hands-on experience with real ghost hunters."

"It certainly is," Jodi agreed. "I'm trying to get a feel for what it's really like going on actual investigations, so I can portray it realistically for my reading audience."

Jason also began filling Jodi in on some of what we'd experienced so far during our investigation. Her eyes widened when she learned of the two separate voices, which had been captured on Rich's video in the empty upstairs room. "Oh, my!" Jodi gasped. "So, please, tell me the details of this. You say it was two different voices, one male and one female?"

Jason said, "We'll actually play the video for you in a little while, before we begin the final part of our investigation. Tonight Keith will be conducting a blessing of this entire house, which will possibly provoke whatever's here into revealing itself. Although you really never know exactly what to expect ahead of time, on any investigation."

Jodi said, "Well, I have to admit that I'm more than a little nervous about tonight. But at the same time, I'm also looking forward to it."

Brian assured her, "Don't worry, Jodi, you'll be in good hands tonight. We'll all do our best to make sure you stay safe."

Without warning, Skippy the African gray parrot suddenly began shrieking, "The bitch is home! The bitch is home!" This caused Jodi to nearly jump out of her chair especially since she happened to be seated right in front of the large parrot cage.

"Aw, jeez," said George Kingston, shaking his head. "Here we go again!" Everyone else at the kitchen table burst out laughing.

Mandy apologized, explaining, "I'm so sorry Jodi! Skippy's obviously excited to have more company here and that's his way of expressing it. He's actually imitating my husband George."

"My goodness!" said Jodi, still laughing while turning around to face Skippy. "That certainly is a beautiful bird. And I'm glad that means he likes me."

Skippy then squawked and whistled suggestively at Jodi, just as he'd earlier been doing to Valerie. Andrew said, "Looks like you've got some competition, Val. He sure likes the ladies, doesn't he?"

Melissa said, "Mom, I've been telling you, we've simply got to get Skippy a girlfriend."

George chuckled and said, "Oh no, not two of 'em in the same house yappin' away."

Immediately after supper, we gathered in the parlor and played the infrared footage for Jodi. She sat spellbound while watching the large screen TV as the metallic sound of a door slamming was heard. With the sound amplified, There was then the audible voice of a little girl whispering, *"They're coming,"* which was followed seconds later by a low, gravelly male voice saying, *"They're here."*

"Oh my God," said Jodi. "Just listening to this is giving me chills!" She watched as on the screen, Jason entered the room and led the others on a thorough search, before leaving to go back downstairs.

There was then the sound of drumsticks lightly tapping, followed by several globules zipping about.

Rich explained to Jodi, "To use a technical term, this is an example of what could be referred to as 'Instrumental Trans-Communication.' What this means is that both voice and visual were transferred through the same media, in this case night video footage." Jodi quickly grabbed her notepad and jotted the term down.

We then began preparing for the night ahead of us by equipping our recording devices with fresh tapes and batteries. Afterwards I sat by myself in the kitchen for a brief session of silent prayer and meditation. At about 8:00 PM, Jason approached me and asked, "You ready for this, buddy?"

"Yes, I suppose as ready as I'll ever be," I replied.

"Good," he said. "Everything's all set to begin the final blessing. Everyone's counting on you and I personally have the utmost confidence in your experience and what you stand for."

"Thanks, Jason," I said.

We all assembled in the parlor to begin the final blessing of the Kingston's 19th Century farmhouse. Before we began, Jason explained to the family and to Jodi, "We're going to begin in the cellar and work our way up. If there is an inhuman spirit involved here, it may tend to retreat from the blessing, so we're hoping to eventually corner it upstairs where the activity is the strongest. We'll choose a particular room upstairs and that's where we'll finalize our cleansing of the house. Does anyone have any final questions before we begin?" Since no one had any questions, the TAPS crew, along with Eric and Jodi, descended into the cellar.

The blessing of the cellar took a little longer than expected, mainly because of the raised structure leading from one section to another. There were a few small crucifixes adorning the walls, which Eric photographed. At one point I nearly tripped over the deer head that was lying on the dirt floor, just as Brian nearly had the previous night. With the aid of a flashlight I took a closer examination of the desiccated deer head, which seemed to stare up at me with its empty eye sockets. Although it had originally been intended for mounting, it had now been discarded and left to rot, most likely by the previous tenants of this house. Also, I was reminded of what Mandy had mentioned to us about the former tenants possibly having practiced animal sacrifice in this house, most likely down here in the cellar.

In each section of the cellar I read from Scripture and pronounced the blessing, while Brian sprayed the walls with blessed water and Eric took pictures of the proceedings.

When we returned back upstairs, Mandy anxiously asked us how everything had gone with the blessing of the cellar. Jason informed her, "Everything went alright. The only difficulty we had down there was maneuvering through that raised space. But the cellar is now completely blessed."

Turning to Mandy, I asked, "By the way, concerning that deer's head lying on the floor down there… was that already here when you moved in?"

"Yes, it was," replied Mandy. "We think it was left by the last people who lived here. In fact, we've been meaning to get rid of it; we just don't go down to that section of the cellar very often. Sorry that it's still there."

"Quite alright," I said. "And I was wondering about the crucifixes on the walls. Did you place them down there?"

Megan answered, "Yes, we did. In fact, when the priest was here he asked why we didn't have any crosses hanging on the walls. So I told him that we put them all down in the cellar, because we're always so scared down there."

Jason announced that we were now ready to begin the blessing of the first floor area. Before we started, Jodi approached me and asked, "Keith, I noticed you're using a Bible. Would you mind sharing with me some of what you're reading during the blessing so I can use it for reference?"

"I'd be glad to Jodi," I said. I then gave her a list of the Scripture passages I was using, which included Psalm 23, Psalm 105, Luke 10: 17-20, Hebrews 9: 11-14, and Ephesians 6: 10-18, among others.

"Thank you very much, Keith," said Jodi.

The blessing of the first floor also went without incident, with the exception of Michael's former bedroom. It was in here that the atmosphere seemed to suddenly thicken and become somewhat oppressive, shortly after Valerie, Brian and I entered the room. Valerie was especially affected by this sensation. However, the oppressive atmosphere within the room instantly seemed to lift as I began reading aloud from the Book of Psalms.

It was then time for us to commence the blessing of the upstairs area. With my Bible open to the 23rd Psalm, I stood at the bottom of the staircase, as my fellow TAPS members gathered with me, waiting for the word from Jason. Addressing Mandy, George, their four children, Eric and Jodi, Jason said, "Now, I have to make you aware that because of the cleansing we've done so far, whatever is here has probably moved upstairs. Our game plan is to eventually corner it in one of these rooms, which will most probably be the in-laws room. But by that time it'll probably be enraged and it may even lash out at us. So this will be the final and most dangerous part of the entire blessing."

I added, "Hopefully we'll be successful and after that it will be all over."

Jason asked, "Again, does anyone have any last minute questions?"

Mandy replied, "No. I understand." George and the three teenagers also nodded in agreement.

Turning to Jodi, Jason said, "Now, it's totally up to you, Jodi, whether you want to remain down here with the family or accompany us upstairs. Nothing may happen while we're up there. But on the other hand, you never know exactly what to expect."

"I want to go upstairs with you," said Jodi, adding, "Just be ready to catch me if I jump, okay?"

"You got it," Jason told her with a quick smile.

After taking a deep breath, Andrew asked, "Alright, are we ready?"

Everyone nodded in agreement.

Brian said, "Let's go for it, then."

Pointing in my direction, Jason firmly directed the other TAPS members, "I want someone in front and in back of Keith at all times, because if this thing does decide to attack it's gonna target him!"

"You got it," said Brian, as he and Andrew instantly positioned themselves just as Jason had told them with Brian directly in front of me and Andrew directly in back.

As we moved forward, Mandy glanced up at me with tears filling her eyes and her hands clasped in front of her. Reassuringly, I lightly squeezed her shoulder and smiled. She smiled back hopefully at me in return.

In single procession with Jason in the lead we began slowly making our way up the staircase. Brian sprayed the walls with blessed water as I began to read aloud, "The Lord is my shepherd; I shall not want. He maketh me to lie down in green pastures. He leadeth me beside the still waters. He restoreth my soul. He leadeth me in the paths of righteousness for his name's sake."

We made it up the entire staircase and arrived at the second floor without incident. I continued reading: "Yea, though I walk through the valley of the shadow of death, I will fear no evil..."

It was then we heard what sounded like a low, subtle grunt from somewhere nearby. Brian instantly came to a halt and said, "Shhh! I just heard something! What the hell was that?"

Jason motioned for him to be silent. After listening for a few seconds, Jason said, "I heard it too. But maybe it was the Kingston's dog Blue."

When the sound was not repeated, Jason motioned for me to continue. "For thou art with me; thy rod and they staff they comfort me. Thou preparest a table before me in the presence of mine enemies. Thou anointest my head with oil; my cup runneth over."

With Jason still leading, we began making our way along the outer hallway of the second floor. "Surely goodness and mercy shall follow me all the days of my life and I will dwell in the house of the Lord forever." After I'd finished reading, Brian sprayed blessed water along the walls of the outer hallway on both sides.

We then entered Melissa's bedroom, which had the graffiti on two sections of the walls. Eric asked us, "Would it be distracting to you guys, if I were to take pictures while you're doing this?"

"No, not at all, Eric," I said. "Thank you for asking."

Brian said, "It won't distract me either. Go right ahead."

"Thanks guys," said Eric.

Brian sprayed the walls of this room with blessed water while I anointed the windows with blessed oil. Rich did a sweep with his

EMF detector, which indicated no unusual readings. After the room had been blessed, I said, "In the name of Jesus Christ, if any of the inscriptions or illustrations on the walls have occult meaning, or have been used in profane worship, we ask that any power now be removed from them. Amen."

Brian, Andrew and Valerie repeated, "Amen."

When the blessing of this room had been completed, we entered the next bedroom, which was the one shared by Megan and Michelle. As soon as we'd entered the girls' bedroom, Rich pointed out to Jodi the hole in the bedpost where the toothbrush had been impaled. "They even showed us a picture of it, stuck right through the hole here," said Rich.

"Wow," said Jodi, examining the splintered hole more closely. "But how could a plastic toothbrush have gone through solid oak without breaking?"

With a shrug, Rich said, "Well, since we weren't here when it happened, we can't vouch one hundred percent for the validity of this. But yes, although it's rare, things like this do sometimes occur. Amazingly, sometimes a glass vase can be hurled across a room and land without breaking."

We repeated the same procedure in this room after which I prayed, "We ask that any lost or wandering spirits be sent to their proper abode and that only spirits which are of God be allowed to enter any of these rooms. Amen." I was of course thinking of the "Indian" spirit that the girls had reported seeing, which was said to resemble their father.

We then continued as a group down the second floor hallway, and entered the vacated room that Melissa had recently moved out of. Rich did a thorough sweep with the EMF and found the readings to be normal. Andrew also used a digital thermometer, and verified that the temperature in this room was 67 degrees. We considered this to be normal room temperature since the room was not currently in use

Jason told us, "We're kind of getting near the end, so I think instead of blessing this room right away, and we'll save it as a neutral spot. Maybe later we'll split up into separate teams. Meanwhile, Rich, you might want to start the infrared running again in the in-laws room. That way we can see if it picks up anything while Keith's doing the blessing, since that's supposedly the most active room."

"Absolutely," said Rich. He and Brian then went down the hallway into the in-laws room to position his video camera on the tripod in the center of the room, exactly as it had been the previous night. Rich also had the insight to place the framed photo of the grandmother on a shelf, within clear view of the camera lens in the event that it might be knocked off while no one was in the room. They then returned to us after shutting the door to the darkened room behind them.

Jodi asked Jason, "Okay so what's going on now? What exactly do you mean by this being a "neutral' room?"

Jason explained to both Jodi and Eric, "If there is an inhuman or demonic entity here in this house, Keith will most likely be cutting off more and more of its access as he blesses each of the rooms. He's also probably pissing it off royally by doing so. In fact, that growl we heard earlier just may have been a warning."

"It's all so fascinating," Jodi commented her eyes like saucers.

Jason continued, "So, as Keith continues blessing more of the rooms, it'll have less places to hide out. So we eventually hope to be able to narrow its access down to two rooms and then corner it. Maybe then we can force it into revealing itself."

Eric asked, "And how would you go about forcing it to reveal itself?"

I answered, "One method is through religious provocation. Demonic spirits usually prefer to remain anonymous, especially when paranormal researchers or clergy are present. In that way, they desperately try to avoid expulsion. Needless to say, forcing them to reveal themselves can be very dangerous."

Jodi shook her head and told us, "I can't help but marvel at what you people do. It's one thing to be here observing but I don't think I could do this myself for any amount of money!"

When we'd all moved back out into the hallway, Jason directed us to split up into two separate groups with himself, Andrew, and Jodi in one group, and Valerie, Brian, Eric and me in the other. "Make sure you contact us immediately if anything starts to happen," Jason instructed our group. "We'll do the same if we start to experience anything."

"Will do," said Brian, setting his pocket radio to the appropriate channel.

Both of our groups ventured down the opposite hallway where most of the unused rooms were located. We then temporarily spit up with Jason's group going into one of the rooms on the opposite side of the hallway a little further down. We entered the next room over to continue with the blessing. Eric quickly reloaded his camera and resumed taking pictures. Everything initially seemed calm and uneventful as I began reciting Scripture. As I continued reading, however, Valerie said, "Excuse me for interrupting Keith, but… is it just me or is the air starting to get kind of thick in here?"

Rich said, "Now that you mention it Val, the atmosphere in here does feel rather stuffy." Rich began doing a sweep of the room with his EMF detector. "I'm getting some spikes," he told us. "One-point-one… one-point-two."

Brian suggested, "Keith, why not try some religious provocation?"

Glancing around the room, I said, "In the name of Jesus Christ, on the authority of His shed blood, give a sign of your presence." When there was no immediate reaction, I repeated, "In the name of Jesus Christ, give us a sign of your presence."

The oppressive atmosphere in the room noticeably thickened, causing Valerie to wince. Andrew said, "The EMF is continuing to spike; it's now at one-point-three."

Valerie turned to Brain and said, "Maybe we should alert Jason and the others as to what's going on."

Brian quickly held up his radio, pressed the side button and said, "Hey Jason? Andrew? Jodi?"

Andrew's voice came back, saying, "Hey Brian, what's up?"

Brian replied, "We seem to be getting some activity in here; I think Keith may have just provoked it."

"We'll be right there," said Andrew.

Then, almost as soon as it had begun, the oppressive atmosphere in the small room began to dissipate. By the time the others arrived to join us, everything seemed back to normal. With a frown, Rich said,

"The EMF readings have suddenly leveled back down. I don't understand it, since I was getting some spikes in here just a moment ago."

Valerie verified that the atmosphere within the room had become noticeably oppressive during the reading of Scripture. Brian told Jason and the others, "Like I way saying, I think Keith may have succeeded in provoking it, especially when he asked for a sign of it's presence in the name of Jesus."

Jason commented, "Well, if religious provocation is having an effect, then it doesn't sound like this could be anything good."

A little nervously Jodi asked, "Do you mean that an inhuman spirit could really be involved here?"

Jason replied, "Well, there is always that possibility, especially considering the fact that the previous tenants may have seriously dabbled in the occult. And if the symbols on the wall over in Melissa's bedroom are any indication, it seems likely that they were." Sensing Jodi's trepidation, Jason placed a comforting arm around her and said, "You know Jodi, anytime this starts to become a little overwhelming for you, it's totally understandable if you'd prefer to remain with the family downstairs. Nothing else may happen, but on the other hand, the worse may be yet to come."

"No, I'm determined to hang with you guys and learn first hand," Jodi reiterated. Turning to me she asked, "Keith, in your opinion why do you suppose whatever's in here is targeting this particular family? Is it just because the spirits resent the fact that a family has moved in here?"

"Very good question," I said. "And one that can't easily be answered. There could be a variety of reasons why whatever entities may be here have been activated. It could be that they're simply opportunistic or 'territorial' as you suggested and they're picking on Mandy and her family just because they're here. But also, certain people and families just happen to be more sensitive to psychic activity than others. I've seen that first hand. And some entities seem to be parasitic in nature, meaning that they literally feed off of the energy put out by negative human emotions. That's one reason they try to generate fear."

Jodi asked, "But if there is an inhuman spirit at work here, what about the Indian spirit that Michelle and Megan and Melissa say they feel comfortable with?"

Rich stepped in to elaborate, "There may be human spirits in this house which are being dominated by an inhuman spirit. The Indian could have been here for years and is making his presence known to the girls because he feels protective towards them. And perhaps that's also why he seems to resemble their father."

"That would make sense," Jodi agreed.

"Also," I added, "there are certain entities which will attempt to deceive people into believing that they're human spirits, whereas in reality, they may never have walked the earth in human form."

After the blessing of this room had been completed without further incident we again split into our separate groups. Jason's team moved into another room across the hallway. Rich, Brian, Valerie, Eric and I entered the next room over from them, where I again began reading Scripture and invoking angelic protection.

In just under an hour, most of the upstairs rooms had been successfully blessed, with the doors, mirrors and windows anointed with blessed oil. Brian radioed Jason's group and reported that we'd experienced no further activity. On the other end, Jason said, "We haven't been experiencing anything at all up here either. Let's regroup and take a break for a few minutes. You guys can meet us over in the main bedroom here."

"We'll be right there," said Brian, before switching off his radio.

Once we were all back together in the main bedroom, Jason told me, "Good job so far Keith. We're actually almost done up here, which means we'll soon be done with the blessing of the entire house."

With a yawn Rich said, "Great. I'll tell ya, I could really use some caffeine right about now."

Nudging him, Valerie said, "I'm not surprised. After all, on your E-mail correspondence you sign your name as 'Caffeine Rich' and 'Jedi Coffee.'"

Smiling, Rich said, "I always need to be charged with a high caffeine level to keep functioning at maximum overdrive."

Jason asked, "How about you, Keith? How are you holding up?"

"Alright," I said. "Fighting off fatigue, but otherwise okay."

Jason then rubbed his eyes and said, "You know, I think at this point we could all use an extended break to get our second wind. Since things seem to be pretty much in control up here, maybe we should go downstairs for a while. I know that I could sure use a pick-me-up."

Everyone was in agreement. Before we began heading back downstairs, however, Rich wanted to check the video camera which he'd left running set on infrared in the in-laws room. Andrew volunteered to accompany him this time. They'd gone down the hallway and into the darkened room, when we overhead Rich say, "What the heck?"

"What is it?" Jason called out as we all rushed down the hallway. "You guys alright in there?"

Andrew switched on the overhead light for us as we entered the room. "Yeah we're okay," he said.

Inside the room, Rich was inspecting his video camera with a puzzled expression. Without looking away from it he explained, "It's just that the camera seems to have somehow shut off by itself about three minutes into the recording time. But it was running fine when Brian and I left it."

Brian verified that this was so. "That's right dude, I checked it out myself."

Rich said, "And everything seems to be in working order now except that it's switched off and the timer reads just under three minutes." With a sigh of frustration he added, "So any activity we might have caught in here while the blessing was going on was lost. At least the picture of Grandma Kingston is still on the shelf where I left it so I didn't miss that."

Jason told him, "Well, it's been pretty quiet up here anyway, so maybe nothing at all happened in this room. In fact right about now I'd welcome a door slamming or something like last night, while we're actually here to witness it. But anyway, Rich, you can set it on again and check on it again when we come back upstairs. I don't know about you but I need to take a bathroom break anyway and at least have some soda or something."

"Ditto," said Rich.

"Me three," said Jodi.

The rest of us all agreed as well.

We went downstairs to the parlor, where Jason informed the anxiously waiting Kingston family, "I'd say the blessing's going successfully so far and we should be able to wrap things up pretty quickly when we go back upstairs."

Brian added, "We had a little activity going on at one point, in one of the upstairs rooms that aren't being used."

Sounding concerned, Mandy asked, "Oh? What kind of activity?"

"Nothing major," Brian assured her. "Just some EMF spikes while Keith was doing some religious provocation and a noticeable thickness in the air, but it didn't last long at all. We're certainly alright."

Rich also gave a little laugh and said, "Plus something may have shut off my video camera while it was recording up in the guestroom. Of course, it could've just been a technical glitch. It's just that I've never had it shut off by itself like that before. It wasn't battery failure, because I had it plugged into a wall outlet."

Mandy also chuckled, and said, "Believe me, appliances going haywire with no rational explanation is nothing new in this house. And I really apologize for the condition that some of those rooms are in. We're intending to fix them up. It's just that so much else has been going on here."

Jason waved his hand and said, "Not a problem. Hopefully after tonight this will all be taken care of and you people can get on with your normal lives."

Feeling refreshed for the time being we returned back upstairs shortly after 11:00 PM to complete the blessing of the last three remaining rooms. Jason said, "Alright, here's the game plan. We'll briefly split up into our two separate teams, while two of the last rooms are blessed. Keith, it's totally your call as to where you'd like to begin."

"Well, I guess I could take care of that last room down the hall and then we could move on to the in-laws room," I said.

"Fair enough," said Jason. "Jodi, Andrew and I will remain in the large spare bedroom and as soon as you're done we'll all group together for the final blessing. Then it's just a matter of waiting to see if anything else happens tonight. And again, be sure to radio us if anything at all unusual happens. We'll do the same if anything happens in here."

Brian, Rich, Valerie, Eric and I headed down the hallway to one of the last rooms where I read aloud from Psalms 23 and 105, as well as from the ninth chapter of Hebrews. Upon concluding, I asked for a sign of any spirits that might be present and waited for almost a full minute in silence. When there was no reaction, I indicated to Brian that he could begin spraying holy water within the room, while I began to pronounce the blessing. However, no sooner had I concluded, then we were suddenly startled by the ringing of the two-way radio that Brian carried, indicating a call from Jason's group.

"Yo, whas'up?" Brian asked into the radio.

Jason's voice said, "We're getting some activity in here. Come meet us in the large bedroom."

"We'll be right there," said Brian. Glancing at the rest of us, he said, "You heard the man. Let's go."

Without hesitation we rushed over to join the others in the main bedroom. From the expressions on their faces it was evident that they'd just experienced something out of the ordinary. Jason was reassuring Jodi, who appeared to be the most shaken. Andrew turned to us and explained, "Something was just in here with us. The room temperature suddenly dropped for a moment and there was what sounded like some sort of vibration, like a low rumbling along the far wall."

"We all felt it," Jodi confirmed. "It was in here and then just as quickly it was gone."

Jason clarified, "We immediately looked out the window, and ruled out any sort of vehicle driving by which might have caused the vibration."

Valerie said, "Keith and Brian were just completing the blessing of the room we were in. Maybe that's what provoked it into revealing itself."

"That's right," said Brian. "In fact, just before we completed the blessing, Keith had just demanded that it give us a sign of its presence."

Andrew said, "Well, it looks like it chose to do so in here. But whatever it was I guess it was just passing through because it seems to be gone now."

With a comforting arm around Jodi's shoulders, Jason asked her, "How're you holding up kid?"

Jodi gave a small laugh and said, "Oh, I'm fine now. I was just taken a little off guard, that's all."

"We all were," said Jason. "That's the way it usually happens in these situations."

No sooner had we begun to relax, then another low vibrating sound could distinctly be heard from somewhere out in the hallway. Jodi gasped and all of our heads instantly turned towards the open bedroom doorway. "Christ," said Brian, "that sounded like a growl that time!"

"It sure as hell did," Jason agreed. "Let's go check it out. Eric and Jodi, are you up to this?" They both nodded in agreement.

Once we'd moved out into the hallway all was silent except for the sound of our breathing. I then said. "Before we do anything else, I'd like to administer a protective blessing over each one of us, if that's agreeable."

"Absolutely," said Jason. "Go for it."

Seeing as no one had any objections, I anointed each person's forehead head with blessed oil in the form of a cross, including my own, then asked everyone to please bow their head for a moment. Raising my right hand, I said, "The word of God according to his Psalmist, David: 'Touch *not* my prophets, nor do my anointed ones harm.'"

"Thank you Keith," said Jodi.

"Yes, thanks for doing that Keith," said Jason. Glancing at Jodi once again he said, "Are you ready for this?"

"Oh yes," Jodi replied. "I'm not about to turn back; not after I've come this far."

We then decided to move on to the in-laws room… not quite certain of what we might find in there after the blessings and religious provocations which had been done in the other rooms. Jason gave the word to cautiously open the door. Slowly, Rich turned the doorknob and opened the door of the in-laws room. As we peered into the darkened interior of the room at first all we could see was the glowing red light of Rich's video camera, mounted on the tripod.

Rich did a sweep about the room with his small flashlight, before he and Andrew stepped in, switched off the night vision on the video camera and then switched on the overhead light, illuminating the entire room. After the rest of us entered the room a quick look around reveled nothing out of place. Not surprisingly the videotape had by now run out. The disappointment in Rich's voice was evident as he said, "Everything in here looks *exactly* the way we left it. Even the picture of Grandma Kingston hasn't budged at all. It sure would've been a prize if I could've captured that flying off the shelf on video."

Coming over and placing a hand on Rich's arm, Valerie said, "I know, it's frustrating. But you know from experience that it's not always going to happen when you want it to."

"You're right, Val," Rich said with a tired smile. "It's just that this is turning out to be a longer night than expected."

And then we all heard *it* again. What sounded like a low, muffled growl had just come from somewhere down the hallway. All eight of us instantly perked to alertness as Brian said, "That sounded like it came from the main bedroom!"

"Let's go," said Jason, leading the way as we all rushed down the hallway in the direction of the large bedroom. No sooner had we reached the main bedroom, than another muffled growl could be heard once again from the opposite direction, almost as if we were listening to a stereo effect.

With perspiration beading on his forehead, Brian exclaimed, "Damn! Where the hell's that coming from?"

Glancing back and forth Jason said, "Whatever the hell this thing is it can play cat and mouse with us like this all friggin' night if it wants to."

I suggested, "It seems our only alternative is to try and corner it somehow."

"Exactly what I was thinking," said Jason. When Jodi looked questioningly at us, Jason explained to her, "Our game plan will still be to try and limit the entity's mobility up here so that it only has access to maybe the last two rooms. And eventually we hope to confine it to one room alone."

"And that's when I can perform the actual expulsion," I said.

Jason added, "Of course the main thing is to make certain that none of us are cornered in the process. That's why it's especially important that no one goes anywhere by themselves at this point."

"Oh, don't worry," said Jodi. "I'm not about to go off wandering anywhere by myself in *this* house."

Eric said, "Trust me, neither am I."

"Alright," said Jason, "theoretically, if this is an inhuman entity we're dealing with then it should now be confined to the last two rooms. Maybe it'll bounce back and forth between the two rooms for a while and then Keith can bless one of these two rooms. Hopefully, we'll then have it trapped in the *one* remaining room."

Another muffled growl was heard causing us all to freeze in our tracks. This time it seemed to come from somewhere directly above us. Glancing up, Brian said, "What the hell? It sounds like it's up in the friggin' attic now!"

"I think you're right," Jason agreed.

Valerie asked, "But didn't we already bless the attic while we were outside earlier?"

Jason replied, "Yeah, but when you think about it, all I did was spray some holy water into that small ventilation window. That may not have been enough depending on how strong the entity we're dealing with is."

Everyone then glanced up at the small rectangular access door to the attic, which was located on the ceiling directly above us. I asked, "Do you suppose it has pull-down steps?"

Still looking up at it, Jason said, "No… it looks too small for that. It's probably just a single board that slides over the opening. But someone has to try and get through there. Mandy told us earlier that it's not safe and that it's basically no more than a crawl space. But all we really need is for someone to squeeze through that opening just far enough to spray some holy water around. "

Stepping forward, I said, "Well then, I guess it's up to me to go up there."

Valerie also volunteered saying, "Since I'm the smallest, I'd probably fit through the opening easier than anyone else."

Jason said, "Well before we decide who's going up there, first we have to see about getting ourselves a step ladder." He then asked Andrew and Valerie to go downstairs and ask the Kingston's if we could borrow any kind of a small stepladder to use to get into the attic.

They returned several minutes later with Andrew carrying a small stepstool in his right hand. Surprisingly the Kingston's had informed Andrew and Valerie that they didn't happen to have a stepladder. They'd apologized and offered the footstool as the best that they could do.

Incredulous, Jason said, "What the-? Aw no, we can't have this! That's not tall enough or steady enough for any of us to risk our necks on. We'll simply have to hoist someone up there by hand." Turning to Andrew he said, "Okay Andrew, you're elected."

"Uh… me?" asked Andrew, taken off guard.

"Yes you," said Jason, with some humor evident in his voice. "You're the most qualified one to go up there. You're the right height and build and you have the proportionate upper body strength. Besides, the floor up there's not safe enough to walk on, so you'll basically just be reaching in and spraying the holy water around. Keith will be assisting you from down here."

"Well… okay," Andrew said with a shrug. "Let's do this."

Jason assured him, "Don't worry, I'll be right here to catch you in case you slip. Me, Rich an' Brian will be steadying you, so there shouldn't be a problem."

"Famous last words," Andrew laughed as he stepped up onto the stool, which had been placed on the floor directly underneath the small access opening. Brian handed Andrew the spray bottle of holy water, which he held onto tightly with his left hand. Rich handed him a small flashlight, which he held in his right. He switched on the flashlight and said, "Okay, I'm ready."

With a combined effort, Jason, Brian and Rich then securely grabbed onto Andrew's legs and hoisted him aloft. I rushed over to help spot him. Andrew reached up and pushed on the board, which covered the opening. It easily fell aside within the attic. Seconds later, he'd managed to secure his elbows on both sides of the small opening, allowing him to pull his torso further up into the attic. We could hear him grunting with the effort.

Concerned, Valerie said, "Andrew, please be careful."

Rich asked, "You okay up there, buddy?"

"Yeah... I'm okay," Andrew replied from above us.

Still reaching up Jason again assured him, "Don't worry, I've got you covered."

"That's reassuring," said Andrew now with his legs dangling free. With a supreme effort he then used his arms to hoist himself up even further, finally twisting his torso about until he rested in a sitting position. Only the lower parts of his legs were now visible as he sat balanced on the rim of the opening. A small cloud of dust and a few pieces of debris dropped down upon us causing us to flinch.

Eric stepped back and took a few snapshots. Jodi nervously tensed her hands into fists as she said, "Ohhh! Please, hold on tight Andrew!"

"I'm holding on as best as I can," Andrew called back. "I think I'm alright now though as long as I stay in a sitting position."

Jason asked him, "What's it look like up there, Andrew?"

"Just a second and I'll let you know," said Andrew. After shining the flashlight at his surroundings and coughing from the dust, Andrew replied, "It's really hard to breathe up here. And there's no real floor... just some rough-hewn beams with the bark still on them. They're most likely the *original* beams, probably well over a hundred years old."

From underneath him I said, "Well, I'll make this as quick as possible. Ready, Andrew?"

"Yep. Go for it, Keith," he said.

Opening my Bible, I then read from Hebrews, Chapter 9, which specifically refers to the Blood of Christ. As I pronounced the blessing

Andrew sprayed a dose of holy water in all four directions of the attic space. "Okay, Andrew," I called up to him, "that concludes the blessing of the attic."

"Okay, then I'm on my way back down," Andrew called back. "Just make sure you guys are there at the ready."

"Not a problem Andrew," said Jason as we all stepped in closer. "I've got you covered man, so go ahead."

Andrew first passed down to us the spray bottle of holy water and the small flashlight. He then braced himself by placing his hands firmly against the edges of the small opening, and once again twisted his body around. Both Brian and Rich began holding onto Andrew's legs as he slowly *and* cautiously began lowering himself down while I also stood at the ready and Jason spotted him from behind. Brian told him, "Easy, now, dude. We got ya. Just a little bit more."

It seemed that Andrew was about to make it down smoothly, when his descent suddenly accelerated. Almost as if he'd just been forcefully pushed from above his body shot out of the attic opening like a projectile seemingly in fast motion with a cloud of dust and debris surrounding him. "Look out!" exclaimed Rich, as Andrew landed with a clump on the floor directly in front of Jason before any of us had a chance to help break his fall.

"Andrew!" Valerie cried out. "Are you alright?"

As we all gathered around him Andrew took a moment to catch his breath, before replying, "Yeah, I think so... just a little winded. I think I snagged my hand pretty good on something sharp though."

After we'd assisted Andrew into a standing position, Valerie examined the palm of his right hand, which was bleeding from a long, nasty scratch. "Oh, my God," she said. "We've got to get that cleaned off right away."

Jodi quickly handed him a wad of tissues, which she'd pulled from her pocket. "Here, hon, take these," she said.

"Thanks Jodi," Andrew told her. Turning to Jason he said with a laugh, "Hey, I thought you were supposed to be ready to catch me from behind in case I slipped." Jason also chuckled, shrugged and said, "Sorry man, but it just happened so fast there really wasn't time for me to do much of anything."

Andrew agreed, saying, "Yeah, I guess there wasn't really time for anyone to catch me, the way I was shot out of there. But anyway it could've been a lot worse!" He let out an expletive, while dabbing the blood.

"Ohh! How bad is it?" asked Valerie.

Andrew replied, "As far as the cut goes I don't think it's really deep enough to require stitches or anything but it's lengthy... and it sure as hell smarts like a bitch. I think I must've cut it on a loose splinter of wood when I fell."

Valerie gave Andrew a quick hug and told him, "We're sure glad that you weren't more seriously injured, hon."

"Thanks, so am I," Andrew laughed.

Brian then asked, "So, what the hell happened up there, dude? It looked like you shot out of there like a cannon!"

"Well, I assume I just slipped on my way out," said Andrew. "But now that you mention it, there was of sort of a pushing sensation when it happened almost as if I was being forcefully ejected. Maybe something really didn't want me up there."

Jason said, "Anyway Andrew, we've got to get that cut washed off and taken care of and fill the Kingston's in on everything that's been going on. Whatever this thing is up here, it's pissed... but at least it now seems to be confined just to this area. It looks as though it's going to be a longer night than we anticipated."

With his uninjured hand Andrew brushed away some of the dust and cobwebs that covered his dark shirt and trousers before we all made our way back downstairs.

As soon as we entered the parlor, Mandy asked, "Is everyone alright? We heard some commotion going on up there."

Jason explained, "Well we just had a slight mishap while Andrew was assisting in blessing the attic. He took a little spill while he was leaning into the small opening in the ceiling."

"Oh my God!" Mandy gasped. "I'm so sorry this happened, Andrew! How bad is it?"

"Oh it's nothing to write home about," Andrew assured her with a smile. "Just a nasty little gash that needs a couple of Band-Aids that's all."

Rushing over to him, Mandy said in a concerned voice, "Well, we've got to get that cleaned off right away and apply some antiseptic so it won't get infected." She then led him to the bathroom as if she were escorting one of her own injured family members.

A short time later while we all sat in the kitchen drinking more coffee Jason explained to the family, "Okay, here's the situation as it stands. So far, we haven't encountered any manifestations of whatever human spirits may reside in this house. However, as you know, we have been dealing with what seems to be an inhuman entity, because it responds to religious provocation."

With her eyes slightly moistening, Mandy said, "You know, I'm actually not surprised. In fact, I've suspected for a while that there may be something more than just ghosts here. Even before the priest came to bless the house, I suspected that."

Melissa said, "Me too. I've always felt that there was something more sinister in this house, than just the Indian spirit."

Rich said, "It could possibly be that the inhuman entity has been keeping the other spirits from showing themselves. Maybe it's even holding them hostage so to speak and preventing them from moving on."

I added, "Most of the rooms upstairs have now been blessed except for two. So we're pretty sure we have the inhuman entity confined to these two separate rooms."

"And which two rooms are those?" asked Mandy.

Jason answered, "The large bedroom that most of us stayed in last night and the in-laws room."

Michael shared a concerned look with his father George, while Michelle, Megan and Melissa huddled closer to their mother. To reassure them, Jason said, "It does seem to be contained up there, because the rest of the house has been blessed and the blessing seems to be effective."

"That's good to know," Mandy said with some relief. "So, what are you planning to do now?"

"Well when we go back upstairs in just a few minutes we'll try to contain it to only *one* room. After that Keith will pronounce the final expulsion."

Mandy smiled, and said, "Again, I can't begin to thank all of you for placing yourselves in the line of fire for us."

By the time we went back upstairs it was nearing 2:00 AM, and time for me to begin blessing the final two rooms. We were all well exhausted by now, despite the caffeine we'd just imbibed. And yet we all knew we had a job to complete before retiring for the night. At Jason's discretion, I first began blessing the larger upstairs bedroom with Brian assisting me. I again began by reciting the 23rd Psalm aloud, followed by a reading from the Gospel of Mark, Chapter 16: "These signs will accompany those who believe: in my name will they cast our demons…." I then asked for a sign of the entity's presence.

"I'm suddenly getting a slight spike over here in this corner," Rich announced while checking his EMF detector.

"Keep going Keith," Brian encouraged me.

As I continued asking for a sign the atmosphere in the room began to noticeably thicken. And then *just* as quickly the air returned to normal. Still glancing at he EMF detector Rich announced, "Now it's back to normal again."

Brian said, "I guess it's gone from this room now. Looks like you've managed to chase it out again Keith. So it's probably now gone to take its last refuge in the in-laws room."

"Well then I suppose it's time for us to take our final stand," I said to everyone.

As soon as the bedroom we were still in had been properly anointed Jason said, "Alright, let's go for it and finally wrap this up once and for all." He then firmly led us out of the bedroom, down the hallway and into the in-laws room.

Assuming the entity we'd been dealing with was now "trapped" inside of this room we were now prepared for the final confrontation. However, before beginning the blessing we were also unexpectedly joined in this upstairs by Michael Kingston who wanted to be present for the conclusion of our investigation and deliverance session. Michael assured us, "Of course I'll do whatever you guys want. But if it's okay, I'd like to be here for this."

We all agreed to have him present. As Jason said to him, "After all, Michael you've already been experiencing much of the activity in this house and you and your girlfriend will most likely be continuing to live up here after we leave right?"

"Yes, that's true, we will," said Michael.

"Then you're certainly welcome to stay up here with us and observe while we do our thing," said Jason. "The only thing we ask is that you don't separate from us or go off by yourself until we're finished."

Michael readily agreed saying that he'd feel a great deal safer being with us anyway.

Rich slipped a fresh tape into his video camera, turned down the lights once again and began recording in night shot. Eric also continued taking photos although by now we were hardly even aware that he was doing so. Before commencing with the blessing of the in-laws room, I said a special prayer of protection over Michael and anointed his forehead with blessed oil in the sign of a cross. I then began by reading Psalm 23 aloud. This I followed with a reading from the Gospel of Luke, Chapter 10 verses 17-20: "And the seventy returned with joy, saying, 'Lord, even the devils are subject to us in Thy name.' And He said to them, 'I beheld Satan falling from Heaven like lightning. Lo, I give you power to tread on serpents and scorpions and on all the power of the enemy and nothing shall hurt you. Nevertheless, do not rejoice in this, that the spirits are subject to you; but rejoice, because you names are written in Heaven.'"

After Brian, Rich, Eric and I had moved into almost completely darkened in-laws room where Rich's video camera was still recording I opened my Bible and prepared to begin. Because of the dull lighting in the room, Valerie switched on the small flashlight she carried and held it close enough for me to be able to clearly see the page. Since Michael's infant son usually slept in this room, I also read an excerpt from the Gospel of Mark, Chapter 10: "Let the little children come to me, and forbid them not, for the kingdom of God belongs to such as these."

After a significant pause I addressed the entity itself. "In the name of Jesus Christ, if there is a spirit in this room with us, give us a sign of your presence."

We then waited in silence for something to happen. Strangely, the room seemed unusually still and quiet. Again, I said, "In the *name* of the Lord Jesus Christ, we demand a sign of your presence."

Even though this was the room in which the entity was supposedly now contained there was still no reaction. Andrew suggested, "It must be intentionally laying low. Keep trying to provoke it Keith."

Although I continued praying and asking for a sign of any spirit entity that might be present nothing revealed itself. By now, we all would have welcomed it if at least the Indian spirit had appeared to us or if the framed photo of the grandmother had toppled off the shelf. But despite the previous activity, nothing now seemed to be happening. Rich finally became somewhat impatient and said to the entity, "You've been putting on quite a show in this house up until now. So why not reveal yourself to us while we're all here in this room?"

Valerie also asked, "Why won't you reveal your presence to us now? Are you *that* afraid of us?"

"Show yourself, coward!" said Brian.

We waited several more minutes but there was still no response. Finally, I suggested to Jason that I conclude the blessing of the room we were in and then pronounce the final expulsion. Jason agreed saying, "We're not getting any response so you might as well go for it Keith. Then I suggest we call it a night. I think we're all pretty wiped out at this point."

Turning to Brian I asked if he was ready. "Sure thing, Keith." he replied. "Let's drive this sucker out once and for all."

Holding onto my Bible I said, "Then in the name of the Father and of the Son and of the Holy Spirit, we bless and sanctify this room. We ask that all wandering spirits be sent to their proper abode and that all restless spirits now be at rest." After Brian had sprayed holy water in all four sections of the room I said, "In the name of Jesus Christ we ask that you give us a sign of your departure." Again, my words were met with only silence.

Brian said, "Maybe it's already gone Keith. You've done a pretty thorough blessing after all."

"You could be right," I agreed. "It could have simply gone quietly."

Rich shut off his video camera and switched on one of the table lamps.

Jason rose from his sitting position and glanced at his watch. "Well it's almost 3:00 AM now," he said. "I'm beat so I'm gonna call it a night. Thanks so much for doing the final blessing Keith."

"You're welcome. Glad to be of service," I said.

Jason then asked Michael, "How are you holding up? Do you feel comfortable sleeping in here for the rest of the night?"

Sitting on his foldout bed Michael replied, "Sure, I'll be fine. Thanks, guys."

Valerie said, "I can go downstairs and let the rest of the family know that it's over."

"I'll go with you," Rich offered.

Jason, Brian, Jodi, Eric, Andrew and I were less than halfway down the hallway with Rich and Valerie slightly ahead of us, when Rich suddenly called us to a halt. "Wait up a moment, guys," he said holding his arm protectively in front of Valerie. "I think I just heard something again."

"Where?" asked Brian.

"I'm not sure," Rich replied. "It was somewhere here along the hallway... but I'm not sure whether it came from one of the rooms or not."

Then we all heard it... another muffled growl, seemingly coming from all around us. Only this time it sounded much more subdued than before. Brian said, "The thing's still up here with us. Even after we blessed the whole friggin' house!"

"But it seems to be considerably weakened," said Jason. "It must be finding this place extremely uncomfortable to be in right now."

I said, "Brian, I'd like for you to please start spraying holy water throughout the entire hallway."

"Alright, you got it, man," he said.

Valerie and Rich quickly returned to the in-laws room and explained to Michael what was happening.

Brian then liberally sprayed holy water throughout the hallway while I again recited Scripture and demanded that any unseen entities that may be present reveal themselves to us now, *or* depart in peace.

When Brian and I were done Jason said to everyone, "Alright, here's what we'll do now. At least one of us will have to spend the rest of the night with Michael in the in-laws room and I'd like a couple of people to stay downstairs with the rest of the family. The rest of us will spend the remainder of the night in one of the bedrooms up here." With a sigh he added, "At this point all we can do is wait it out and see if anything else happens tonight. That should tell us whether the blessing's taken full effect."

It was now after 3:00 AM. Since all of us were by now fairly exhausted we wasted little time in retiring for what remained of the night. Rich and Valerie went downstairs to join George and Mandy and their three daughters who were all spending the night together on the first floor. Upstairs, Brian would be staying in the in-laws room with Michael in case anything else were to happen before dawn, while the rest of us retired to one of the smaller bedrooms.

With a comforter and a blanket I bedded down on the floor and soon began nodding off. I had only just begun to doze off, however, before the ringing of Jason's small radio roused us all from our momentary slumber. Stretched out upon the room's only bed, Jason placed the radio to his mouth and said, "Yeah."

In the darkened bedroom we could all clearly overhear Valerie's voice saying, "Jason? Sorry to bother you but we seem to have some activity going on down here."

In a groggy voice Jason asked, "What is it, what's goin' on?"

Valerie replied, "Well, both George and Mandy said that their bed was just shaking with them in it."

"Uh-huh," Jason acknowledged.

"So, what should we do?" asked Valerie.

Still half-asleep Jason simply answered, "Chill…."

Wearily, I pulled myself up off the floor and grasped for the bottle of holy water, which I'd left beside me. With the comforter wrapped about my shoulders, I began shuffling towards the bedroom door. "Good man, Keith," Jason mumbled.

"Sure thing, Chief," I said with a light chuckle.

"Someone go with him," said Jason. Andrew also rose and began following close behind me.

Fortunately the hall light had been left on, which enabled us to make our way without the aid of a flashlight. Once downstairs Valerie and Rich met up with us just outside George and Mandy's bedroom. There was a single small kitchen light on, dimly illuminating the immediate area. Andrew asked Valerie, "How're they holding up?"

Valerie said, "Well they're alright but they're also a little shaken up by what just happened. And they're afraid to go back to sleep."

Rich added, "Anyway, thanks for getting up and joining us down here guys."

"No problem," said Andrew. He then turned to me and said, "Well I guess it's your call Keith as to what our next move is."

I took a moment to peer around the corner into the Kingston's main downstairs bedroom. George and Mandy sat next to each other on the bed in their thermal pajamas. They both looked at me with frightened yet expectant expressions on their faces. On the floor beside the bed, Michelle, Megan and Melissa were huddled beside each other in sleeping bags also wide-awake and looking frightened.

My heart went out to the family and I felt myself becoming angered at what they were being put through. "Let's move over into the kitchen," I whispered to Andrew.

Rich also offered to join Andrew and I while Valerie said she didn't mind going back to the bedroom to stay with the Kingston's. "Thanks, Val," said Rich giving her a quick hug.

"That's alright," she said with a tired smile. "Maybe if I manage to calm them down enough we can all get at least a little sleep."

Once Rich, Andrew and I were in the dimly lit kitchen, I explained to them in a hushed tone, "I'm going to attempt one last expulsion. We assume that the inhuman entity's power is weakened so it should be done now before it has a chance to regain strength."

Rich said, "So maybe those last growls we heard upstairs and the shaking of the bed just now were just a final display of its remaining power."

"Yeah, like a final, desperate intimidation tactic," said Andrew.

"Exactly," I said. "So by the grace of God this will be successful."

"Okay, Keith," said Rich. "We're ready whenever you are."

189

Keeping my voice as low as possible to avoid further alarming the family I said, "In the name of the Lord Jesus Christ, may any unseen entity which is present in this house, which is not of human origin, depart from here. And let mighty and holy angels of God, who will watch over this family and protect them from harm, also fill this vacancy. In the name of Jesus Christ I ask that a sign of departure be given."

As we waited in silence all that could be heard was the faint whistling of the chill winter wind at the windows from outside. Now raising my voice just a little, I said, "It is not by my own authority I ask this, but by the authority of the shed blood of Jesus Christ. May holy angels escort all wandering spirits that are here into His divine presence and in the name of Jesus, I again ask for a sign of departure."

Once again we waited in silence. Several seconds had passed when I momentarily felt a chill, as if a cold breeze had suddenly passed by. Glancing at Rich and Andrew I could see by their expressions that they'd also just experienced it. Rich was beginning to comment on it when our attention was suddenly diverted to a vibrating sound right there in the kitchen with us. Glancing to our immediate right, the three of us were astonished to witness the large metallic parrot cage beginning to slide across the floor towards us! Within the cage, beneath the cloth that was covering it, we could hear the startled Skippy wildly flapping his wings. And then after the cage had moved perhaps only a few inches it suddenly stopped.

At first, Rich, Andrew and I stood transfixed to the spot, with the only sound being that of Skippy still agitated within his covered cage. Andrew said, "Tell me that you guys just heard and saw the parrot cage move by itself."

"Oh yeah," said Rich. "Damn! It figures that something like that would happen just when I'm not videotaping."

"That's the way it usually is more often than not," I commented.

Then there was a sudden and noticeable change in the atmosphere of the room. Andrew asked us, "Hey, do you feel that? Or is it my imagination?"

"No, I feel it too," said Rich. "It's like the air in here has somehow lightened."

Andrew said, "You're right. It almost feels like a purification of some kind. What do you make of it, Keith?"

Facing my two friends squarely I said, "I believe that we've just been given the sign of departure we asked for... which hopefully means it's over."

Late the following morning, while we were all getting ready to leave, Jason and I spent several minutes in the parlor, speaking with the Kingston family. All the while in the background, Skippy kept up a lively rapport with us by reciting a telephone conversation he'd obviously memorized word by word. Mandy told us, "It's absolutely amazing that the parrot cage moved by itself last night. I've checked the floor and it was only moved about three inches but still... that parrot cage along with the stand weighs at least two-hundred pounds!"

George said, "Trust me, it does. Me an' Mike have moved that whole thing a number of times."

Jason explained, "Well an inhuman spirit tends to have much greater abilities than a human spirit would. Even though this one was presumably in a weakened state it still had the ability to move a two-hundred pound object even if it was just a few inches."

Mandy asked, "So, is the inhuman spirit gone now completely?"

Jason and I shared a glance before I answered, "I believe that it's gone from this house and that it's in a nullified state. But now it's also up to you people to keep it at bay."

"Do you mean that there's a chance it could come back?" asked Mandy.

Jason said, "We'd be lying to you if we said we had a definite answer to that. But what Keith means is that to prevent it from possibly returning, you're all going to have to work together as a family to help maintain a positive atmosphere in this house."

"Exactly," I said. "Now I know you people don't dabble in the occult so there's no need to worry about that."

"No, we certainly don't," said Mandy sharing a laugh with the rest of her family.

Michael said, "Believe me we've had enough trouble without inviting more in."

"Good attitude," said Jason. "Believe me we've had to deal with situations where people have intentionally invited hostile spirits in even knowing the potential danger."

"Now you people are of the Catholic faith correct?" I asked.

"Yes," said Mandy. "We haven't been to church in awhile, but we've been meaning to get back."

"It's totally your decision, of course," I said. "But if you're so inclined to begin attending again than that could help. It could be a boost to your faith."

Mandy agreed. "You're right. It certainly couldn't hurt."

Melissa then asked, "What about the Indian spirit? Is he still here?"

Gently, I explained to her and her sister, "When an expulsion is done, it's not like you can pick and choose which spirits remain and which ones stay. During the deliverance session I prayed that *all* spirits be sent to their proper place. And no human spirit really belongs in this house either; they're meant to move on as well. It's not a good thing for a human spirit to be wandering in a state of unrest."

Jason added, "And there's also the possibility that the human spirits here were being held against their will by the inhuman one. And besides even if the Indian spirit was in fact watching over the two of you what happens when you both grow older and eventually move out of the house? Once it's purpose in being here is gone, instead of passing on properly it may be trapped in a state of confusion."

"Unless, of course it was an angelic spirit," I added.

Melissa reached over and clasped her sister Megan's hand in hers. "I guess you're right," she said. "Thank you for explaining that to us."

Michael then said, "Y' know it's too bad you guys aren't gonna be here another day. There's a movie house in downtown Skowhegan that's said to be really haunted."

Jason laughed and told him, "Thanks Mike but I think we're all 'investigated out' right about now and we have a long drive ahead of us. Maybe next time we're in the area."

As it came time for us to make our departure, Skippy became extremely excited at all the commotion and bustling about which was taking place. Each time either Jodi or Valerie would walk by, he'd let out a suggestive whistle.

We then said our final good-byes to the family. With tears in her eyes, Mandy embraced each of us and said, "I can't thank you people enough for all you've done for us."

"Not a problem," said Jason. "Just promise you'll keep in touch and call us no matter what just to let us know how you're all doing."

"Oh, don't worry we'll keep in touch," Mandy promised.

Eric told the family, "I'll be sure to send you copies of the photos I've taken here."

"Oh yes, thanks so much, I'd love that," said Mandy.

"And thank you for all your hospitality," said Eric.

George Kingston also went around shaking our hands and giving each of the two ladies affectionate hugs. When he came to Jodi he said, "So I guess you'll be heading back to New Hampshire now, right?"

Jodi replied, "Oh yes, my husband and kids will be waiting impatiently for me. Plus, after all that I've experienced this weekend, I'm anxious to start getting my notes together for '*Second Glance*.'"

"Again Jodi, I think that's such an appropriate title," said Mandy. With a sniffle she turned back to us and said, "And you people be careful on your way back to Rhode Island."

Jason said with a laugh, "I'm sure it will be a lot less treacherous on the way back then it was getting here. It certainly looks like a perfect day out there for our trip back home."

George assured us, "Believe me you guys got nothing to worry about. The roads around here will be perfectly cleared by now."

From his large parrot cage, Skippy suddenly began shrieking his own farewell: "The bitch is home! The bitch is home"

"That parrot's so friggin' awesome!" Brian exclaimed with a grin.

CHAPTER 17

Ghost Magnet

E VERY SO OFTEN in the course of our paranormal explora-
tions, we come across someone who we define as a 'ghost
magnet.' By this, we refer to an individual who for some
unknown reason, usually through no conscious fault of their own,
seemingly attracts spirits to him or herself. Quite often this person is
of the female gender, perhaps because females, in general, tend to be
somewhat more sensitive on a psychic level than males. One such
individual is Kristyn Gartland, a native of Massachusetts who also
happens to be a paranormal investigator with The Atlantic Paranormal Society. However, when I first met Kristyn she was actually
a client who had asked for our assistance. I was a member of TAPS
at the time.

It was during the month of October in the year 2001 when Kristyn first contacted us. At the time she was a single mom living in an
apartment located in Reading, MA. According to Kristyn, she had
been aware of the presence of spirits around her since she was a
young girl. The spirits would frequently make their presence
known, either by touching her or playing mischievous little pranks
around the house while no one else was at home, such as turning
water faucets on and off, moving small household objects such as
salt shakers, etc.

Over the years, Kristyn became accustomed to the sprits letting her know they were around. Even as a single mother alone with her 6-year-old son, Kristyn found that this sort of mild activity did not really bother her. In fact she sometimes assumed that the spirit of her recently deceased grandmother was perhaps simply letting her know that she was still watching over her and her grandson.

Lately however, the spirit activity had taken on a disturbing new twist, in that her 6-year-old son was now also being affected. He happened to have an imaginary friend in the form of a young girl, whose name was Jenny and who he described as having long hair and wearing a long dress. Of course there is nothing really unusual about a young child having an imaginary playmate. However, he also said that his friend Jenn said she lived in the large cemetery, which was located directly across from their apartment building and that her ears were bleeding.

When Kristyn asked her son how old Jenny was, he replied without hesitation,' She tells me she's eight. And she was sick before she went to live across the street." Now her son had certainly never visited that cemetery. However, out of curiosity, one recent afternoon Kristyn took him across the street for a walk through the cemetery grounds. He quickly led her down a certain path, until they arrived at a large granite monument, upon which the beautifully carved life-size image of a young girl was who matched her son's description. "That's her, Mommy!" he'd said, excitedly tugging on her arm. "That's my friend Jenny and she says hi!" Sure enough the grave belonged to a young girl named "Jenny" who had died a few decades ago at the age of eight. Shortly after this her son began waking up screaming in the middle of the night saying that there were also two other children there in the darkened bedroom with him.

Not only that but Kristyn had recently caught a brief glimpse of what appeared to be a little child, most likely a young boy, wearing a nightshirt, running down her hallway. Unsure of whether he was real or a spirit form she followed him down the hallway and into one of the vacant bedrooms. There she saw the little boy crouching behind the bed, peeking at her until he suddenly vanished. "Just one second he was there and the next he wasn't," Kristyn said over the phone.

Another unnerving incident had occurred while Kristyn was taking a shower. Although her son was not home at the time she suddenly heard a large bang from somewhere in the apartment. She immediately turned the shower off, quickly wrapped a towel around herself and went out to investigate. She found no explanation for the noise. However upon returning to the bathroom there was an imprint of a man's face on the steamed mirror. And on one of the moist shower walls someone had clearly written the word "Hello." Kristyn said, "I know it sounds crazy but I was actually more angered than scared when this happened. I really felt as though my privacy was being invaded."

Kristyn mentioned several other things that had been happening in her apartment such as windows opening by themselves, disembodied whisperings, sudden cold spots, TV channels suddenly changing and the heater being suddenly turned off all with no apparent logical explanation. Nor were she and her son the only ones who were experiencing unusual things in the apartment building. At least a few other tenants in the building mentioned that they had also felt a strange presence in their apartments. One couple with a small baby had even reported arriving home to find a tablecloth taken off the dining room table and placed in another room neatly folded.

Kristyn and her best friend had also recently used a Ouija board in an effort to contact some of these spirits but had been frightened away from further using it after they'd begun to receive hostile messages. They had also been given the names of two children, Michael and Laura. Shortly after this Kristyn's son claimed to have been talking with two new friends. He said they were a boy and a girl named Michael and Laura even though he hadn't been home when the Ouija board was being used, ruling out the possibility of having overheard these names. Michael and Laura were obviously the "other children" that her son was now seeing in his bedroom.

After taking down Kristyn's info and her address we agreed to investigate her case making it a priority because there was also a young child involved.

We arrived at the apartment house in Reading early on a Saturday evening in mid-October. Our crew of investigators this evening consisted of TAPS founder Jason Hawes, tech specialists Brian Harnios and Rich Einig and myself as a spiritual consultant. We also had Theresa with us, a member-in-training at the time. Kristyn welcomed us in with a warm smile, obviously relieved to have people there who would not automatically judge her as merely being delusional.

Kristyn was a 26-year-old woman with a lively personality with fair hair and blue eyes. Her sense of humor was evident from the start. "I hope y'all are hungry because I've put out a lot of snacks for you," she told us. Kristyn had even written out a humorous menu for us on a chalkboard, which listed such imaginary delectable as "spirit soufflé" and "orb pie." We could see that we were going to get along with this lady just fine.

Kristyn also sported some brightly colored body illustrations. "Nice tats," Brian complimented her admiring the ones adorning her upper left arm and shoulder.

"Oh, thanks," she said with a laugh. "At first, I wasn't quite sure *what* you were referring to."

Kristyn explained to us that her son was staying with his father so he wouldn't be in the way or upset that people were here looking for "ghosts" in his home.

She also informed us that recently her boyfriend had seen three unfamiliar children standing in the hallway, just in front of the doorway. They were dressed very plainly in old fashioned, dingy clothes. I asked, "Did they say anything?"

"No, they simply stood there staring at him," said Kristyn. "Before he had a chance to say anything, they'd simply vanished."

Jason asked, "And how did that make him feel?"

Kristyn replied, "To be honest, it freaked him out. He found it very disturbing, suddenly seeing three children in the apartment that he didn't even know. And then when they vanished he realized they weren't even *living* children."

We then asked Kristyn if she'd mind giving us a tour of her apartment, to which she readily agreed. She informed us that her roommate, a young male college student who rented a single large room in the apartment adjoining the parlor, was also absent this evening. Jason asked, "Has he experienced any of the activity going on here?"

"Oh, he's pretty much a skeptic, actually an atheist and hasn't really experienced anything," said Kristyn. "But he's not here as much as I am. And besides because he's such a skeptic he really wasn't interested in being here tonight."

She showed us the main bathroom, where the imprint of the face had appeared in the condensation on the mirror and the word "Hello" had been written inside the shower stall. "Honestly, I felt more angry than afraid when that happened," she told us. "I know it sounds funny but I didn't want them to see me naked."

"That's understandable," said Jason. "Who wants to feel as though an invisible presence is watching them in the shower?"

Brian commented, "That's enough to give anyone a case of the he-be ge-be's."

"You got that right," said Rich.

Kristyn also showed us where she'd seen the appearance of the little boy and where he had run and hid inside the bedroom before vanishing. Outside of the bedroom was the hallway, where Kristyn's boyfriend had also witnessed the three unfamiliar children. While we were still in the bedroom, I commented on the multiple angel decorations in her bedroom and throughout her apartment. Kristyn said, "Oh that reminds me. I don't know if this is significant but there's this little angel statue that I have that seems to keep moving around from place to place. I keep it up here on a self, too high for my son to reach, but I still keep finding it in different places. And just the other day, I found it on the floor next to my bed, with one of the little feet broken off."

She reached up to one of the top shelves upon which an array of knickknacks were displayed and took down a small, white porcelain angel. She also held up a tiny left foot with her other hand. Another thing that Kristyn pointed out to us was a large, gold colored ceramic sun hung on her parlor wall. She explained, with a sigh, "I know it sounds crazy, but sometimes this ceramic sun starts shaking on its own. My boyfriend and I have both seen it happen, always at night."

Jason asked, "Has your roommate ever seen it shake?"

Kristyn replied, "No, but he'd probably just scoff at it even if he did."

When the tour of the apartment was finished we all gathered together inside Kristyn's parlor to for a more detailed interview. She reiterated that her problem with attracting spirits seemed to be generational and inherited from her mother's side of the family. In fact, until recently it hadn't actually presented much of a problem at all. But now that her son was being terrified, and her own personal privacy was being invaded, she very wanted help with her situation. Jason said, "So, you mentioned that your son has supposedly been communicating with a little girl named Jenny correct?"

"Yes, that's true," said Kristyn. "As I explained to Brian, when I took my son to the cemetery and we found her marker, he stated saying excitedly, 'That's her, Mommy, that's Jenny!' And he also tells me that Jenny's ears are bleeding and that she always talks with her hands, which leads me to believe that she may have been deaf. "

"That's so sad," said Theresa. "And you say that Jenny was eight years old when she died and that she's buried in the large cemetery *right* across the street?"

"Yes that's correct," said Kristyn.

"In fact, one reason I think I might be having so many problems with spirits here is because the front part of this building is actually built right over what used to be part of the cemetery."

"What?" asked Theresa in astonishment.

Kristyn explained, "You see before this apartment house was built the cemetery originally extended right over to where we are now. But when this area was developed a number of years ago and the street out front was put in the cemetery was moved back and a lot of the graves were relocated. And so this building was actually built right over where the front section of the cemetery used to be. Of course, needless to say, I was never told about this when I first moved in."

"Oh, jeez!" said Brian. "No wonder you've got problems here."

Jason agreed, saying, "That could definitely be a contributing factor."

I then asked, "Kristyn could you tell us more about what happened when you and your friend were using a Ouija board in this apartment?"

Slightly blushing, she said, "I confess. Guilty as charged. But it was only because my best friend and I wanted to contact some of the sprits here to see if they were friendly or needed help, like that little girl Jenny. Or we thought that maybe it could even be my grandmother. In fact, we did seem to have contacted two children, a boy named Michael and a girl named Laura. But we stopped as soon as it started giving us bad messages."

I asked, "What sort of bad messages were you and your friend getting?"

"Threatening ones, saying that it hated my guts and that it was going to do me harm," said Kristyn. "But we learned our lesson after that and we haven't touched it since."

Rich asked, "Where is it now? Do you still have the board?"

"Yes, I've hidden it away in a closet where my son won't find it," said Kristyn.

I explained, "The thing about Ouija boards or similar devices used for divination is that there's no guarantee just who's going to come through. It could be deceptive sprits posing as lost souls."

"Well I'm afraid I had to learn that the hard way," said Kristyn. "But after what happened I'll certainly never be using it again."

I told her, "A lot of people make that mistake. In fact, as teenagers my brother and sister went through a similar experience after they'd played with a Ouija board."

Kristyn went on to say that she was very close to her maternal grandmother and that she still felt a spiritual connection with her. I asked, "So, you feel that your grandmother is here with you?"

"Oh yes, I know she is at least in a literal sense," said Kristyn.

We all looked at each other in silence for a moment, wondering exactly what Kristyn meant. "I'll show you," she said reaching up to her mantel and taking down a small ornate container. She opened the lid and took out what appeared to be a rolled up plastic sandwich bag stapled at each end, which contained her grandmother's ashes. "We're eventually going to have her ashes interred," Kristyn explained. "But for now, they're here with me. That's another reason I though that my grandmother might be hanging around here watching over me and her great-grandson."

Brian laughed, and said, "I was wondering what you meant when you said she's still here in a literal sense. I was hoping she wasn't stashed somewhere in a closet!"

After the interview was concluded, Jason decided that he and Rich would remain with Kristyn setting up equipment in the apartment while Brian, Theresa and I would go across the street and visit the cemetery. We'd of course stay in close communication with each other through our portable radios. Brian was given the responsibility of videotaping our cemetery excursion with the video camera set to IR. Before we left Kristyn said, "I've actually got some pictures of Jenny's monument which I took just recently. They may help you to identify it more easily."

She showed us several pictures of the monument with the life-size relief of the little girl carved on it. A few of the photos had been taken at night with a flash camera. Theresa said, "That's so beautiful. We should be able to find it pretty easily. I'd like to ask too, do you think the spirit of the little boy also came from the cemetery?"

Kristyn replied, "Well as I had told Brian over the phone my son has mentioned the names 'Michael' and 'Laura.' He said that Michael was being mean to him but that Jenny told him that she'd protect him. And of course both the names 'Michael' and 'Laura' came through on the Ouija board although my son would have no possible way of knowing that. So, my guess is that they may very well be buried somewhere over there."

Once we'd gone across the street and entered the darkened cemetery we found Jenny's monument without much difficulty. Up close this figure of a young girl, nearly life-size and expertly carved into the granite stone in relief was even lovelier than it had appeared in Kristyn's photographs. She was depicted with angelic features, with hair and clothing the style of several decades earlier. She was also shown wearing some sort of rain or snow boots on her feet. "What a beautiful little girl she was," Theresa commented.

"Yes she was," I agreed. "I'd really like to come here in the daytime to get a better look at this monument."

Videotaping the monument from top to bottom, Brian said, "I'd like to take a look at this in daylight, too. I'll tell ya, her family must have been very well off to afford this to be made."

Theresa said, "And she must have been quite a special little girl too very much loved by her family. They obviously wanted her to always be remembered. I wonder if she may have been deaf since Kristyn's son mentioned that she communicated with her hands and that she was bleeding from her ears."

"Or perhaps that may have had something to do with the way she died," I suggested.

At the bottom of the monument there was inscribed a lovely set of verses attributed to Jenny herself. Theresa and I placed our tape recorders at the base of the monument and began a brief EVP session. Theresa asked, "Do you have any messages for us Jenny?" She paused and asked, "Are you friends with the little boy who lives across the street?"

After we'd completed our EVP session at Jenny's monument we wandered about the cemetery for the next fifteen minutes or so shining our flashlights on various headstones in search of young children with the names of Michael or Laura. However, it soon became evident that the cemetery was much too large for a thorough nighttime search.

Brian was taking some more footage when his portable radio sounded. "Hi, it's Jason," said the familiar voice.

"Yo, what's up Jason?" Brian asked into the radio.

Jason asked, "How's it going over there?"

Brian replied, "We found Jenny's monument and Keith and Theresa did an EVP session there. Now we're just looking among the headstones but not much else is happening. Anything going on over there?"

"Yes, Rich's hair was just pulled by something unseen," said Jason.

"Really?" Brian asked in astonishment. "Well, we're heading back there now anyway. Over and out." Brian then told us, "Guys, they're having activity over in the apartment. Rich had his hair pulled by something invisible. I think we should be heading back there." We agreed.

Back inside Kristyn's apartment, Rich had obviously been taken completely off guard by his experience. He told us, "It was as if an invisible hand suddenly came up from behind me, and ran its fingers through my hair." With a laugh, he added, "I sure as heck wasn't expecting it."

Sounding relieved, Kristyn said, "At least now someone else has experienced something here so you know I'm not crazy."

"Never thought you were," said Jason.

Kristyn was also anxious to know if we'd obtained any evidence at all from the cemetery. A few of the pictures taken with Theresa's digital camera did reveal multiple orbs although we had to consider these inconclusive at best. We listened to the audio recording we'd taken but there were no evident examples of EVP.

Brian then hooked up the video camera he was using to Kristyn's TV so we could watch the footage he'd taken while we were inside the cemetery. Unexpectedly the first several minutes of footage consisted of an upside-down view of Brian's left sneaker stepping along the ground with a rhythmic crunching of gravel.

Jason asked, "What the-? Brian, did you just take several minutes worth of footage of the ground?"

"Oops, sorry," Brian apologized. "I didn't even realize I was filming the whole time."

"Hey well, at least you didn't leave the lens cap on," said Jason.

The footage of Jenny's monument came out clear but with no definite indication of anomalies. A few brightly illuminated specks flew by which we were able to positively identify as insects.

After watching the video footage we spent some time taking turns listening through a pair of headphones while utilizing a microphone amplifier that Rich had set up, which would augment any ambient sounds in the immediate area. After Rich had been listening for a few minutes, Jason broke the silence by asking him, "Are you picking up on anything?"

Rich shook his head and said, "That's a negative."

We all took turns listening for a while longer, including Kristyn who thought she could also hear a slight whispering at one point. However nothing definite was heard.

Next we split up into two groups to begin checking the other rooms in Kristyn's apartment. Brian and I were taking readings and photos in the spare room rented by Kristyn's roommate, who had wished to be absent for the investigation this evening. We observed that the roommate was an avid collector of science fiction paraphernalia, including a plastic alien skull, an "X Files" poster and various other decorations. Brian commented, "Jeez, this guy *sure* is into aliens."

"He does seem to have a penchant for them doesn't he?" I said in agreement.

As Brian was walking past the partially opened bedroom closet he witnessed a sudden dark flash of movement followed by the door swinging partway open by itself. "Holy crap!" Brian exclaimed. "Dude – did you just see that?"

Brian Harnois reacts to a closet in which
he'd just seen a "shadow figure" dart by.

I quickly snapped a couple of pictures before coming over to where Brian was closely inspecting the closet door. Together, we attempted to recreate what we'd just witnessed by opening and closing the door partway and then letting it go. But the door would not move again on it's own. Brian then suggested that we alert the others to what had just happened.

Once everyone else had joined us in the spare room, Jason and Rich also attempted to move the closet door in a way that would indicate some sort of spontaneous spring action, but their efforts also proved unsuccessful. Jason asked Kristyn, "Have either you or your roommate ever noticed the door swinging open on it's own before?"

"No, I haven't and he's never mentioned it to me," said Kristyn. "Of course he claims to be such a big skeptic. But I think he would've told either me or my boyfriend about something like that."

Brian said, "I'm telling ya, that freaked me out just now, because I was right next to it when it happened."

Jason then said, "Well I think we should set things up in here to see if we can pick up on anything."

Minutes later, Rich had his sound system connected in the room and Brian had he video camera pointed at the closet door. Rich noted, "Room temperature is presently seventy degrees, even."

We lowered the room lighting significantly by switching off all the lights except for one desk lamp and then waited in silence. After several minutes, Kristyn took a turn listening with the headphones while seated on the bed. It was not long before she said, "I think the *whispering's* back."

Rich asked her if he could take a listen.

"Yes, I'm getting some whispering too… very faint… I can't understand what it's saying, though," he said.

Jason also took a turn, but the whispering had stopped. Removing the headphones, he said, "I'm not getting anything. Maybe we should try asking some questions."

Kristyn put the headphones back on as Rich and I switched our tape recorders on. Rich asked, "Is there anyone here in this room with us? If so, could you give us a sign of your presence?"

Brian asked, "Could you open the closet door for us again?" After a wait of several seconds, Brian looked around at the rest of us and asked, "Is it me, or did it suddenly become a bit warmer in here?"

Rich checked his temperature gage and said, "Ambient room temperature is now seventy-two, which means it's just gone up two degrees."

Brian said, "I don't know if it's my imagination but something about the air in here suddenly feels a little thicker."

"I feel it too, very slightly," said Rich.

Still seated on the bed, Kristyn suddenly took the headphones off and doubled over with a groan. "Ooooohh... I don't feel so good," she said.

Concerned, I asked, "Kristyn, what's wrong?"

"I don't know," she said, her eyes filling with tears. "All of a sudden, I just feel really nauseous. I don't know why but it just came over me."

Fortunately Kristyn recovered quickly. Jason decided that we should conclude our session in the spare room and take a short break in our investigation. Before leaving the room, he asked Rich to use his EMF detector to scan near the headboard of the bed directly in front of where to where Kristyn had been sitting. Rich announced, "I'm getting a slight fluctuation right here. Something's setting it off."

"I'm *not* surprised," said Jason. "There's an electrical outlet right below which is undoubtedly what's causing it."

As we gathered together in the parlor, I asked, "How are you feeling now, Kristyn?"

"Much better thanks," she said. "I really apologize for that, I don't know what came over me."

Jason said, "Please don't be sorry. There's of course an electrical outlet right in back of the headboard close to where you were sitting. And I was thinking that might have had something to do with what happened. Has your roommate ever complained about suddenly feeling ill in there?"

"No, he never has not since he's been here," said Kristyn.

Jason then explained, "Well, here's what our next steps will be. We'll review whatever evidence we've collected here tonight and let you know our findings. As it is now based on what you've told us combined with what we ourselves have experienced tonight, we feel there could be some sort of paranormal activity going on here."

207

Kristyn smiled, and breathed an audible sigh of relief. "Again, thank you guys for believing me and not thinking I was just a fruit-cake," she said.

"Not a problem," said Jason. "Now, if you'd like us to we'll return next weekend for a follow-up. As we explained to you over the phone, Keith would be willing to perform a spiritual cleansing inside of your apartment, if you so desire."

"Oh, yes, I'd really like the activity to stop, mainly for my son's sake," Kristyn readily agreed.

Brian said, "In the meantime, whatever you do, don't fool around with the Ouija board again."

"Oh, trust me, I won't," said Kristyn. "I've learned my lesson especially after what happened the last time."

Theresa reminded her, "Also, please don't hesitate to contact us during the week if you need to."

"I sure will," Kristyn told us with a smile. "After all you guys are my new lifeline."

Before leaving, we asked Kristyn if she had any questions. "Yes, I do have one," she said. "When you come back and do the cleansing next week what about the other apartments in this building? I mean, at least half of this entire building is built over what used to be cemetery grounds."

Jason and I shared a glance with each other before he explained to Kristyn, "Well, that's the unfortunate thing about apartment buildings. We can cleanse your apartment, which should expel any negative entities in *here*. But unfortunately, since these entities can't be destroyed, they'll simply move on to someplace else. And as you said at least some of the other tenants in this building is also experiencing problems."

I added, "All you can do, if anyone else in the building mentions having problems is to tell them about us."

Over the course of the following week, we reviewed our data from Kristen's apartment. We unfortunately detected no trace of EVP on the audio recordings we'd taken. Also, not unexpectedly, the closet door in the spare room had failed to move on its own while the video camera was trained directly on it. However, in one of the photos that I had taken in the roommate's room immediately after Brian had seen the shadow, there was something that caught my attention. It was an angled shadow, visible in the lower right corner of the photo. Of course, this did not necessarily mean that the shadow was anything of paranormal origin. Most likely it was merely a shadow cast by the flash of the camera, against some sort of obstruction within the room. However, it was at least something. I'd simply have to wait until returning to attempt to recreate it.

We did receive a call near the end of the week from Kristyn, who wanted to give us an update on the activity that was taking place in her apartment. She informed us that Jenny, Michael and Laura were still visiting her son. In fact, he claimed that Michael was still being mean to him, but that Jenny was helping to protect him. One other somewhat peculiar thing had happened over the course of the week. This involved the small porcelain angel statue that previously had its foot broken off. Kristyn had found it lying on the floor one again and somehow, the foot seemed to have reattached itself.

TAPS arrived early the following Saturday evening, with our team consisting of the same members as the previous week. Kristyn reported having experienced only minor activity throughout the week, although one night, at approximately 3:00 AM, she'd briefly glimpsed what appeared to be a reddish ball of light floating over the left side of her bed. She'd instantly reacted by switching on her night table lamp but whatever it was, was now gone.

I asked to see the little angel statue from her bedroom and briefly inspected it. The foot was indeed reattached, with only slight hairline cracks less than halfway around the ankle and no visible residue of glue. If someone had reattached it, then they'd certainly done an expert job.

With little delay we began our follow-up investigation, which would be immediately followed by a religious cleansing of her apartment. Originally, because some of the other tenants were also experiencing inexplicable problems in their apartments, Kristyn had made an arrangement with her landlord for us to cleanse the basement as well. However, Kristyn informed us that the landlord had suddenly and mysteriously changed his mind earlier that very day.

"That's unfortunate," I said. "Less work for me, but as Jason explained anyone else who's having problems will simply have to personally contact us."

Just as on the previous investigation, Kristyn's son was spending an overnight with a family member. Her roommate was again away for the evening. Brian asked, "Oh, by the way, Kristyn did you mention anything to your roommate about his closet door swinging open by itself while we were here?"

"No, I didn't," said Kristyn. "He'd definitely refuse to believe it even happened anyway. That's just the way he is."

Inside the spare room, Brian again used verbal provocation in an attempt to get the closet door to swing open on its own, but his efforts proved to be unsuccessful. I also searched the room for something that might have caused the shadow effect, which had come out in the photo I'd taken. However, I was unable to find anything in the room that might have caused it, at least not from the angle I'd taken the photo.

We then sat as a group in Kristyn's parlor to again attempt communication with whatever spirit entities might be present with us. Kristyn was also ready with her own camera to try to capture any possible evidence. After dimming the lights and switching on our tape recorders, we were ready to commence. Rich and Theresa were taking turns manning the video camera, while Brian was monitoring the sound system. Jason said, "I think if anyone wants to start asking questions, now is the time, before Keith begins the blessing."

Theresa asked, "Jenny, are you here with us tonight? If so, can you give us a sign of your presence?"

We waited in silence for several seconds before Rich asked, "Is there anyone named Laura here?"

I asked, "Is there someone named Michael here?"

Following another several seconds of silence we heard a clicking sound. "That's weird," said Kristyn. "My camera just went off by itself."

"Is it supposed to do that?" asked Brian.

"No, it's not and it's never done that before," said Kristyn.

Theresa asked, "Is there a child named Laura here? If so, did you just switch Kristyn's camera off?"

We sat in silence, waiting for something else to occur. Brian, who was listening through the headphones, broke the silence by asking us, "Is anyone whispering in here?"

We all looked at each other and shook our heads no.

"Well, there's somebody whispering," said Brian. "I can't make it out, though."

Rich next took a turn with the headphones to see if he could decipher what was being said. After we'd spent another ten minutes or so asking questions and leaving spaces of several seconds for a response, Jason asked," Rich, you getting anything else?"

Rich shook his head and removed his headphones. "No, not now. Just like last time I was getting what sounded like some very quiet whispering but it stopped."

Jason said, "Alright Keith, if you're ready, we may as well start the cleansing."

"Yes, I'm quite ready," I told him.

Jason explained to Kristyn, "Now, when Keith does the cleansing it's part of the investigation as well, because we might get activity then."

Kristyn asked, "Why, what usually happens?"

"Every case is different," said Jason. "But the cleansing can also act as a form of religious provocation because you're coercing something to leave."

I added, "And as we explained to you last week, we can only try to remove it from your apartment *not* from the entire building. However, I will do an anointing outside on the main front entrance door of the building."

Jason asked her, "Do you have any questions before we begin?"

"Just one," said Kristyn. "Do you think that whatever's here could be more than just human spirits? I mean, you mentioned that something else could come through by using the Ouija board."

Jason said, "Honestly, we can't yet say for certain at this point. But we'll make sure to do a thorough cleansing so if anything here is really negative, it should be expelled."

Kristyn suddenly became teary-eyed and said, "I sometimes can't help feeling that this is all my fault. I should've known better than to fool around with a Ouija board in the first place, especially since I seem to be some kind of a freaking 'ghost magnet' or something."

I gently touched her arm and told her, "Please don't blame yourself Kristyn, you couldn't have known."

Kristyn managed a smile and thanked me for not judging her.

With Brian assisting me, I began the cleansing in the spare room. After reciting the 23rd Psalm out loud, I anointed the windows with blessed oil, while Brian sprayed the room with blessed water. Before anointing the closet door, I said, "In the name of Jesus Christ if there is a spirit in this room give us a sign of your presence."

When there was no response after a wait of about ten seconds, I went ahead and anointed the closet door. "Whoa," said Brian checking his EMF meter.

"What is it?" I asked.

"There's something in here," said Brian. "The EMF's cooking up a storm. I guess something didn't like you blessing the closet."

"Apparently not," I said. "It's a good thing that Kristyn's roommate is such a skeptic, for *his* sake."

Before leaving the room, Brian liberally sprayed the closet with blessed water while I anointed the door that connected the room to the parlor.

The cleansing of the bedrooms and the parlor went without incident. I of course did a spiritual sealing of Kristyn's son's room, reading aloud from the Gospel of Mark, Chapter 10, verses 13-16, where Jesus takes the little children in His arms and blesses them.

As a group, we then moved into the small kitchen. Rich took a seat at the table and found his chair to be somewhat unsteady. Kristyn warned him, "I'd be careful if I were you. One of the legs is a bit wobbly. In fact, I was meaning to throw it out before you guys came over tonight but it just slipped my mind with everything else that's been going on."

"Thanks for the warning. I'll be careful," Rich assured her, while unsteadily shifting his weight in the chair.

With the overhead kitchen light lowered I quietly began: "The word of God, according to His Psalmist, David: 'Touch not My prophets, nor do My anointed ones harm.' In the name of God, if there is the spirit of a child here, please give us a sign of your presence."

We waited in silence to see if there would be some sort of reaction. When nothing happened I said, "In the name of God, if there is an inhuman spirit here, then give us a sign of your presence *now*."

We again waited for a period of about three seconds... when the silence was suddenly broken by a crashing sound within the room. As it turned out, the wobbly leg of the kitchen chair that Rich was sitting in, had spontaneously given way at that exact moment causing him to tumble to the floor. Kristyn gasped and Brian exclaimed, "Rich! Are you okay over there, dude?"

"Yeah, I'm... fine," he said with a laugh. "Just a little startled is all. I should've been expecting that."

Once we found out that Rich was all right, we all cracked up with laughter, realizing the humor of the situation. Jason said, "We couldn't have timed *that* more perfectly if we'd planned it."

Brian and I next went downstairs to anoint the front entrance door of the apartment building, since this was obviously the section of the building that had been built directly over what was once part of the cemetery grounds. Both Kristyn and Theresa came downstairs with us as well. After anointing the inside of the door, Brian and I stepped outside onto the top front doorstep.

While tracing the sign of the cross on the outside of the door, I said, "May mighty and holy angels guard this dwelling and all who inhabit it." I also added a brief prayer, in Latin, for any restless spirits that might be present: "Pie Jesu, qui tollis peccata mundi, dona eis requiem. Pie Jesu, qui tollis peccata mundi, dona eis requiem. Angus Dei, qui tollis peccata mundi, dona eis requiem, sempiternam." ("Merciful Jesus, who takes away the sin of the world, grant them rest. Merciful Jesus, who takes away the sin of the world, grant them rest. Lamb of God, who takes away the sin of the world, grant them rest eternal.")

Just before I finished reciting this prayer, I suddenly overheard what sounded like a distressed scream coming from somewhere right around us. I looked at Brian who was looking at me with a wide-eyed expression. "You just heard that too?" I asked him.

"Yeah, I did," he said. "What the hell was that, dude? It sure sounded like a scream but it seemed to come out of nowhere."

No sooner did we step back inside than it became evident that both Kristyn and Theresa had also heard the scream. With her voice trembling, Kristyn said, "Alright, what was that? Tell me that you guys heard that too!"

"Yeah, we sure as hell did," said Brian. "We just heard a scream while Keith was praying right outside there."

Theresa said, "We just heard it too, but it sounded weird, like it was coming out of the air all around us." Both Kristyn and Theresa explained that they'd also suddenly felt a warm rush of air moving past them at the same moment that they'd heard the scream.

"I would interpret it to be a sign of expulsion," I said. "So, what say we go upstairs and explain to the others what we've just experienced?"

"Sounds like a good idea," said Kristyn who seemed anxious to move away from the doorway.

Back upstairs, we reported to Jason and Rich what we'd just experienced. I also played the recording of the phantom scream, which came out surprisingly clear. Kristyn said, "It gives me a chill just listening to it again."

"Me too," said Theresa.

I told Jason, "Hopefully this was a sign of expulsion. In fact, to me it feels very tranquil in here now."

Everyone else agreed that the atmosphere within the apartment *did* seem to have noticeably lightened. Kristyn breathed a sigh of relief and said, "Thank you guys, so much! It does feel calmer in here. And I know it's not just my imagination either."

Before leaving Kristyn's apartment we decided to do perhaps half an hour of evidence review. We watched the footage of our investigation inside of Kristyn's parlor, which had been taken in night shot. At one point during the footage the camera was trained on Brian with

Theresa standing beside him. Brian was asking for a sign of spirit presence when suddenly, what appeared to be an illuminated orb came into view and began floating around Brian's face. We couldn't even say for certain whether it was actually a small, condensed ball of energy or a round dust particle, although we were able to rule out it being an insect. The small globule began lightly bouncing off of Brian's face, monetarily disappearing up his left nostril. We just couldn't help finding this amusing, especially since Brian had been completely unaware that a small speck of something had just traveled up his nose. Rich asked him, "Brian, you didn't feel anything?"

"No, I didn't feel anything at all," he said.

As we continued to watch the monitor the globule left Brian's nostril and eventually floated away. Some of us had actually been wondering if the globule, or whatever it was, would continue up through Brian's nasal passage and come out the other side. Also, since Brian apparently had no sensation of it, I was wondering if he had sneezed would it have possessed enough substance to shoot out?

Before leaving we asked Kristyn if she'd like us to dispose of the Ouija board for her. Kristyn replied, "Oh yes, please do. I'd really appreciate it if you'd take it with you." She was obviously quite anxious for us to take it out of her apartment. As Kristyn took it out of one of her cupboards where she'd had it hidden, she said, "This is one thing I certainly want nothing more to do with."

Brian assured her, "Don't worry Kristyn. We'll dispose of it, so that no one will have any trouble with it again."

Jason added, "Keith is going to perform a blessing over it first and then we'll take it with us when we leave. Once we have the board home we'll dispose of it by burning it."

"Good," said Kristyn. "I'll never be bringing one of those into my home again that's for sure."

It was a plastic coated, glow-in-the-dark brand of the Mystifying Oracle. After anointing the board with a liberal amount of blessed oil and blessed water, I said, "In the name of Jesus Christ, may any unholy element which may be attached to this board be removed. Let any evil influence associated with this inanimate object be rendered powerless. Amen."

"Thanks Keith," said Jason.

In a determined voice, Brian said, "Now when we get this home we'll literally burn the *hell* out of this board."

Kristyn told us, "Again, thank you all so much for what you've done. Hopefully, both me and my son will be able to sleep a lot easier at night now."

Jason said, "Things should be a lot calmer in here after tonight. Just make sure you call us if the activity starts picking up again."

Kristyn assured us that she would.

(Note: I personally do not recommend the burning of Ouija boards as this could possibly cause a backlash of activity. The best methods for disposing of a Ouija board that has been used for spirit communication, is to either bring it to church authorities or to bury it after it has been blessed or to contact someone knowledgeable in disposing of such objects.)

Later on during the following week, while reviewing some of the audio recording I'd taken inside Kristyn's son's bedroom, I discovered a brief EVP. On the recording I could hear my own voice saying, "All children of God are welcome to come into the light." I then said to Brian, "We have angels of God watching over us," to which Brian responded, "Oh, no question." There was then the sound of a quick electronic squeak or glitch, immediately followed by a male voice clearly saying *"Amen."* It is interesting to note that when an EVP is recorded, either an electronic sounding squeak or a tapping sound will occasionally be heard just before the EVP itself.

The activity inside of Kristyn's apartment did considerably lessen following the spiritual cleansing we performed. Aside from a few random knocks and light flashes here and there, things were relatively quiet. It would be nice to be able to say that things remained that way for Kristyn, but unfortunately, they did not. Less than a year later, when she moved across town into another apartment, the activity she'd previously experienced slowly began to start back up again in her new residence. It was not long until Kristyn again contacted TAPS, and requested an investigation followed by a spiritual cleansing. TAPS member Fran Ford also accompanied us on this investigation.

When we arrived, Kristyn explained to us all that she'd been seeing orbs of light shooting through various places in her apartment, especially underneath the stairway leading up the second floor. Not only had the footsteps and knocks returned, but Kristyn had also seen what appeared to be a dim face with reddish, glowing eyes floating over her within her darkened bedroom. I asked her, "Approximately what time of night did you see this face hovering over you?"

"It was right around three A.M.," she replied. "Just like in my other apartment, that's when these things usually happen. And for whatever reason, I always seem to wake up at that time."

Jason asked, "Now, has your son being experiencing anything since you've moved in here?"

Kristyn replied, "Actually he hasn't mentioned spirit children visiting him like he did in our last apartment. But the other night, he came in and climbed into bed with me, saying that there was something in his room with him. And he hasn't done that for months."

Kristyn also informed us of something else, which might have accounted for some of the activity she was experiencing in her new apartment. "It seemed that in her back yard, crushed headstones from an abandoned cemetery have been used as landfill," she said.

Fran gasped, "Oh, my God!"

Kristyn said, "Of course, just like my last experience, my new landlord never bothered telling me anything about this when I first moved in."

I commented, "You would think that would be sort of illegal, using old headstones for landfill."

"Yeah, I'd think so too," she said. "But apparently, I seem to attract these sort of situations."

Although the debris from the headstone had recently been removed from the backyard, Kristyn was still continuing to experience haunting phenomena.

I asked, "You talk to the entities sometimes right Kristyn? Once in awhile, offhandedly?"

"Yep. Quite frequently when I'm cleaning," Kristyn said with a laugh.

"What do you say?" I asked.

Kristyn said, "I just talk to them like I'd talk to someone in the house. Just like, 'Hey, what's going on?' And when I'm in bed and I feel their presence, I try to pretend that I'm not nervous and that I'm not having a hard time falling asleep. But obviously they know."

I did give Kristyn a word of caution about giving too much recognition to certain *unknown* entities, especially in situations where demonic spirits could possibly be involved.

We then continued with the investigation, followed by the religious cleansing. This time, a reporter from the Boston Phoenix had asked to be present, since he was doing an article on paranormal investigation teams and their methods. I conducted the cleansing of Kristyn's apartment in the same manner as I had in her *former* apartment.

However, unlike in her previous residence, no overt activity took place during the religious provocation or the cleansing and reporter Chris Wright remained a skeptic. At one point during the evening, Rich spotted an illuminated, traveling object on video, which Rich was hopeful would turn out to be an anomaly. Upon closer inspection, though, the would-be anomaly turned out to be nothing more than a swirling moth, which had appeared to be illuminated by the infrared. In the article that appeared in the Boston Phoenix, Kristyn was humorously described as "a blond-haired, blue eyed, elaborately tattooed 27-year-old."

Before leaving, I made certain to bless the backyard as well, where the crushed cemetery stones had been used for landfill. The blessing itself fortunately proved effectual which was the main reason TAPS was there in the first place. Once again, the activity in Kristyn's apartment considerably lessened. Her now 7-year-old son was able to sleep in peace without being disturbed by any spirit activity. I also left a vial of blessed water with Kristyn, which she afterwards kept at the ready on the nightstand next to her bed.

Things remained spiritually calm for Kristyn throughout the next three years. We remained in touch with her, and, because of her personal experience in dealing with paranormal situations, Kristyn developed an intense desire to begin investigating the paranormal herself. She also wanted to be able to assist people who were experiencing these types of situations, the way she and her son had been helped.

Jason eventually invited Kristyn to join TAPS as an investigator-in-training. She quickly proved herself to be a valuable member of the team and before long was appointed to the position of full investigator. Although Kristyn had originally been a victim of paranormal phenomena, she was now able to investigate haunted locations and to assist other people seemingly without spirits attaching themselves to her.

It was not until she moved again that entities began manifesting themselves to Kristyn, and the activity was *again* confined to her new apartment. (By this time, of course, Sandra and I had split off from TAPS and formed New England Anomalies Research.) Sandra and I, along with Chris Finch of N.E.A.R. arrived at Kristyn's new apartment in Massachusetts on a snowy winter evening and were met there by our friend Mike Dion of New England Paranormal. Kristyn welcomed us in and proved to be a gracious hostess as always. As usual, Kristyn's son was out for the evening.

We decided to begin our investigation that with an EVP session. After I'd set my own tape recorder and placed it inside of Kristyn's son's empty bedroom, we all went inside of Kristyn's bedroom to begin our session. We began by asking the standard questions, pausing at least ten seconds in between each question to allow an answer to be recorded. "Do you have a name?" asked Mike.

"What is your purpose here?" asked Sandra.

Suddenly, a *low rumbling* sound could be heard within the otherwise silent bedroom, causing us to become alert. We were quickly able to locate the source as coming from Kristyn's digestive tract. "Sorry guys," she apologized with a laugh. "That was just my stomach growling."

"Jeez, Kristyn," said Mike. "Didn't you eat?"

Kristyn said, "Yes, so I guess I must just be digesting now."

As soon as we'd all quieted down again, we resumed the EVP session. "Do you mean harm to this family?" I asked.

Once again, on cue, a deep growl emanated from Kristyn's stomach. Since it was plain to see we wouldn't be making much progress in the master bedroom we decided to take a break.

Later on, after Kristyn's tummy has settled a bit, we continued our EVP session in the kitchen and in the parlor. Sandra and I then performed the religious cleansing throughout Kristyn's apartment assisted by Chris. Aside from some minor temperature fluctuations we detected no overt phenomena during the cleansing.

We did obtain some rather interesting results from our EVP sessions that evening. Naturally, we had to discount the "demonic growling" sounds taken inside the main bedroom, which were in reality nothing more than gastric eruptions.

But on the recording I'd taken inside of Kristyn's son's empty bedroom, recorded on analog, a voice could be heard plainly whispering: *"Want... out."* I can only speculate as to exactly what message, *if* any, these words were meant to express. Perhaps the entity wanted us out of what it may have considered "its" territory. Or perhaps it felt trapped and wanted out itself. It could be that this was merely a residual playback of sorts. Or it could also have been a ploy for sympathy by an intelligent *yet* deceptive spirit.

In the kitchen, Mike Dion captured a digital recording that, while not a voice, was interesting nonetheless. It was the distinct sound of a metal pipe dropping onto a concrete surface with a slight echo to it. Of course, no metal pipe had been dropped at that moment; also the floor of Kristyn's apartment was covered with soft tile. To make such a sound anywhere in her apartment would have been virtually impossible. We could only speculate as to whether this noise could also have been residual.

Fortunately, the blessing we performed was apparently successful.

Over the next two years, Kristyn Gartland moved again twice. And in both apartments the paranormal problems again picked up, shortly after she'd moved in. As with the other apartments, the spirit activity seemed to be centered primarily around her and to a lesser extent, her son. Kristyn requested that Sandra and I perform a cleansing in each place, both of which had a positive effect.

During our blessing of her most recent apartment, Kristyn, Sandra and I were upstairs on the second floor together and were commenting upon the bathroom décor. As usual I was recording on audio. When the tape was played back we found an EVP, which was clearly a breathy male voice. As far as we could it make out, it seemed to be saying: "*Oh, Jees-ah.*" While this is of course open to interpretation, it may have been a sigh of exasperation or perhaps expressing its displeasure at us being there to again help Kristyn.

It goes without saying that each time Kristyn moves into a new residence, we are now automatically expecting a call from her and we gladly agree to assist. Now that her son is a bit older, he rarely experiences the phenomena, aside from an occasional rapping on the walls or the sound of disembodied footsteps. Kristyn continues to function as a full investigator for TAPS and fortunately, never seems to have a problem with anything following her home. We also sometimes good-naturedly tease Kristyn and tell her that if we ever want the Amityville house to be genuinely re-haunted, we'll simply have her move into it!

CHAPTER 18

Voices From Beyond

IT WAS LATE June of 2002 and the TAPS investigation team was on the scene of a case in Mansfield, Connecticut. It involved a family who less than two years before had moved into a 130-year-old farmhouse, in which the husband was reportedly being repeatedly attacked by something unseen. In fact on one recent early evening the husband and wife had been standing outside in the yard and the husband had begun verbally berating the spirits to his wife. Suddenly, he'd been roughly shoved from behind, causing him to trip into a small rut in the lawn and breaking his ankle. As a result of his injury, he was unable to return to work for at least several weeks.

Since the husband and wife were not particularly religious, they'd requested that we basically document and verify the activity they were experiencing in the house, as opposed to performing any type of religious cleansing. Our friends and fellow investigators Bill and Nancy Washell, who had temporarily relocated from Maine, had been instrumental in bringing us to the attention of this couple and were also there with us on this particular evening. There were rumors that at least part of the property the house had been built on also contained an Indian burial ground although the exact location was not listed on the Mansfield town historic records.

Shortly before 8:00, Jason Hawes, Grant Wilson, Shelly King, Bill, Nancy and I were up in the attic, taking photos and recording for EVP. According to the clients, a small Cassio keyboard which was in the attic had been spontaneously playing by itself at various hours, even unplugged and with the batteries removed. The family had also overheard muffled voices and shuffling about, even when the attic was known to be vacant. While we were all up there, Shelly was walking through the attic when she hesitated at a certain point. "I'm getting the impression that there's something right here," Shelly said to me. She indicated the space immediately in front of her.

Rewinding my audio recording and playing it, I instantly found a response to her statement. A voice softly said, "*Right.*"

Nancy also felt her wrist being roughly grabbed by something unseen while up there. When she reviewed her own audio recording from the attic, she discovered a rather harsh sounding male voice, telling her in no uncertain terms to "*Get out. Get down!*"

A short time later, while Jenn Rossi was taking audio recordings downstairs in the dining room, she happened to capture an EVP of an young child mournfully crying. The wailing was so distinct and pathetic sounding that it reduced both Jenn and the female homeowner to tears upon listening to it. Meanwhile, I decided to rejoin Bill in the attic, who was alone taking video recordings and trying to establish spirit communication. I apologized for intruding and asked, "Are you getting much of anything, Bill?"

"No, just a little orb activity here and there," he said. "But you're welcome to join me and see if we can get any response."

Taking a seat on the floor next to him I switched my own small tape recorder back on again and began an EVP session with Bill. We asked a series of questions and together tried to prompt the spirit into playing the Cassio keyboard. After fifteen minutes or so of Bill and I attempting communication and getting no apparent response, Jason, and Grant rejoined us upstairs. Jason announced to us that, unfortunately, the wife had just been called into work at 4:30 AM the next morning, meaning that we would have to cut our investigation short this evening.

Grant also informed us that both he and Shelly had witnessed a shadow figure illusively darting around downstairs in the master bedroom. When I asked him if it was still down there, Grant explained that it instantly moved out of view every time they'd tried taking a photo of it and that finally it vanished altogether.

"It doesn't want to be filmed," I speculated.

Since this was shortly before the Forth of July some young kids then began lighting off fireworks nearby, which was unfortunately spooking the family's horse outside in the pony corral. One particularly loud firecracker went off from just outside the property. Pretending to be shot, Grant doubled over and groaned.

Before leaving that night, Grant, Shelly and I made one *final* attempt to communicate with the shadow entity that had been darting about in the downstairs master bedroom. "I don't think it's going to appear to us again tonight," Grant said with a sigh. "It seems to be dodging us as if it thinks that we're some kind of threat to it, like we're trying to make it leave."

"That's not what we're here for," I said.

"No and that's what I'm trying to tell it," said Grant. Addressing the entity, he said, "We're not trying to harm you, or make you leave. We simply wish to communicate with you." But there was no response.

We then packed up our equipment. The husband and wife thanked us and apologized for the fact that we had to leave so abruptly. Jason said, "No need to apologize. We understand you have an early morning tomorrow. So, we'll go over our evidence this week and let you know our findings."

The very next morning, Jenn was shocked and surprised to find that the child's wailing she'd recorded only the night before had now completely vanished from her audiotape! The sounds of her own voice asking questions were still there, as well as the voices of family members and other investigators in the background. But somehow, only the EVP itself was now gone, although it had been very clear when she'd played it for the rest of us. As I half-jokingly told Jenn at the next TAPS meeting, "Well, it seems as though the spirits in the house had only let you borrow the sound of a child crying and then decided to take it back."

"Yes, it seems that's exactly what did happen," Jenn agreed.

When I reviewed my own audio recordings, I discovered another interesting EVP that had been recorded up in the attic. It was right after Grant had explained to me about the elusive shadow figure darting about in the master bedroom downstairs. At the point where I commented, "It doesn't want to be filmed," a distinctly female, in a breathy, almost sensuous tone, could then be heard saying, *"Let's go down there. Let's go there. Aaaahhhh…."* In the background, Grant could be heard moaning while pretending to be shot, when that firecracker went off.

I found the breathy quality of this EVP of particular interest. As was sometimes the case with other examples of EVP, there was the definite sound of respiration taking place, although this was presumably the voice of a disembodied entity. Also, the fact that it was apparently interacting through conversation would classify this voice as intelligent, as opposed to residual. It certainly presented another intriguing aspect to the mechanics of Electronic Voice Phenomena.

When we telephoned the family in Mansfield and shared our findings with them, they immediately invited us back for a follow-up investigation. One week later, TAPS members Rich Einig, Fran Ford, Renee Laverdiere, Jenn Rossi and I arrived at the 19th Century farmhouse in the early evening. The couple informed us that the situation was somewhat worsening; especially the overall feeling of oppression the husband was experiencing. He was also going through somewhat of a depression, since the injury to his ankle was forcing him to stay home on sick leave from his construction job. The wife was also feeling increasingly overwhelmed with an oppressive feeling whenever she had to be downstairs in the basement.

During our first hour there we did spend some time taking recordings in the basement. Although the wife joined us in the basement, at one point she became overwhelmed with a feeling of sorrow, burst into tears and had to rush back upstairs. While we were still down there, Jenn, Fran and Renee also began experiencing a sensation of vertigo, as if the concrete floor beneath them was somehow shifting.

Back upstairs, Rich and I ventured up into the attic to troll for more EVPs, while Jenn spent some time conferring with the family.

Fran and Renee were both in a spare room on the first floor, which also served as a sewing room. Renee had her back turned to Fran, when suddenly she heard her name being called. *"Renee."*

Renee turned around and asked Fran, "Did you just call me?"

"No I didn't," she said.

"Yes you did, I *just* heard you," said Renee. "I swear, somebody just called my name."

"Well, it wasn't me," said Fran.

At that moment, they both plainly heard a female voice within the room call out, *"Renee."*

After standing there in silence for a moment, Fran asked, "Okay, we both heard that right?"

Renee nodded. Unfortunately they did not have a tape recorder going at the time but at least they'd both heard the voice, which provided verification for their report.

Rich and I were able to capture some minor EVPs in the attic, which included a voice softly whispering *"Yes"* in response to our having asked if there was a presence among us. We then rejoined Jenn, Fran and Renee downstairs who were also sharing their findings with the family especially about the disembodied voice that had called out to Renee in the sewing room.

Privately, I spoke with the wife in the dining room. She broke down crying during our conversation and confessed that she believed it was just a matter of time until the spirits in the house did her husband in. "I know whatever's here wants him gone so it can have me all to itself," she said through her tears.

"Who do you think it is that wants him gone?" I asked.

"Jonathan," she relied. "That's the name I've given to the spirit I see in my dreams. So I'm convinced it's just a matter of time until my husband's taken from me."

Although she and her husband were not religious, I reminded her that she didn't have to be a victim in her own house and that certain steps could be taken to counteract the spiritual attacks against her husband. I also informed her that if they should ever decide to move, they could take precautions against any spirits following them. At the

end of our conversation she smiled and appeared somewhat reas-
sured.

Before we left that evening, Fran also gave the family some advice
about "saging" their house for protection.

Fortunately, the Mansfield case ended on a positive note. The di-
lemma involving the apparent spirit attacks against the husband was
eventually resolved. We remained in contact with the family and
advised the husband and wife to verbally make peace with whatever
spirit entities might be co-existing with them in their home. Together,
as a couple, they did verbally address the spirits telling them. "If this
is Jonathan or whatever your name is, or your names are, we wish to
live here in peace with you. Neither of us wishes you any animosity.
We only ask that you respect us as the present owners of this house.
You are welcome to stay here as long as you do no one any further
harm."

The attacks on the husband completely ceased after the couple
verbally made peace with the spirits in their house. Although some
phenomena continued indicating that the sprits were still there, the
family now at least felt comfortable living in their home. And so, we
at TAPS considered this case to be a success as some measure of
closure was brought to the family.

The husband and wife continued to live in this house for another
three years, until they eventually relocated to be closer to the husband's business. To our knowledge, neither "Jonathan" nor any of the
other spirits followed them when they moved.

CHAPTER 19

The 'Mothman' of Brayton Cemetery

IT WAS NEARING 3:00 AM and a brilliant full moon shown overhead, as Richard and Rose, both in their early twenties, cruised along the familiar stretch of Post Road in Warwick, Rhode Island. The year was 1975, late summer and Richard and his then-wife Rose were on their way home from a social occasion with friends. Before long they had entered the section of Warwick known as Apponaug, which included the downtown center of the city.

Rose, who was slouched in the passenger's seat, was beginning to doze as her husband Richard continued driving along Post Road. Just up ahead, she could see some of the polished headstones of Brayton Cemetery glinting from the moonlight. She gave a yawn and slightly shifted her position in the seat. As they were passing the cemetery Rose caught a sudden flash of movement up ahead. Blinking and quickly becoming fully alert, she could see someone, or *something*, standing near the outskirts of the cemetery grounds.

"Rich... what's that in the cemetery up there?" asked Rose. "Do you see it?"

Richard replied, "Yeah, I do. It looks like someone standing there, dressed in white."

Whoever or whatever it was, it appeared to be rather tall. And as it came closer into view, they could see it starting to raise both arms. Or were they... wings? Richard instinctively slowed his speed, both to get a better look and as a precaution in case the figure were to suddenly jump out in front of them. As it was, the figure was standing very close to the raised stonewall which bordered the historical cemetery.

And then, to their astonishment, the tall, whitish figure suddenly lifted itself several feet into the air and lurched forward. Richard, slamming on the brakes scarcely had time to react. He and Rose watched as the figure sailed across Post Road, perhaps twenty-five or so feet in the air directly in front of their car. They both craned their necks to look, as the solitary figure swiftly glided past their car, finally disappearing out of sight into the darkness across the street. "Rich, what the hell was that?" Rose asked her husband.

But Rich was equally baffled. "Whatever it was, it's clear out of sight now," he said, glancing into the rearview mirror as he drove along.

Rose said, "It sure as hell looked to big to be a bird. I mean it was definitely man size!"

After that night, although they'd traveled along that familiar stretch of Post Road past Brayton Cemetery many times, Richard and Rose never again saw the 'Mothman,' as they later referred to it. Richard, who also happens to be my wife Sandra's older brother, first related the story to me many years later. The figure that was seen that night flying over Richard's car has been described as having the appearance of either a large, light-colored bird or moth-like creature or perhaps even an American Indian. But whatever it may have been, both witnesses claimed that it appeared to be close to human-size and that it had become airborne, launching itself from the edge of Brayton Cemetery and swooping directly across Post Road.

Although to my knowledge there have been further sightings of the 'Mothman' of Warwick since Richard's and Rose's encounter in 1975, Brayton Cemetery is still known for reports of paranormal activity. Some of this activity mysteriously seems to center around the grave of a young girl, located near the far end of the cemetery. However, there have also been reports of people being repeatedly touched on the shoulder right outside of Brayton, as well as the sound of a young girl sighing.

In fact, during the early days of The Atlantic Paranormal Society, Brian Harnois would sometimes utilize Brayton Cemetery as a "training ground" for new members; especially those who'd never participated in an on-location investigation before. During one of these training exercises, Brian, Rich Einig and two new investigators who were present experienced an unusual sighting, when they suddenly heard a deep growl coming from the wooded area, which borders the far end of the cemetery. They were suddenly startled, as a dark shape was sighted in the same location from which the growl was heard. The dark form then seemed to separate, as two small, unidentified animals came *whooshing* past them, running is opposite directions. Brian defined these as a "Watchers," or spirit entities that watch cemetery grounds. He later speculated, that he him may have had a momentary encounter with something akin to the legendary 'Mothman' of Brayton.

As to exactly why Brayton Cemetery may be associated with some paranormal activity, one can speculate on at least a few possible reasons. To begin with, one has to simply study the history of the cemetery. Named after Chief Justice George Arnold Brayton (August 4, 1804 - April 21, 1880), it is a rather large cemetery in which the graves from at least four other smaller cemeteries were combined. As the City of Warwick became less rural and the population increased over the years, many of the older homesteads that their own family graveyards were demolished, meaning of course that the graves had to be relocated. Also, some of these *new* graves inside of Brayton Cemetery were moved from a local "poor asylum", and at least several of these graves remain unmarked to this day.

Brayton Cemetery is also located very closely to running water that possesses a high mineral content. Some theorize that this may possibly serve as an energy source for any spirit entities that might be present.

Another unfortunate element as to why this particular cemetery may be haunted is because of the evidence of vandalism and cult activity, which had occasionally been found there. For this reason, negative energy may have been attracted to this particular cemetery, which is often the case where previously consecrated ground has been defiled.

Of course, there is also the possibility that American Indian graves, already existing on the location, may have been violated to make way for the multiple burials within Brayton Cemetery. This could perhaps account for the 'Mothman' having somewhat resembled and American Indian.

And so, at least for the present, the 'Mothman' remains a mystery, along with the other unexplained phenomena throughout the grounds of Brayton Cemetery. On many a moonlit night I have driven along Post Road though Apponaug past this cemetery, half-wondering if a tall, whitish winged figure just might spring from the cemetery grounds and swoop directly in front of my car. But thus far, my brother-in-law's experience has yet to be repeated. And although I'm certainly not holding my breath in hopes that it will, I've also learned to expect the unexpected.

In the meantime, much effort has recently been made by a local private landscaping team to maintain the upkeep of Brayton Cemetery. They have indeed been very successful in restoring the cemetery to its original serene beauty. If anyone is planning on visiting this cemetery, please do be respectful and respect the currently enforced rule of limiting your visits to the daylight hours. Brayton Cemetery, also known as Warwick Historical Cemetery 34, is located along Post Road in the Apponaug section of Warwick, RI.

CHAPTER 20

A Case of Demonic Oppression

BECAUSE OF THE high demand of scheduling involved with the TV series "Ghost Hunters," Sandra and I eventually decided it was best to branch off from The Atlantic Paranormal Society and found our own organization, which we named New England Anomalies Research or NEAR.

A few other former members of TAPS, including Chris Finch, my brother Carl, Andrew Graham and Lisa Dowaliby, also decided to join us. However, we of course continued to work with TAPS as demonology consultants and specialists with inhuman hauntings. One such situation that we were asked to assist with occurred in October of 1994, when an emergency call came in from a family living in Salem, New Hampshire. The case involved a single mother, her two young children and her husband, all of who were living in an apartment in which they felt there was an unseen, hostile, presence. Due to the severity of what they were reportedly experiencing and because the young children were being effected as well, TAPS decided to make this case a priority.

Since most of the TAPS personnel would be busy filming during this particular weekend, and Carl had a prior commitment, the investigation crew consisted of Mike Dion, Lisa Dowaliby, Kristyn Gartland, Sandra and myself. Sandra and I had specifically been asked to be part of the investigation team to determine if the activity occurring in the client's condo may be of inhuman origin. We'd also been requested to perform a religious cleansing at the conclusion of the investigation, regardless of whether or not we found any activity.

Upon our arrival in Salem, at the client's request we first met up with her and her family in the parking lot of a nearby shopping mall. The reason for this was that her landlord was supposedly very reticent about having any sort of "ghost busters" inside the condo, meaning that the actual reason for our being there had to be kept secret. A light rain had begun to fall as we stepped out of our vehicles and introduced ourselves to the family, who seemed both delighted and relieved to meet us. The mother, whose name was Leigh, was a slim, attractive young woman, who wore her short blonde hair in a pixie-cut. "Thank you so much for coming, and I'm sorry we had to meet outside here in a parking lot," Leigh said apologetically.

Mike Dion said, "I understand that there's a privacy issue involved, about having investigators at your condo. Is this true?"

Leigh replied, "Oh, yes. It's mostly because of the landlord. He absolutely refuses to allow us to have anyone having anything to do with the paranormal in our apartment. So, that's why I have to make it look like we're just having friends visiting with us tonight."

Leigh then introduced us to her two young children, a boy and a girl, who were ages six and eight respectively. She also introduced us to her husband Cliff, a husky, soft-spoken young man with dark hair and a short beard, and to her mother, who would be taking Leigh's two children to stay with her during our investigation. Since the children had reportedly both been scratched and poked by something unseen while in the apartment, I asked Leigh if she would like me to do a quick blessing over them before they left. "Oh yes, please, by all means," she said. I then took out a small vial of blessed oil, anointed the foreheads of her two children in the shape of a cross and said a brief prayer over them.

"Thank you so much for doing that," said Leigh.

Leigh's mother smiled and said, "Well Leigh, I guess you're in good hands for tonight. These seem to be very nice people, and I'm so glad they've come all this way to help you."

We told Leigh's mother and the children it was a pleasure to meet them. Leigh then kissed her children good night, before asking us to follow her and her husband the rest of the way to the condo.

Upon our arrival, we were requested by Leigh to try not to be too obvious or to look like we were here on official business. For this reason, we laughed and joked with Leigh and Cliff on the way up as if we were all old friends. We later brought our cases of equipment up through a back entrance. Even with these precautions, however, we soon noticed neighbors from across the street looking at us from their windows.

Once we were inside long enough to relax for a few moments, Leigh placed her arms around me and closed her eyes. I could feel her body trembling. "I'm so glad you people are here to help us," she whispered. "We've felt so alone and isolated in what we've been going through."

Supporting her slight weight in my arms, I told her reassuringly, "Yes, we understand and we're going to do all that we can to help you tonight."

Several minutes later we were in the process of unpacking some of our equipment, when Leigh became so emotionally overwhelmed, that she suddenly collapsed onto the parlor floor in a dead faint. We rushed over to assist her. Fortunately, Kristyn Gartland happened to have some basic first aid knowledge and was able to tend to her. Leigh soon began to recover and was instructed by Kristyn to sit up with her head lowered between her knees for a few more minutes until her light-headedness began to abate. Her husband Cliff explained to us that this had happened before, when she would become overwhelmed by stress.

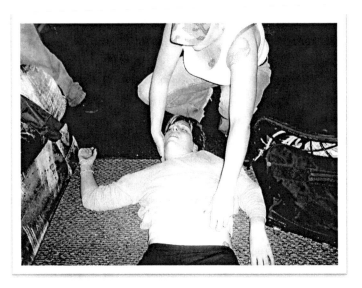

Leigh, a client in Salem, N.H. momentarily collapses from emotional stress.

At the moment Leigh had fainted, Lisa Dowaliby noticed that the indicator on the EMF meter she was holding happened to jump slightly. Curious, she thought, although she could come up with no logical explanation for why this would have happened.

When Leigh felt fully recovered, she sat beside her husband on the parlor sofa as we gathered around to begin the interview with them. We told Leigh to take her time and just relax and to take a break whenever she felt the need. Leigh thanked us, but said she was feeling much better and that she really wanted to get the whole story out.

Leigh and Clifford explained that the problems seemed to stem from the time they'd first moved into the condo. Initially, the phenomena they experienced seemed relatively benign. Silverware, car keys and other small items would be rearranged or missing altogether. Sometimes the missing items would turn up in odd places later on; where Leigh and Clifford knew they hadn't left them.

At first they blamed everything on the two children playing pranks although the children always insisted they had nothing to do with what was being misplaced. The daughter then claimed that one of her favorite dolls was being moved around in her bedroom by itself and that it frightened her. Leigh and Clifford naturally assumed their daughter had an overactive imagination… that is, until they witnessed the doll siding across the bedroom bureau by itself.

They promptly disposed of the doll outside in the dumpster. When it came back the next day, Clifford drove to a landfill located out of the city and disposed of it there. This time the doll did not return. Shortly afterwards their daughter began receiving painful scratches on her face and body, almost as if they were being inflicted as punishment for the doll having been discarded.

Shortly afterwards the son began waking up in the morning with the same type of painful scratches his sister had. The family also began hearing loud scratches and rapping sounds in the walls at all hours of the night, which frequently kept them awake. Heavy furniture would be found rearranged in the morning in ways that would be impossible for the young children to have had a hand in. There were many other problems that developed in their apartment as well, such as sudden icy cold drafts. Sometimes these drafts even seemed to cause a chill throughout the bodies of the family members, almost as if something had just passed right through them!

In the bathroom, the sink faucets would sometimes turn on by themselves and neither Leigh nor Clifford seemed to be able to take a shower without the shower curtain seemingly being yanked down on them. There were often sudden, nauseating odors within the rooms, similar to either sulfur of rotting meat, which were beginning to make Leigh and her family sick.

They alerted the landlord to these odors, who had their place inspected to see if a small animal, might have died either in the walls or under the floorboards. However, nothing could be detected which might be causing these disgusting odors. Worse yet the landlord began blaming the family for loud noises, because some of the other tenants were now beginning to complain, saying that the noises were coming from their apartment. The landlord even threatened to evict them if the noises continued.

To compound things the family began experiencing a endless string of bad luck, which included unexpected financial expenses such as one car problem after another. Although both of their vehicles were relatively new and in good condition, it soon seemed that every other week at least one of their cars was in the repairs shop. Sometimes it was both cars, which caused them to have to rely on other family members and friends for transportation. There were health issues as well. Leigh was beginning to experience frequent dizziness and fainting spells within the apartment. She went to see her family physician, which had blood work done on Leigh. When the results came back normal her physician attributed these fainting spells to emotional stress and prescribed a mild sedative.

And then, despite Clifford's young age, early 30's, he soon suffered a mild heart attack. Clifford blamed this on his own stress level, brought about by what they now believed to be supernatural activity they'd been experiencing within their condo.

When Leigh and Clifford had finished relating the details of what they'd been going though, Mike said, "Not to sound obvious, but having you considered moving out of here?"

Tearfully, Leigh replied, "Yes, we've considered it. We love this place and we don't want to move, but we feel that we may have to anyway. It's convenient for Clifford's work and we could never get another place like this for the amount we're paying now."

"I understand," said Mike.

Leigh wiped her eyes with a tissue and said, "Also, there's something else. We've been doing some reading up on this sort of thing and we understand that if we do move and this is something like a demon doing all this, then there's a possibility that it could even follow us. Is that true?"

Mike glanced over at Sandra and me. "Well," I explained, "there are no absolutes about this. It depends upon a number of factors, sometimes having to do with the laws of attraction and invitation as well as how vulnerable or sensitive a person is. But, although it won't definitely happen, I do have to say that it is a possibility."

Leigh again wiped her eyes and slowly nodded as her husband placed a comforting arm around her.

Since Mike was leading the interview, he then asked, "Have either of you ever dabbled in the occult or used a divination device such as a Ouija board?"

Clifford shook his head no.

Leigh replied, "I did once or twice when I was a kid but nothing much happened."

Mike asked, "To your knowledge has there been activity experienced by any of the other tenants in this building?"

Leigh perked up. "Actually, there has. When our landlord told us that some of the other tenants were complaining about us, I got kinda' bold and went over and started chatting with the lady who lives across the hall. She and I have talked with each other before. And when I asked if she's ever experienced anything unusual since she's lived here, she told me yes, she had."

"And what exactly has she experienced?"

"Pretty much the same things we've been experiencing, although not as severe. She said she and her family heard knockings and scratches on her walls and things get moved around sometimes, and that she just feels really creepy in there. She doesn't like to be alone there, ever."

After Mike had jotted this down in his notes, he asked, "Do you know any of the history of this condo including before you lived here?"

"I don't know anything definite," said Leigh. "But I've heard rumors from some of the other tenants that there were people who were involved in occult practices living in some of these apartments. It's even possible this was one of them."

Clifford added, "There's also rumors that this place was built over an old Indian burial ground. But that can be said about a lot of places."

"Those factors could certainly be significant," I said.

Mike asked, "To your knowledge, has there been any sort of religious blessing done in this condo, Christian or otherwise?"

Leigh replied, "We actually tried to get a pastor in here to bless the place. But somehow our landlord found out about it and he threatened to have us evicted if we had the pastor in here."

"What?" asked Mike, "Why in the world would he do that?"

Leigh explained, "Because he doesn't want his condo building getting a reputation for being haunted, because he thinks it'll scare tenants away. That's why we had to sneak you guys in here tonight."

Lisa said, "Why, that's preposterous! You pay rent here and you have the right to have anyone over here that you please."

"Lisa's right," said Kristyn. "I think your landlord's just bluffing. In fact, I'd check the lease if I were you."

With a sigh, Leigh said, "Well, you're probably right. He sure isn't a very good landlord. But we're both so exhausted from fighting all this stuff."

Mike then asked Leigh and Clifford, "Is there anything either of you would like to add about what you've been experiencing here?"

Leigh and Clifford looked at each other before Clifford said, "No, I think that pretty much covers it."

Leigh asked, "Do you think you can help us?"

"We'll certainly do all that we can," Mike assured her. "First, we'll set up our equipment, then we'll begin our investigation, which will take at least a few hours. And afterwards, Keith and Sandra will perform a religious cleansing, as you've requested."

"Yes, we'd definitely appreciate that," said Leigh.

Fortunately we only had five rooms to deal with counting the bathroom. After we'd finished setting up our equipment, Mike began taking thermocouple readings in the kitchen, to measure any possible fluctuations in the ambient temperature. At one point, although Mike was standing still, there was a sudden drop in the room temperature surrounding him. "Hey, guys… the temperature just dropped four degrees right over here," her announced.

It then returned to normal. After we'd noted the change, there were no further fluctuations while we were in the kitchen.

We then split up into two teams, with Mike and Kristyn comprising one team and Lisa, Sandra and myself in the other. While Mike and Kristyn were in the master bedroom taking recordings, Lisa, Sandra and I began exploring the other rooms. Meanwhile, Leigh and Clifford were content to stay with each other in the parlor.

Sandra, Lisa and I checked the bathroom faucets for any obvious leaks or for anything that might cause them to spontaneously turn on by themselves. After testing them several times we realized the faucets were relatively new and tight. I commented, "These seem to be in pretty good condition. I don't see anyway that they'd just turn on by themselves."

"You're right, they seem pretty sturdy," Sandra agreed.

Next, Lisa reached over and gave a slight tug on the shower curtain bar. It came loose, causing her to have to catch it in time before it clattered down into the tub. "Well, I guess that debunks the shower curtain being thrown at them," she said. "You practically just have to touch it and it falls."

"Good call, Lisa," said Sandra. "We actually have the same exact problem with our shower curtain at home."

In the master bedroom Kristyn and Mike were continuing with their audio recordings, when the bedroom door, which was open by a few inches suddenly closed twice *and* reopened twice on its own. Thinking that someone was just outside the bedroom, Mike asked, "Is someone there?"

There was no reply. Mike went over, opened the door and glanced out into the hallway. "There's no one out there," he told Kristyn over his shoulder. "And there's no one else in sight."

"That's freaky," said Kristyn.

Several minutes later we again gathered in the parlor. Kristyn and Mike were explaining what they had just experienced in the master bedroom… when suddenly; the sound of a door slamming came from that direction. Startled, we all glanced at each other. "What was that?" asked Kristyn. "Mike and I were just in the main bedroom and we're all in here now, so the bedrooms are empty!"

Sitting on the sofa with her husband, Leigh looked truly terrified. Mike then said, "Let's go see if we can find the source of that noise. But I need at least one person to stay here in the parlor with the family."

"I'll stay with them," Sandra volunteered.

"Thanks Sandra," said Mike. "We should be right back."

Mike, Kristyn. Lisa and I found nothing amiss or out of place in either of the two bedrooms. The closet doors were securely shut and the bedroom doors were open just as they'd been left. Obviously, no one had been in either of these two rooms when we'd heard the slamming noise. Lisa did an EMF sweep in both bedrooms but found no unusual readings. Also, Mike's thermocouple registered no unusual fluctuations in room temperature. Mike concluded, "If there was something in either of these two rooms it seems to be gone now."

Meanwhile, in the parlor, Sandra was speaking calmly with Leigh and Clifford, when Leigh's face suddenly took on an alarmed expression. Concerned Sandra asked, "Leigh? Is everything alright?"

Leigh said, "I can suddenly feel the spirit presence. I'm usually able to tell when it's nearby."

Sandra quickly switched on her tape recorder. "Where do you sense it is right now?" she asked Leigh.

"It's over in the kitchen," Leigh replied. Seconds later Leigh grabbed onto her husband's arm and said, "Now it's just moved into this room with us!" Both Leigh and Clifford appeared terrified.

In a determined voice, Sandra then addressed the spirit by saying, "In the name of Jesus Christ, by His shed blood, you will be put down… and nullified."

Aside from the bubbling of the fish tank filter, there was silence in the room for the next several seconds. Leigh then said, "I don't feel it in the room any longer. I think it's gone."

The rest of us soon returned to the parlor. Sandra and Leigh explained to us what had just occurred, Mike suggested that we do a quick review of our audio recordings. Nothing was heard in the form of EVP until the very end. When Sandra said, "In the name of Jesus Christ, by His shed blood, you will be put down," a mocking male voice on the recording was heard to clearly whisper, "*Put me down.*" When she said, "and nullified," the same voice again mocked her by saying, "*Null-i-fied.*"

Before concluding our investigation and commencing with the religious cleansing, the five of us gathered in the master bedroom to compare notes. Because of the EVP that Sandra had captured on her tape recorder, Mike and Kristyn decided to attempt one final EVP session in the master bedroom. The overhead light in the bedroom was extinguished, leaving only a nightstand lamp on, which bathed the room in a soft glow. Mike began by asking, "Is there an entity present in this room with us?"

After a pause Kristyn asked, "Did you cause the bedroom door to open and close by itself?"

Lisa next asked, "Are you the entity that was with us in the parlor earlier?"

A few more questions were asked, when suddenly, Mike witnessed what appeared to be a small, dark mass scoot across the bedroom floor in front of him. "Whoa!" he exclaimed. "Did anyone else see that?"

Kristyn replied, "I just caught a quick glimpse of it too, Mike! It was kind of like a dark blob and it moved very fast across the floor."

"I'm glad at least someone else saw it," said Mike. "Otherwise, I might've thought it was my imagination getting the best of me."

"It wasn't *your* imagination, Mike," said Kristyn. "Trust me on that."

We then concluded the session and separately listened to our audio recordings, which this time yielded no results in the form of EVP.

As a group we sat in the parlor with Leigh and Clifford and discussed our findings up to this point. We had separately listened to our audio recordings from the master bedroom, which this time yielded no results in the form of EVP. However, there were the two examples of EVP, which Sandra had earlier captured in the parlor, as well as the small shadow form, which both Mike and Kristyn had both just witnessed in the master bedroom. Mike told Leigh and Clifford, "So, based upon the evidence we've collected so far we do concur that there *is* paranormal phenomena taking place here."

Leigh smiled and said, "Well, thank you for confirming that we're not crazy, and that we haven't just been imagining all this."

Mike assured her, "Believe me, clients tell us this time and time again."

It was time for Sandra and I to begin the religious cleansing. Leigh decided to accompany us through part of the blessing, while her husband Clifford remained in the parlor with Mike and Kristyn. We began by blessing the kitchen and the bathroom, which went smoothly and without incident. It was not until we reached the master bedroom that a certain amount of heaviness could be felt in the atmosphere. Since we could all simultaneously feel the heaviness,

Lisa checked her EMF meter. "I'm getting some slight spiking," she said. After checking the outlets and appliances in the bedroom, she added, "There seems to be a rather high energy output in this bedroom, including over by the headboard."

Sandra commented, "This could be possibly be causing episodes of TLE."

"TLE? What's that?" asked Leigh.

Lisa explained, "TLE stands for Temporal Lobe Epilepsy. Now, please understand Leigh, we're not saying that you or any members of your family have epilepsy."

"But with some people," said Sandra, "a certain amount of voltage output, especially within an enclosed room, can sometimes trigger symptoms that may appear to be paranormal experiences, when in fact they are not."

Lisa said, "But it's not necessarily anything you have to worry about. We just have to take all possibilities into account."

"I understand," said Leigh.

Suddenly, Lisa noticed something peculiar. "Leigh, what's that on your face?" she asked.

"What? What do you mean?" asked Leigh, bringing her hands up to her face.

"On your left cheek," said Lisa. "It looks like a small cut, or scratch."

Leigh took her left hand away and glanced at it. Sure enough, there was a small amount of blood on the tip of her fingers. "Oh, God," she said. "You're right, I'm bleeding." She then rushed into the bathroom.

Fortunately the scratch was only superficial and only deep enough to cause a small amount of bleeding. Sandra and Lisa, as well as Leigh all agreed that it had seemed to suddenly appear.

As soon as Leigh came into the parlor, dabbing the scratch with a tissue, we informed the others what had just happened. Lisa said, "Keith, Sandra and I were just with Leigh and she definitely didn't have that scratch only a moment before."

"That's right," Sandra agreed. "It was as if it just suddenly formed there."

Concerned, Kristyn asked her if it hurt. Leigh replied, "No, not really. It's just a little sensitive when I touch it, like a cat scratch. It reminds me of exactly what happens when my kids get scratched."

Kristyn suggested, "Maybe it was meant to be taken as a warning."

Before we continued with the blessing, I took my small vial of blessed oil and used it to trace the shape of a cross on Leigh's forehead, while quoting from Psalm 115: "Touch not my prophets, nor do my anointed ones harm."

"Thank you," said Leigh. "I do feel better now." She then went into the parlor to join her husband.

Mike placed his hand on my shoulder and said, "It looks like you and Sandra have your work cut out for you tonight, Keith."

Sandra and I next decided to bless the children's bedroom, which was located to the left of the master bedroom. As we entered the bedroom, I asked, "Sandra, would you please begin by reading from the Gospel of Mark, Chapter 10?"

Sandra then recited from Mark, Chapter 10, verses 13-16, about Jesus taking the children into His arms and blessing them. (While later reviewing this potion of the audio recording, Sandra and I discovered what sounded like a faint voice whispering *"little children"* just before Sandra said these words.)

After the children's bedroom was blessed and anointed, Sandra and I gathered together with the rest of the group in the parlor for the final blessing. Both Leigh and Clifford sat on the sofa as Sandra read Psalm 91 aloud, followed by Psalm 23, as well as various Scripture passages from the New Testament. When Sandra had finished reciting these passages, I asked for a final sign of any spirit presence, before pronouncing the final expulsion. Leigh mentioned that she could feel something building within the room, like a thick pressure. Once again, I prayed for the protection of everyone present, before saying, "In the name of Jesus Christ, on the authority of His shed blood, I bind all spirits, which are of an unholy nature. May they be cast out from these rooms and may mighty and holy warrior angels of God be sent here to watch over Leigh, Clifford, and their precious children. May all lost and wandering spirits also find rest and be sent to their proper abode. This we pray, in *His* name. Amen."

Leigh announced to us that she no longer felt the oppressive presence. "It's gone now, I can feel it," she said. "In fact, it feels so much more peaceful in here as if a weight's just been lifted."

Sandra said, "We've been told that before, so I'm glad that it seems to have had a positive effect."

Mike told Leigh and Clifford, "And you know that you can always get in touch with us, day or night if anything starts to reoccur."

"Thank you, so much," said Leigh, embracing us all in turn. "I don't know what I would have done, if you people hadn't come out here to help us tonight."

Clifford also shook hands with all of us, saying, "Yes, thank you for everything you've done to help us. We really do appreciate it."

Suddenly we heard some kind of commotion from outside the condo, which caused Leigh to rush over to the front picture window and glance out. Kristyn asked, "What is it Leigh, what's going on out there?"

Leigh replied, "Oh-oh… it looks like some kind of fight's starting up out there. That's actually not unusual in this neighborhood, especially on a weekend night. It can get pretty rowdy around here sometimes, especially when people have been drinking."

The rest of us joined Leigh to glance out the picture window and saw that there was indeed some sort of altercation going on in the street down below, with more and more of the neighbors coming out from their houses to see what was going on. Fortunately these neighbors were still up the street a way. Since Leigh advised us that the police would probably be called into the situation, we decided to make our departure without further delay. "I'm so sorry this had to happen while you people were all here," Leigh apologized.

Mike told her, "No, it's not your fault. We understand that these things happen. Considering the situation, though, I think we should get going, while the getting's good."

Everyone else agreed. We quickly said our final good byes to Leigh and Clifford and then went outside to begin loading up our equipment in an orderly fashion.

We had no sooner begun loading our equipment into our vehicles than the local police arrived to break up the neighborhood ruckus. They temporarily blocked off the street, preventing anyone to from entering or to leaving and began taking names of everyone there. Fortunately, Clifford and Leigh came outside to join us and explained to the police officers that we were friends who were simply visiting with them. After checking our identification the police accepted Clifford and Leigh's explanation and decided to allow us to be on our way. Both Clifford and Leigh profusely apologized to us for the inconvenience and again thanked us for all we'd done to help them that night.

During the drive back home, Sandra, Lisa and I speculated that the general hostility in Leigh and Clifford's neighborhood might have contributed to the negative activity within the condo. There are certain types of entities that seem to literally feed off of the energy produced by negative human emotions, and this may indeed have been the case here. In fact, it brought to my mind the Biblical story of Jesus casting out the evil spirits from the demoniac who identified himself as Legion, because of the numerous evil spirits that resided within him. I even speculated that expelling the entities might perhaps have influenced the reaction among the inhabitants of the immediate neighborhood that night.

We of course kept in touch with Leigh. Throughout the first several weeks following our visit, things remained relatively calm inside the condo that she and her family shared. The children were no longer scratched or terribly frightened and Leigh's anxiety level lessened considerably. However, as the neighborhood disruptions began to increase in frequency, the paranormal activity within the condo gradually began to pick up once again, suggesting that there may indeed have been a correlation between the two.

Family problems between Leigh and her husband began to develop as well. Some months passed and we were considering a return visit to the condo in Salem, New Hampshire. But because of repeated disagreements with their landlord, Leigh and Clifford eventually decided to relocate altogether. For awhile after moving they did continue to experience some very minor activity, which they felt they were able to tolerate, as long as the children were no longer being attacked or frightened. Over time this minor activity also ceased. The last time I communicated with Leigh, she and her family were doing well. She wished her story to be told, in the hopes that it may be beneficial to others that are experiencing a situation similar to hers.

CHAPTER 21

Conclusion

IT WAS A SEASONABLY warm early May evening in 2009, as Sandra and I began quickly setting up for our class at the Bay State Paranormal Center. The title of our class that evening was Demonology 102, and the classroom was already filling up fast. Among those in attendance was our friend Alison Oborn, the Co-Founder of Paranormal Field Investigators in Adelaide, South Australia. Alison had also previously been a guest on our paranormal TV talk show, *Ghosts R NEAR*.

Finally we were ready to begin. Elizabeth Russell, the director of Bay State Paranormal, introduced us to the class and we were welcomed with a round of applause. Most of those in the room this evening were already very familiar with us, many of them having taken our Demonology 101 class a few months earlier.

Sandra efficiently ran the power point presentation, as I began by giving a concise definition of what a demonologist is. "Essentially, a demonologist is someone who studies the history, theology, nature and activity of the demonic realm, and is able to apply this knowledge... hopefully in a *constructive* and positive way. In researching the paranormal, eventually an investigator will encounter forces that exist outside the human and fall into the sphere of the inhuman, or preternatural. This includes the demonic and angelic realm.

"What originally started me on this path was the fact that unexplained occurrences would sometimes happen in the house where I grew up. There were things such as unexplained laughter and unintelligible chatter outside of my bedroom window at night. Objects sometimes mysteriously vanished and occasionally one of us would be touched or even pushed. Now, it's not as though these things were happening constantly... but every once in awhile, something a bit bizarre would occur. My brother also witnessed a full-bodied apparition of a woman in our basement, on more than one occasion."

Sandra and I went on to discuss some of the many possibilities to rule out before coming to a paranormal or demonic conclusion in a given case. For example, those scratching sounds in walls or in the attic are much more likely to be caused by small rodents, rather than something paranormal in nature. We explained that there are also many other things to take into consideration prior to reaching for a paranormal explanation, such as Pareidolia, the mind creating something familiar out of chaos, also known as Simulacra or Matrixing. At this point, I made reference to an informative article on Pareidolia, which our friend Alison had written for the Paranormal Field Investigators website. We also covered hypnopompic and hypnogogic hallucinations, TLE (Temporal Lobe Epilepsy), as well as other possibilities.

We focused on how and why individuals would attract an inhuman attachment to themselves or their homes as well as some protective steps an investigator can take before becoming involved in a potentially malevolent haunting. Blessing and clearing techniques were also discussed. A Biblical perspective was emphasized as Sandra and I related various examples of how we were able to protect others and ourselves in situations involving demonic spirits.

We spoke at length about the potential dangers of communicating and summoning the demonic, such as through the use of Ouija boards and automatic writing. The question that I posed to the class was, "Could these be methods of spirit communication which invite 'possession'?" I then elaborated, "Actually, Ouija boards and automatic writing devices in and of themselves are not dangerous. The same type of spirit communication can just as easily be accomplished by using an overturned wineglass on a waxed table.

The danger lies in the fact that the individual using such devices is opening up his or her psyche to unknown forces and inviting these forces to take over at least part of his or her motor control. In other words, they're literally asking an entity to manipulate their hands just enough to move this indicator, or pencil, and spell out a hidden message. By doing so, they are granting permission for an unknown spirit to infiltrate their life. And demonic spirits can often be much more difficult to get rid of, than they were to initially bring in. Keep in mind that demonic spirits can and often *do* masquerade as human spirits, especially departed loved ones."

My brother Carl, who was also in attendance, added to the discussion by relating some particulars of an exorcism he and I both participated in back in the early 1980's, in which a 14-year-old Hispanic boy's personality was periodically being taken over by what was seemingly a demonic entity. This condition is commonly referred to as "transient possession," meaning that the individual is not in a constant state of possession. Carl explained, "Not only was this boy displaying radical personality changes, along with extremely accelerated motor control, but the possessing spirit was also able to manipulate inanimate objects, such as heavy furniture. Also, there would always be a sudden, noticeable change in the atmosphere within whatever room he happened to be in just prior to him going into possession."

"That's a very significant point," I said. "One thing to always look for in identifying a potential case of demonic possession, is extraneous phenomena taking place, which would obviously not be happening in a case of multiple personality disorder, or an dissociative identity disorder."

I also spoke about the potentially very dangerous practice of provoking demonic entities to get a reaction. "One thing which I strongly disagree with," I said, "is the way provocation is often portrayed in the popular media. For example, you often see the lead investigators on TV shows charging in and starting out by challenging any demonic spirits that might be present to reveal themselves, usually through a series of insults." I then began acting out a typical challenge for the class, saying, "C'mon out an' show yourself, you gutless coward! Show me what you got!"

From the titters and nods from those in the class, I could tell that many found this routine to be very familiar. I told everyone, "Let me make it clear, that I do *not* recommend taking this approach on investigations, especially where demonic spirits may be involved. You may very well not only be endangering yourself but also others who are present."

Then came the evidence part of our class, which began with Sandra playing some examples of EVP, recorded in a demonically infested house located in Brooklyn, New York. These included a male voice ominously saying, "*Walk show*," and "*Smokers... hot!*" The same male voice was also recorded saying the name "*Beatrice*," which, as Carl explained, turned out to be the name of a missing person from a past generation in this house.

We then played some video clips for the class, which began with footage of Fr. Bob Bailey, a Catholic priest who I'd been training in demonology, performing his first deliverance session in a case that Sandra and I had taken him on. This was followed by footage of a rather solid-looking "globule" flying in Sandra's direction while in the basement of the Brooklyn house as well as footage of myself performing a religious cleansing in the same basement. We next showed footage of a woman who was undergoing a state of transient possession, taken at a residence in Lewiston, Maine; it was a case that Sandra, Brian and I had been called in to assist with.

Near the end of the class, Sandra and I held a question and answer session, during which several pertinent questions were asked. One member of the class asked, "Are you able to tell if you're dealing with just one demon or with multiple demons?"

I replied, "Usually we can, although this can sometimes only be determined during a deliverance session. It is very helpful if we have the opportunity to work with someone who has the spiritual gift of discernment."

Someone else asked, "Where exactly do demons come from? Do they come from Hell?"

I answered, "Demons exist in a separate dimensional plane, which Jesus described as a state of 'wandering through dry places, seeking rest, and finding none', (Matthew 12: 43-45). In the King James Bible, the word 'Hell' is sometimes translated from the word Sheol' simply meaning the grave, or 'Gehenna,' which was a place of burning refuse in Jesus' time."

Another person asked, "When you are using an EMF detector while on a case, what would you consider to be a significant reading?"

Sandra replied, "well, getting a reading at all on an Electric Magnetic Field detector simply indicates that electrical equipment is operational, such as an alarm clock. This is similar to what we talked about earlier, concerning the possibility of temporal lobe epilepsy, causing some people to experience feelings of paranoia or of being watched. I've come across information on websites claiming that a reading of two-point-four, to two-point-seven, means there's a ghost present. Personally, my opinion is that if you're getting any kind of reading at all, I'd advise the client to either move the appliance or move the bed."

A member of the class named Kevin further suggested, "It's also a good idea to establish a baseline first and then go from there, when taking EMF readings."

"Exactly. That's a good point," I agreed.

One of the final questions asked was, "Do all demons recognize a certain church or figurehead as an authority?"

"They do seem to acknowledge a Higher Power and are adverse to virtually anything that represents goodness and holiness. Regardless of culture, they also seem to respond to the name of Jesus Christ."

In conclusion, I asked everyone in the class to remain silent for a moment, as I said a brief prayer of protection for everyone, due to the subject matter we'd been discussing. "In the name of our Creator, and of all that is positive and holy, we ask for that nothing which is negative be allowed to follow us from this place, only that which is of a positive nature. We ask for traveling mercies and divine protection as we leave for home this evening. Amen."

"Amen," everyone said in unison.

During our own drive home that evening, I complimented Sandra on just how well she had done in helping with the class presentation and also on how attractive she looked. "Thank you, dear," she said.

"It was certainly a very responsive class tonight. And I'm glad that everything went alright, despite how exhausted we both were."

Sandra and I then began discussing our itinerary for the upcoming week ahead of us, which (along with our daytime employment) included another taping of our paranormal talk show Ghosts R N.E.A.R., with our friend Shannon Sylvia as our guest. The following evening, we were scheduled to participate in a paranormal investigation at "haunted" Old Slater Mill in Pawtucket, as part of a combined PFI/NEAR investigation, while Alison was here visiting with us from South Australia. The evening after that, we were slated to do a two-hour interview as the guests of Dark Plains Radio. This, on top of the multiple telephone calls and emails we'd be responding to, many from people from throughout the country asking for advice and assistance. And of course, most importantly would be spending as much time as possible with our son, Keith Jr.

Sandra humorously commented, "The 'N.E.A.R. Jet' would certainly come in handy right about now!"

Sandra, Paula Donovan and Lisa Dowaliby relax after a taping of the talk show, Ghosts R N.E.A.R.

Breinigsville, PA USA
15 December 2009

229288BV00004B/66/P